STAGING
PREMODERN
DRAMA

STAGING PREMODERN DRAMA

A Guide to Production Problems

LEE MITCHELL

GREENWOOD PRESS

WESTPORT, CONNECTICUT
LONDON, ENGLAND

Library of Congress Cataloging in Publication Data

Mitchell, Lee
    Staging premodern drama.

    Bibliography: p.
    Includes index.
    1. Theater—Production and direction.   2. European
drama—History and criticism.   I. Title.
PN2053.M56   1984   792'.0232   83-5624
ISBN 0-313-23685-2 (lib. bdg.)

Library of Congress Catalog Card Number: 83-5624
ISBN: 0-313-23685-2

First published in 1983

Greenwood Press
A division of Congressional Information Service, Inc.
88 Post Road West
Westport, Connecticut 06881

Printed in the United States of America

10 9 8 7 6 5 4 3 2 1

PN
2053
M56
1983

Contents

	Preface	*vii*
	Introduction	*xi*

Part One: General Points Regarding Production

1.	Characteristics of Early Drama	3
2.	Problems in Transforming the Text of a Classic Into Performable Material	11
3.	Typical Problems of Casting Premodern Plays	23

Part Two: The Greeks

4.	Special Problems of Producing Greek Tragedy	37
5.	*Antigone:* A Problem of Balance	53
6.	The *Electra* of Sophocles: A Problem of Proportion	65
7.	The *Trojan Women:* A Problem of Emotional Tone	77

Part Three: History: Tragical and Romantic

8.	The *Tragical History of Doctor Faustus:* A Problem of Impact	91
9.	The Spanish Theatre and Lope de Vega	105
10.	*Fuente Ovejuna:* A Problem of Language	111

Part Four: Later Comedy

11.	The Satires of Jonson and Molière	127
12.	*Volpone*: A Problem of Contrasts	129
13.	*The Alchemist*: A Problem of Tempo	137
14.	Molière's Art and Some Typical Problems in Staging his Plays	153
15.	*Les Fourberies de Scapin*: Problems of Sequential Progression	163
16.	*Tartuffe*: A Problem of Clarity	169
17.	*She Stoops to Conquer*: A Problem of Coherence	183
18.	*The Rivals*: A Problem of Style	199
Appendix A.	Notable Productions of the Premodern Plays Discussed Here	213
Appendix B.	Additional Premodern Plays Suitable for Modern Production	217
Bibliography of Production Aids and References		221
Bibliography of Texts and Translations of Plays Discussed Here		225
Index		229

Preface

My obsession with premodern drama began very early in life. During childhood I was fortunately situated where I was able to attend the best professional productions and I saw a great many. Before I was through high school I had seen six *Hamlets,* including Barrymore's. By the time I reached adolescence I was being allowed to work backstage in various modest capacities, a rare privilege for a teenager. The natural next stop was the degree program in drama at Carnegie Tech where freshmen cut their teeth on Greek tragedy. Eventually I joined the faculty in theatre at Northwestern University, enabling me to work on the classics under favorable conditions before knowledgeable audiences. During World War II, as an officer in the corps of engineers, I worked first in the Pentagon drawing up plans for expedient stages and afterward in the Southwest Pacific getting theatres built for troop entertainment—over fifty, all told, varying in seating capacity from six hundred to ten thousand. The virtue of this assignment was that with plentiful manpower and earthmoving machinery I was able to experiment with every stage shape and seating arrangement from Greek to Elizabethan. Upon returning to Northwestern I initiated a course in Production of Premodern Drama, followed by others in Advanced Stage Directing and Directing for the Open Stage. The labs of the directing courses proved ideal for experimentation. I think I can honestly say that I have witnessed more attempts to solve the problems of presenting the court scene in *Volpone,* the table scene in *Tartuffe,* and the revelations in *Electra* than any person alive. School holidays were spent catching up on plays in New York, while summer vacations passed in a round of Shakespearean festivals such as those at Stratford, Ontario; Stratford, Connecticut; Ashland, Oregon; and Antioch, Ohio. Upon reaching retirement age at Northwestern I was offered an appointment as Distinguished Professor of Theatre at Western Kentucky University which provided for more frequent visits to the theatrical centers of Europe.

The thing that struck me after I had seen certain premodern plays a considerable number of times was how much of value in specific know-how was being lost between productions. One production of a classic could succeed brilliantly but the next production of the same play only a decade or so later might miss all the fine points which the previous one had achieved. On the opposite tack, an ambitious and handsomely mounted production would sometimes fail because of mistakes (duly noted by critics) only to be followed a few years later by another superproduction making all the same mistakes and falling equally short of the audience's expectations. Some of this is no doubt due to vanity—the desire to be "original" (a thing not wholly possible with a revival)—and some, perhaps even more, to ignorance of the true nature of the material and what others had done to enhance or denigrate it.

One small book cannot remedy very much of this. The subject of premodern drama is enormous; an encyclopedia could scarcely encompass it all, but I can make a beginning and this is what I am attempting.

One cannot truly know a drama one has never seen on the stage. Describing a play from a study of the text is like describing a symphony from a reading of the score. The plays described in this book, with one exception, are plays I have seen many times on many stages and have also produced, often several times, with competent casts. There is no better way of understanding production problems than by putting a play to the test of audience response. The descriptions here are not, however, of the "this is how I did it" variety, for in every instance problems that frustrated me were solved later by others and are reported accordingly.

Of course, nothing a person does is ever entirely original. Every inspiration is based on something seen or heard in the work of others. My interest in premodern drama gained tremendous impetous from the influence of B. Iden Payne, E. Martin Browne, Thomas Marc Parrott, George Fullmer Reynolds, and Moody E. Prior. The kernel of many an idea expressed in this book will be found in the writing of one or another of these men. But teachers are not the only ones from whom one learns. One's own students contribute more than most people realize. From the first I kept fairly copious notes of my discussions with students; and now, looking over these, I find certain names credited with remarkably perceptive observations: Walter Kerr, Charlton Heston, Gerald Freedmen, Jack Clay, and Marshall Mason, to name only a few. Lively exchanges with colleagues count, too. The number of these is quite beyond computation, but certain ones remain unforgettable. Among them are H. Darkes Albright and William P. Halstead, my collaborators on *Principles of Theatre Art* (first published in 1955), Bergen Evans, Charles Shattuck, and Robert I. Schneideman. But beyond all teachers, students, and colleagues is the debt I owe to my wife, Maurine Morgan Mitchell, whose interest and encouragement has made pleasurable the task of putting into order the results of years of note taking.

This habit of note taking originally grew out of the need to remember especially perceptive points in regard to interpretation, mounting, and stage business (as well as things to avoid should I ever have the opportunity of staging a production of my own), and afterward as material for discussion in the pre-modern drama course. The idea of putting it all into book form came later. Now I find myself wishing that I had been more methodical in recording dates and names, and more systematic in preserving and filing programs and play reviews.

The long time it has taken me to put this book together is due to the enormous amount of material that had to be sifted, organized, and condensed. In order to get it in hand I began by dropping as much as I could of information easily available elsewhere: stage history, textual criticism, elementary points of directing, and finally, all detailed discussion of Shakespearean production.

I will be very much surprised if anyone agrees with all I have to say. Theatre is a highly individual art. Those who have worked on any of these plays will certainly have different ideas of their own. I hope, though, that every reader will find something of value: some new approach, some previously unnoticed hazard identified, or some useful suggestion for solving a difficult problem or two.

Introduction

Few of us enjoy the opportunity to share in the production of a really great play, one of the caliber of *Antigone, Volpone,* or *Tartuffe,* more than a very few times in the course of a long career; and when such an opportunity is at hand, it is natural to want to make the most of it.

Great plays are not easy to do. Our own efforts are measured against a standard set by the most talented actors, directors, and designers of past generations. But the challenge is irresistible. Wholly successful productions of classics are few, making us feel that we can do better, that we can solve problems others have missed. To take a single example: *Macbeth* is acknowledged as a masterpiece, but it seldom plays as well as it reads and successful productions of it are rare. Therefore, it has never lacked producers and it probably never will. Fortunately for the gifted newcomer, the most successful production cannot continue forever; after a few years it will be time to make a new attempt.

We have no Shakespeare on Broadway today, no Sophocles, no Lope de Vega, no Ben Jonson, and yet no contemporary playwright seems likely to approach them in artistry. We can, however, bring to modern audiences the best theatre art of the past, taking advantage of the vast amount of scholarship that has accumulated around the question of authors' intentions and conditions of original presentation, and at the same time capitalize on the virtues of indoor production and the superior developments of modern theatre craft.

Our objective ought to be to bring to today's audiences the full value and truth of the original without falsification or cheapening by underestimating the capacity of moderns to exercise their minds and emotions. To revive a premodern play in the exact form in which it was originally produced (even assuming that we always know what that form was) would of course yield nothing but an historical curiosity. Modern audiences, accustomed to a different kind of theatre, different nuances in characterization, and often a different language as well, require some adaptation of material if the author's intention is to register. The overall problem then is to find a mode of presentation that will prove most satisfying to our contemporaries while remaining true to the original.

What adaptations need to be made? The first one that comes to mind is the matter of translation, obvious enough for a play composed in ancient Greek or seventeenth-century French, less obvious perhaps but equally worthy of attention for plays composed in Elizabethan English. Another is the need to supply actions missing in the text as most of the plays were originally printed without stage directions. A third, which soon becomes obvious, is the need for cutting to performable length plays published, as was customary, with all the lines that had ever been spoken in various productions during the author's lifetime. And finally, for some of the earlier plays, there is the need for reduction in scale of works composed for performance before audiences of thousands to a size that will not overwhelm an audience of hundreds. These are the most readily apparent adaptations. Others will become apparent as we look more closely at the characteristics of early drama.

Today we have many directors eager to use the classics as springboards for innovative stagings, cutting lines and characters, adding new ones, rearranging scene sequences, and trying hard to bring forth something the like of which no one has ever seen before. At the same time we have scholars who write perceptively about the plays without having seen them on the stage, treating characters as if they were constant from production to production, lines as if they were invariably audible, and the sequence of scenes as if it were inviolable. Their comments can be valuable to one trying to understand the text but confusing to one trying to understand what he has seen on the stage.

Can these conflicting attitudes be reconciled? Probably not. But it ought to be possible to produce a Molière comedy, a Greek tragedy, or an Elizabethan romance bearing a reasonable resemblance to the play the spectator has paid to see and to do it in such a way as to leave most of the patrons satisfied in a manner not too distant from that which the author might plausibly have intended.

No two theatre workers will ever agree as to how this should be accomplished. Nor need they. But they do need to recognize previous producers' problems. Let one example suffice. A favorite of playwrights from Sophocles to Sheridan is the silent character who is also the center of attention. In the printed play this character, who has no lines, is invisible to the reader and often overlooked by him. Yet in performance all eyes are fixed on such a character while the lines of the speaking characters take second place. In studying the script for production it is possible to review volumes of commentary without ever noticing the dramatic possibilities of this central, silent character.

Each director has a unique problem in reaching his audience with the material the author has provided. In order to do this he must first decide what the author intended and then find means of getting it across to his audience. The basic problem is simple enough; it is the material that is dense. But, by drawing upon the experience of others, it is possible to identify particular problems crucial to the success of the production, analyze them, and compare the various solutions adopted by men of genius. It is possible to determine which solutions have succeeded and why. Finally, he can study the noble failures and try to discover where they went wrong.

Ignorance of the errors and triumphs of previous producers is probably the principal cause of failures in the production of premodern drama. One reason for this is that it is practically impossible for a busy theatre worker to see all the productions he ought to see. If he is working steadily most of his time is spent preparing and running the plays from which he derives his livlihood. If he is working independently on Broadway or the West Coast he needs to be available for whatever opportunities come his way. This limits his travel to see particular plays in other production centers such as London and Paris. Of course there are always the libraries, but reading about plays is not the same as seeing them, especially when it comes to nuances such as pace and pointing. The result is that the best and busiest theatre artists do not always know what others have done to solve the problems that can make the difference between success and failure in a particular instance.

This is why I have chosen to go into such detail on matters of staging, setting, lighting, costuming, and properties—elements of production not usually given much attention in discussions of the more elevated aspects of premodern drama.

Inevitably perhaps my approach is conservative: novelty, while a potent factor in compelling audience attention, is short lived. The novelty that electrified yesterday's audience is a soporific for today's. The basic problems attendant in making sure that an audience sees, hears, and understands never change, however. I realize of course that there are many interpretations of these plays, but interpretation is not my main concern. In Sophocles' *Electra*, for example, there are many ways of viewing the characters' motives, but no matter how one views them the play loses power if Clytemnestra's corpse is not positioned on the stage in such a way that all members of the audience can immediately recognize her when Aegisthus removes the covering. It will also lose power if Electra's lament over the urn is not entirely heard and understood. Seeing, hearing, and understanding, these are the basic necessities. Making sure that they are provided is the first responsibility of director, designer, and actor.

A play seen for the first time begins with nothing more than an impression of time and place, then grows scene by scene, episode by episode, into a rich and complex experience. Indeed, it may be so rich and so complex that we cannot fully appreciate it until we have seen it several times, seen several productions, and studied the text in the light of our memories of the performances. The more familiar one becomes with a really great play the more interested one becomes in the art of making it go as it should and the particular problems that have to be solved before a satisfactory whole is achieved.

Here then are the problems. Not all of them, perhaps, for there must be many that I have yet to discover and new ones will certainly come into being as theatrical tastes and modes of production continue to change. In order to provide a frame of reference, I have prefaced the discussion of problems with a description of the characteristics that set off early drama from the drama of our own time. This is then followed with a detailed treatment of eleven premodern plays: *Antigone*; *Electra*; *The Trojan Women*; *The Tragical History of Doctor Faustus*; *Fuente Ovenjuna*; *Volpone*; *The Alchemist*; *Les Fourberies de Scapin*; *Tartuffe*; *She Stoops to Conquer*; *The Rivals*. All of these are plays which I have staged myself at least once and seen in more than one really first-class production of the caliber of the Comédie-Française or the National Theatre of Great Britain.

With such a broad subject the material is certain to range from the simple and obvious to the complex and elusive. I think it likely that every reader will take it differently according to his experience and the degree of his sophistication in regard to the subject.

No attempt has been made to provide a balanced picture of any particular kind of drama or historical period. My subject is theatrical production, not theatre history or dramatic criticism. With one exception (*Fuente Ovejuna*, by Lope de Vega) the plays discussed are those most often produced and hence most available for analysis in terms of production possibilities. Appendix A lists notable modern productions of these plays. Not all of those plays that could be produced profitably are considered in the text, but a list of additional premodern possibles appears in Appendix B.

The omission of Shakespeare's plays from those considered in detail requires some explanation. Originally I included several, but by the time the first draft of the manuscript was completed, the Shakespearean element so overbalanced the subject it became evident that the common practice of considering Shakespeare's plays separately would have to be followed. This is not as great a loss as it might at first seem, for there are far more excellent treatments of Shakespeare's stagecraft than there are for any of the authors dealt with in the book as it now stands. In the discussion of general production problems various of Shakespeare's plays are referred to because I have taken my examples from works most likely to be familiar to the reader. There are also several books on Shakespearean production parts of which are applicable to the whole of Elizabethan theatre practice; these are included in the bibliography.

PART ONE

General Points Regarding Production

CHAPTER 1

Characteristics of Early Drama

It is often difficult for a director or designer of modern drama to adapt his artistry to the very different demands of premodern drama. Modern practice, influenced by the cinema, has accustomed us to attach much greater importance to the physical environment of the performance, and modern stage lighting, so highly responsive to control, has carried us far beyond the basic requirement of visibility which was all that a Greek or an Elizabethan could have hoped for.

Early authors' ideas about the nature and purpose of drama must have made their plays in performance strikingly different from anything we can call modern. One of the most characteristic differences, the notion that every work of temporal art, whether in drama or music, must have a distinct beginning and end, shows up in the popularity of the prologue-epilogue frame which continues for twenty-four hundred years, contrasting strongly with some of our best modern plays which begin casually and end abruptly, incompletely, or unresolved—more lifelike perhaps but aesthetically less satisfying. Another characteristic is the way of conceiving of plot as a linear sequence of cause and effect, so different from many of today's plays which develop circularly with flashbacks and interpolations as episodes surrounding a central thought or character in such a way that one may often not know what the play is about until it is more than half over. A third characteristic is the frequent use of direct address, whether in soliloquy, aside, prologue, epilogue, or choral interlude. Some modern playwrights have recently returned to this (although more often as a narrative than as a dramatic device). Closely related to direct address demanded by the script is the premodern actor's habit of seeking proximity, playing as close to his audience as physical conditions permit. Proximity was no doubt encouraged by the shape of the open stages for which most early dramas were written, which tended to put the actor more nearly among his auditors than in front of them.

The characteristics I have noted so far are generally applicable to all occidental drama up to the middle of the nineteenth century. Other characteristics are conspicuous in early drama but become gradually less so in later dramas. Describing any of these is like shooting at a moving target. Living drama evolves. The more vitality there is in a period of great drama such as the Greek or the Elizabethan the more swiftly it changes. I shall begin therefore with earlier drama and point out the characteristics that mark it. By the beginning of the seventeenth century some practices which had once been universal began to give way to innovations while others simply faded from the picture.

EXPLICITNESS

The explicit nature of early drama is one of its greatest distinctions; it stands at the opposite pole from modern drama which tends to gain much of its interest from suggestion and implication: actions shown and lines spoken which imply more than they show or tell, and this implication of hidden significance enhances the whole. Premodern drama, in contrast, generally attempts to be as explicit as possible. Important decisions and actions are usually shown as completely as the skill of the playwright allows. Characters describe themselves to us and explain their motives, and both self-description and self-explanation agree with what we see them do. We are told in advance what is going to happen and after the event we are told what took place. Superficially, this way of presenting life may seem to be somewhat naive. But this is only the first impression. When all is shown in this way the revelation of character and evolution of plot are enabled to go much further, especially in tragedy, than is possible in later, less forthright forms of drama. In comedy a comparable forthrightness has the happy effect of precipitating the characters headlong into the surprises and reversals which are the sources of our delight. The turns of the plot may be masked from their participants but never from the audience. Modern directors often overlook this characteristic, not realizing that in comedy a surprise is usually much funnier when the audience knows what is ahead while the characters do not. In *Volpone*, for example, every sign indicates that Celia is incorruptible. Only her husband and her would-be seducer believe otherwise. Volpone's failure to recognize her indifference to the pleasures he promises and Corvino's readiness to believe that she is unfaithful form the base of the comic effect. If the director allows her, as many do, to show the slightest sly interest in Volpone's advances, the scenes, although still amusing, are not nearly as funny as they ought to be. The same is true of Elmire's attitude toward the advances of Tartuffe. The joke is on Tartuffe, who cannot believe that Elmire can resist him. The assurance with which she traps him into revealing his true nature not only enhances the absurdity of his efforts but heightens the comedy when her husband, stunned by the discovery of his friend's hypocrisy, fails to come to her rescue as Tartuffe's persistence intensifies. A director experienced solely in modern drama might encourage us to wonder whether Elmire is entirely sincere—this is what one would expect in modern comedy in a similar situation—but by doing so he would blur the irony and diminish the comic effect by trading superior knowledge for guess work.

POETIC DICTION

Another great distinction of premodern drama is in the nature of the language. Whether in Greek, English, Spanish, or French, there is little inclination on the part of the author toward anything resembling everyday speech. By far the greatest number of premodern plays are written in verse. Those which are not actually set down in verse form are couched in language which is poetic in imagery, diction, word order, and everything except rhyme and meter. Falstaff's lines, for example, are written in prose, but in performance they sound like the same highly colored language used by the others who speak in verse. Even when regional accents are used the general character of the language is poetic and vivid rather than plain, rich and articulate rather than prosaic.

From the turn of the century until the late twenties the prevailing fashion in the speaking of verse in plays was to vary the rhythm and break up the longer cadences so as to make the lines sound more like everyday speech. In part this was a carryover from the rather slow delivery necessitated by the poor acoustics and enormous size of nineteenth-century theatres, and in part from the growing popularity of realistic prose drama which influenced the acting style in general. Today poetic language is generally treated as such except in television or in the theatre by a director who has not done his homework.

INTEGRAL MUSIC AND DANCE

Premodern drama is not only poetic but also in almost every instance lyrical, embodying music and dance as elements intrinsic to the total aesthetic effect. In our time it is natural for us to think of "legitimate" drama as being primarily spoken and therefore distinct from opera which is sung and ballet which is danced. But in premodern drama such distinctions are inapplicable. We know for a certainty that ancient Greek drama, both comic and tragic, was sung, chanted, and danced as well as being occasionally spoken.

Opera and ballet came into being as offshoots of drama only a few hundred years ago. Before then practically every play featured music and dance. What would *The Tempest* be without Ariel's songs, the grotesque dance of the monsters, the epithalamium of the three goddesses and the dance of the nymphs and reapers? Or *Othello* without Desdemona's lovely "willow" song and Iago's jolly "Canakin clink, clink?" *Volpone* contains three ballads sung by Nano, as well as the beautiful "Come, my Celia, sung by Volpone himself. Lope de Vega's *Fuente Ovejuna* has at least four dances and as many songs, including a duet by hero and heroine, choruses by the townspeople and odes by the minstrels. Even the plays of eighteenth-century England include ballads: the toast to the Three Jolly Pigeons in *She Stoops to Conquer* and the spirited "Here's to the maiden of bashful fifteen" in *The School for Scandal*.

The modern director will improve the quality of his premodern production if he makes sure that the music and dance are not skimped or glossed over. These lyrical elements are integral; they are not trimmings which he is free to use or not as he chooses. They demand good orchestration, good instrumentation, intelligent choreography, and thorough rehearsal.

MALE PERFORMERS IN FEMALE ROLES

Throughout most of premodern times, from the beginnings well into the seventeenth century, all acting parts, male and female, were written to be played by men. Neither Sophocles nor Shakespeare had ever seen a woman on the stage, nor had they—as far as we know—ever considered the possibility of a woman playing Jocasta or Lady Macbeth. All such parts were played by boys or men in the company, probably those with the smaller frames and lighter voices.

It is difficult to describe in detail the effect this might have had on the treatment of female character, but a few broad generalizations may be made. In the comedies of Aristophanes it is not hard to imagine the comic grotesquery which men would give to the characters of Lysistrata and Myrrhine, or to the women in the *Thesmophoriazusae*. Men playing women in comedy tend to exaggerate traits that appear to them as feminine foibles. Something of the same sort might be expected in the impersonations of the Nurse in *Romeo and Juliet*, Lady Would-Be in *Volpone*, and Margery in *The Shoemakers' Holiday*.

On the other hand, great care would have to be taken with the serious heroines such as Antigone, Cordelia, and Vittoria Corombona in order to make sure that no note of absurdity would creep in to spoil their serious scenes. The audiences were predominently male, and men in the mass tend to see sex as a subject of unlimited hilarity. In serious drama therefore the psychological aspects of love would have to be emphasized. The sexual nature of the feminine characters and of their relationship with the men would have to be soft pedalled lest some slight slip turn the play inside out. Granville-Barker illuminates this problem in the introduction of his *Prefaces to Shakespeare* when he says that "Shakespeare's studies of women seem often to be begun from some spiritual paces beyond the point at which the modern dramatist leaves off." What he says of Shakespeare is equally true of Sophocles and the other Greek authors of tragedy. In this respect one might imagine that the treatment given heroines in oriental drama, most of which is still performed by men, might be instructive as to the style and discretion with which women's parts were once played by men in the drama of the western world.

My own guess is that in our time, when women's roles in these plays are performed by real women the comedies probably lose a good deal of their bawdy vitality while the women's parts in the more serious works—tragedy, history, romance—gain subtlety and emotional power. At the same time, Granville-Barker's parting advice is worth committing to memory: "Let the usurping actress remember that her sex is a liability, not an asset. Shakespeare has left no blank spaces for her to fill in with her charms."

OUTDOOR DAYLIGHT PERFORMANCE

The final characteristic that applies to most popular drama up to about 1600, although its influence continues much longer, is that the playwright composed his work to be performed out of doors in broad daylight. All the plays of antiquity were produced in outdoor theatres, several of which have been restored so that today we can occasionally see plays performed in them and see how they work out. The inn-yard theatres of the Elizabethan and Spanish are known in general to everyone. Indoor performances did not become commonplace until well into the seventeenth century.

A poet writing for outdoor performance would have to provide lines that would carry above the inevitable sounds of wind, traffic, children playing, sheep bleating on the neighboring hillside, and disquieting thunder. He might also, especially in England, have had to provide in his play some places where the performance could be interrupted, in case of a sudden change in the weather, without destroying the continuity. Furthermore under ordinary conditions of outdoor performance he could not count on the undivided attention of his audience all of the time and so in order to make sure that everyone could follow the story he would be inclined to overwrite somewhat, repeating or elaborating important exposition and points upon which the plot turned. One result of this is that most early dramatists after the Greeks tend to give us a great deal more play than we need, especially for an indoor performance where the audience is shielded from distraction and able to concentrate.

The natural advantages of outdoor performance are probably beyond recapture in any indoor situation. The feeling of openness and freedom with the consequent holiday spirit is certainly one of them. For the Greek theatre the magnificent views of valley and mountainside beyond the acting area can scarcely be recreated indoors. In all outdoor theatres, Greek as well as Elizabethan, the resonance which open air gives to the human voice makes poetic diction quite natural.

Being out of doors, the plays were necessarily performed by daylight. If one of the scenes was supposed to be taking place at night the audience had to be told in advance by someone coming on with a torch. Torches, candles, and lanterns conventionally symbolize darkness in the texts which have come down to us. Lady Macbeth enters for her sleepwalking scene carrying "a light." Banquo, hurrying home after sundown, is preceded by Fleance carrying a torch. Desdemona and Imogen both have bedside candles lighted. Brutus in his tent sits reading by the light of a taper.

When drama moved indoors candles and oil lamps made it possible for the audience to see. But candles are not easily dimmed on cue (although Italian scenic artists succeeded in doing so for their court spectacles) so that both stage and auditorium remained lighted throughout the performance as brightly as was possible with the illuminants of the time. As a result we have a situation in which the actor is always able to see his auditors and their reactions, an immense advantage, as every public speaker knows. Even more interesting is the fact that the spectators are able to see everything that goes on in the supposedly dark scenes even when the characters are unable to do so. Thus the audience sees Fleance escape after the torch is struck out of his hand by his father's assailants while the supposed darkness conceals him from them. In *Othello*, when Cassio is ambushed in the dark by Roderigo, we are able to see what Roderigo cannot: that Cassio is wearing a cuirass which will frustrate the blade of his would-be murderer.

Comedies seldom have night scenes, but every once in a while we are confronted with one where darkness, being imaginary, poses especially difficult problems for both actors and lighting technicians. There is one of these in *Midsummer Night's Dream* and another in *She Stoops to Conquer*.

The plays of ancient Greece have come down to us without stage directions so we do not know how many might have used torches to symbolize darkness. There are several—*Antigone*, *The Choephori*, *The Trojan Women*, and Sophocles' *Electra*—which seem to begin before dawn and can be played effectively with torches. The *Agamemnon* actually opens with a description of night giving way to daybreak.

CHANGING CHARACTERISTICS

Early in the seventeeth-century performances began to be moved indoors, at first in Spain through the roofing over of outdoor theatres, then in England by the erection of "private" theatres, and finally by the building of popular theatres of increasingly greater seating capacity. With the spectators protected from the weather a more continual repertory came into being. Artificial light made possible performances in the evening instead of during the working day. Enclosure of auditorium and stage shut out much extraneous noise and probably encouraged closer attention to the performance.

Beginning in Spain we see women in plays for the first time, usually in romantic leads. By the middle of the seventeenth century the practice had spread to France and soon afterward became common in England. Men continued to play the hags and harridans well into the eighteenth century but the appearance of women in roles of high tragedy heralded a change in interpretation which has continued to our own day.

Music and dance continued to be frequent components but gradually became less important. Some plays, such as *Tartuffe*, contain neither. In others, like *She Stoops to Conquer* and *Le Malade imaginaire*, they appear as additions or interpolations.

Invention rather than familiarity of plot had always characterized comedy as contrasted with tragedy. But as the comic playwrights of the seventeenth and eighteenth centuries more completely mastered the lessons of their Roman models, plots with unpredictable endings came brilliantly into being. The technique of such plotting is basically simple. Starting with some misunderstanding such as might arise from mistaken identity, disguise, or deliberate deception, the playwright contrives a workable conclusion, then fills in the space between with as many contretemps as his ingenuity can contrive, positioning them in the progression according to effectiveness with the funniest ones furthest along so that as the play unfolds each scene exceeds its predecessors and the confusion grows as the evening goes on. When all the comic possibilities have been exhausted the solution is uncovered, the characters rejoice, and the play ends.

The use of a plot in which the outcome cannot be foreseen by the spectator encourages the dramatist to insert a few surprises along the way, sudden turns in the progression or changes of direction counter to the expectation of the audience. For example, in *The Alchemist* the outcries of Dapper from inside the house surprise the audience as much as the characters in the street outside. In *Tartuffe* the reaction of Tartuffe to Damis' denunciation is quite unexpected and the suspense generated by Orgon's failure to emerge from his hiding place under the table is genuine. In *The Rivals* Lydia's disappointment upon discovering that her dear Ensign Beverley is actually Jack Absolute, although typical of her, is quite unexpected.

CHAPTER 2

Problems in Transforming the Text of a Classic Into Performable Material

When one begins to be interested in producing a premodern drama he soon discovers that the play exists, not in one text but in many, often quite different from one another. Plays that have been with us a very long time, as these have, have undergone much editing, many printings, and many public performances, every one of which has introduced some variation or "improvement." In order to gain a clear view of the author's intention one has to compare the various texts and through them attempt to discern the original.

COMPARING TEXTS AND TRANSLATIONS

Plays of the Elizabethan age have come down to us in a wild variety of texts. Only a few, like *The Tempest* and the works of Ben Jonson, were carefully printed from authors' manuscripts. Most of the texts which we now have are the result of editors' collations of different texts: authors' "fair" copies, playhouse scripts dog-eared with use, and pirated versions compiled from actors' side-books and memories. When these are placed side by side one printing will often supply what others lack or make sense of lines otherwise unintelligible.

A play composed in a language other than English is likely to be found in a number of different translations, made at different times by different translators having different ideas as to what expressions in English most effectively convey the author's intention.

Yet a translation which seems to express the author's intention has met only the first of several requirements. The requirement for the actor is that the lines be eminently speakable. The requirement for the audience is that the lines be understood without difficulty, that the ear be pleased with their sound, and that they linger in the mind as music does after they have been heard. These qualities are not easily achieved, especially in a translation, but they are qualities which are present in the original and the best translations generally manage to convey the quality of the original as well as its sense.

What is true of a Greek classic is equally true of one by Molière or Lope de Vega. The problems of rendering a play into English may differ with the language but the ultimate objectives in regard to actor and audience remain the same.

In comparing translations one quickly becomes aware of the influence of the dramatic taste of the translator's own time upon vocabulary and style of expression. Lines in comedies which were originally couched in something like vernacular seem to have a deadly affinity for English slang and this dates them badly after a few years. Tragedies which in the late nineteenth century were translated into elaborate theatrical language are now often put into speech at the extreme opposite, seeming almost telegraphic in terseness. Occasionally the favored English usages prove hospitable to certain foreign works, as the language of eighteenth-century England still does to Molière's comedies, but this is exceptional.

In some of the Greek plays no single translation comes close to expressing the true quality of the lines in actable terms. Lines that look splendid on the page sometimes turn out to be tongue twisters impossible for an actor to speak with a straight face. In this case the only recourse for the director is to consult other translations. If at this point he can enlist the aid of a classical scholar possessing an intimate understanding of the original the result will be better. Fortunately a great many translations are in the public domain. If the production is based on one which is still under copyright it must of course be produced exactly as printed and the author's royalty duly paid.

In the process of selecting a text one is certain to come across numerous adaptations and "versions" prepared by writers who could not read the original language. These must be treated with extreme caution. Occasionally in comedy one will be useable. In tragedy a careful translation is practically always better.

CONTINUITY AND TEMPORAL PROGRESSION

One of the most consistent characteristics of premodern drama is the continuity of its action: continuity from scene to scene and often from act to act also, uninterrupted by blackout, drop curtain, or time out for scene changes. In early drama scene follows scene in unbroken progression, sometimes with one intermission, sometimes with none. The settings indicated by editors: "A Plain Before the Walls of Troy," "Venice, a Street," "The Countryside Near Cuidad Real," or "A Room in Orgon's House," are nothing more than interpolations to aid the reader. The drawing of a curtain to cover the changing of scenery or properties was unknown to drama until the end of the seventeenth century, and, except for court masques, infrequent for a hundred years more. When the locale of the action was significant it is mentioned in the lines. Otherwise no reference is necessary. When a transition from one locale or unit of action to a different one is effected it is usually provided for in the lines. Variety in the progression from unit to unit is attained by contrasts in tempo, scale, or character of the units juxtaposed.

Continuity is unbroken, with each scene following directly upon the heels of its predecessor. In Elizabethan and Spanish drama the characters of one scene will be making their entrances while those of the preceding scene are still on their way out. The last line of one scene is the cue for the first line of the next as if they were both lines in the same scene. This ties the whole sequence together so that we become less conscious of scenes as separate units and more conscious of the progression as a whole.

In Greek drama the alternation of chorus and episode provides variety. In Elizabethan and Stuart drama a lively scene of action is often followed by a quiet one, a scene with many characters by a scene with few. In French seventeenth-century drama a *liaison*, or linkage, achieved by continuing one or more characters into the succeeding scene, reinforces the continuity; when none continue and the stage falls empty it serves as a signal that the act has ended and another is about to begin.

Pauses between acts are characteristic only of later periods of premodern drama. They seem to perform a function comparable to that of the pause between the movements of a symphony, separating the phases of the work to remind us that it has clear-cut parts and is composed according to a definite plan.

Any properties or scenery that need to be changed are best changed without curtain or blackout or interruption of the lines. The audience quickly becomes accustomed to this and no loss of illusion is suffered. Modern productions that separate the scenes by means of blackouts or curtains chop the play into pieces and make it seem slow. Even worse is the practice of holding up the action while costumed actors change set dressings with little bits of cunning byplay, for this not only interrupts the progression but introduces an element foreign to the continuity intended by the author.

There is no reason why elaborate and elegant settings cannot be used, but they must be designed in such a way that the change from one to another can be effected without interrupting the progression or interfering with the audibility of the lines. In the court masques of Shakespeare's day there were many such changes or "revelations" achieved through sliding, folding, or revolving scenic units, and the same devices can be used today where, in certain plays such as *The Tempest* and *Doctor Faustus*, impressive visual effects enhance the whole.

PREPARING THE TEXT FOR PERFORMANCE, ABRIDGEMENT

Cutting of lines becomes necessary when the text is too long to be performed within comfortable limits. It ought not to be practiced for any other purpose: not to "improve" the plot, reduce the size of the cast, nor simplify the designer's problems. The plays are classics of long standing, widely known and well-loved. Their authors are the greatest our culture has produced. We who stage their works are interpreters, not playwrights of comparable talent. It is absurd to think that we can improve the creations of genius by cutting and slashing the texts according to some individual notion of perfection. Granville-Barker, in the introduction to his *Prefaces to Shakespeare*, expresses the principle very well:

> We cut and carve the body of the play to its peril. It may be robustly, but it may be very delicately organized . . . and some of us, perhaps, are not such very skillful surgeons; nor is any surgeon to be recommended who operates for his own convenience.
>
> . . .
>
> The blue pencil is a dangerous weapon; and its use grows on a man, for it solves too many little difficulties far too easily.

Fifty or sixty years ago it was common practice, when producing any premodern play, to "adapt" it to the proscenium stage and elaborate settings by cutting the text to a fraction of its original length and rearranging the scene sequence to reduce the number of set changes. Several intermissions of fifteen and sometimes even twenty minutes were often needed to change the scenery. In the 1928 production of *Macbeth* for which Gordon Craig designed the settings, nearly an hour of the more than three-hour performance was occupied in changing the massive sets, an hour which had to be gained by abridging the text.

In recent years the development of theatres with open stages and vomitory entrances has made possible such swift and continuous progression that the need for such cutting has been greatly reduced.

Another development even more recent has weakened the impulse to doctor the script. This, for better or worse, has been the change in taste as to language acceptable in public performances. Today the four-letter words are no longer shocking and it is no longer necessary to excise the Elizabethan bawdry for fear of offending the audience. Much of Aristophanes' comedy may still seem gratuitously coarse but it no longer makes the play unproducible.

This leaves us with only the problem of the play's length, for once we realize that problems of staging, translation, and interpretation cannot be solved honestly by cutting we see that a great many premodern plays require no cutting at all. The plays of the Greeks, for example, are quite short. Some of them are scarcely longer than long one-acts. The average Greek tragedy, even when performed in English, seldom fills more than two hours. The longest one, Sophocles' *Electra*, takes only a little more than two and a half hours with one intermission. Molière's plays come in all lengths, but none is longer than the average modern play. Plays of the Spanish Golden Age, as well as those of the English Restoration and eighteenth-century are almost uniformly two and a half hours in the playing.

The only period therefore in which plays consistently need cutting for length is the Elizabethan. We would not even have any problem with these if the texts were printed as performed on the stage, but except in a few instances they are not. The printed versions of most Elizabethan plays, like those of most contemporary plays published in hard cover, contain all the lines the author wrote, plus variations and alternative lines composed for different productions and different casts. The object of the publisher, then as now, was to give the reader his money's worth, not to give him the mere text of the play he had seen on the stage; and to give the journeyman actor who purchased the book as addition to his library of possible parts all of the lines he was likely ever to have to memorize in any of the roles he might be hired to play. The result is that many of the printed plays are over a thousand lines longer than can be performed in a normal evening in the theatre. Some are twice as long. The Second Quarto of *Hamlet* carries on its title page the boast that it is "enlarged to almost as much againe as it was," that is, twice as long as the First Quarto which is generally believed to have been pirated from a playhouse copy. Thus we are often faced with the problem of making a performance script by reducing the text to two-thirds its original length without violating the author's intention.

The principles according to which plays can be cut down in length without destroying the author's creation are fairly well known and generally agreed upon. Here are three of them:

1. Retain all the scenes in the sequence in which they exist in the original. Each scene is an integral part of the progression, contributing to plot movement, to variety, and to general aesthetic effect. Cutting out a scene or changing its position in the progression weakens the total effect.

2. Retain all plot elements in the original proportion. If the play has three plots, like *The Tempest*, all three must be treated in order to maintain the variety and balance of the original. If it has two plots, like *The Changeling*, or *A Woman Killed With Kindness*, then the balance between them must be retained in the way that the author composed it.

3. Retain all characters in their proportional importance. There are many characters which at first seem superfluous (Reynaldo in *Hamlet*, Sir Politic Would-Be in *Volpone*, Furnace in *A New Way to Pay Old Debts*). But every one of these has a purpose. It is much better to keep all the characters and double-up the acting assignments to reduce the number of actors needed; this will give the minor actors more to do while the audience will feel that it is finally seeing the whole play.

The cutting need not be the same in all roles as long as the balance is kept. Hamlet's part, for example, can be cut nearly in half before anyone in the audience will begin to miss anything. The actor's feeling in the matter may confront the director with a problem of a different kind, a problem of diplomacy which each director is going to have to solve in his own way.

One has to be very careful in trimming parts whose function it is to link scenes and bridge time lapses. Elizabethan playwrights are not always as careful as they might be in their treatment of these connective scenes. Often close study is necessary in order to discover the provisions for indicating passage of time in what seem at first glance to be trivial lines.

When one finally begins to cut, which lines should be the first to go? Obviously those which are most likely to be misunderstood because of changes in vocabulary or pronunciation. An instance of this is Desdemona's line in *Othello* (IV–iii–12): "He says he will return incontinent." What she means is that he says that he will return immediately. The meaning of the word "incontinent" has changed. To leave it as is merely confuses an audience.

Next to go are the tongue twisters which trip and betray the actors, lines like Chapman's "Shrink up his cursed eyes With tortuous darkness, such as stands in hell . . ." or Webster's ". . . cities plagued with plagues."

Third, in order of dispensability, are most of the puns, especially those which crop up in the middle of serious speeches or tragic scenes. A good example occurs in *Julius Caesar* (III–i–204) where Antony, mourning the death of Caesar, exclaims:

> Here wast thou bay's brave hart;
> Here didst thou fall; and here thy hunters stand,
> Sign'd in thy spoil, and crimson'd in thy lethe.
> O world, thou wast the forest to this hart;
> And this, indeed, O world, the heart of thee.

THE ART OF INTRALINEAR CUTTING

When a play is several hours overlong one is going to have to cut more than obscurities, tongue twisters and puns in order to reduce the work to performable length. Fortunately Elizabethan playwrights tend to fill their lines with parenthetical additions, multiple dependent clauses, interjections, digressions, and illustrations far beyond need. Some, as in the plays of Ben Jonson, are put in to make the play appear more scholarly in print than would have been possible in performance. Many of the "who," "when," and "where" clauses, multiple metaphors, and parenthetical comments can be cut without altering the sense of the line or impairing its poetic quality. The technique by means of which this is accomplished is called "intralinear," that is, cutting *within* lines to reduce the length of a speech without spoiling its rhythm or sense.

Here is an example from *Volpone* (III–viii–239): Celia's plea to Volpone as it might be read in performance. Six lines have been cut from a speech originally twenty-one lines in length.

> If you have ears that may be pierced—or eyes
> That can be opened—a heart that may be touched—
> Do me the grace to let me 'scape: —if not,

Be bountiful and kill me.
I am a creature hither ill betrayed,
By one whose shame I would forget it were:
If you will deign me neither of these graces,
Yet feed your wrath, sir, rather than your lust,
And punish that unhappy crime of nature,
Which you miscall my beauty; flay my face,
Or poison it with ointments for seducing
Your blood to this rebellion: anything
That will disfavor me, save in my honor—
And I will kneel to you, pray for you, pay down
A thousand hourly vows, sir, for your health. . . .

The speech has been reduced by nearly one-third, but it would be a very rare member of the audience who could spot the excisions. As for the actor, the deletions have certainly made the speech easier to speak and its spirit easier to put across.

The art of cutting a classic for performance is not mastered overnight. It takes practice and close study of the cuts that have been made in great productions of the past, tempered by close listening in the theatre and hurrying home to compare the lines just heard with those in the book.

A play can be said to be well cut when the most knowledgeable member of the audience misses nothing in the performance of a work he knows and loves, and when the average well-read playgoer feels that he is seeing and hearing the play just as it came from the author's hand.

Plays in iambic pentameter generally average about an hour of performance time for each thousand lines of verse. Commercial productions of classics therefore are likely to total nearer two thousand than three thousand lines. Productions of the summer festival theatres are usually longer and more complete. Productions by university theatres can be any length; the nearer they come to embracing the whole printed text the more completely they fill their educational function. There is a limit however to the length of the performance an audience can be expected to endure, and this length is not much longer than three hours. Exceptions to this rule are rare and seem acceptable more as novelties than as regular practice. John Barrymore's *Hamlet*, with one intermission, lasted until nearly midnight and was seldom tedious. Maurice Evans' production of the uncut First Folio *Hamlet* ran about four and a half hours. That this length would be acceptable with other less well-known plays, such as *The White Devil* or *A New Way to Pay Old Debts*, I very much doubt.

Intralinear cutting is like pruning a tree. One cuts off twigs and suckers, trims out dead wood and crossed limbs, trying to maintain the shape of the tree and leaving uncut the branches with the best buds or most promising fruit.

For an example, here is the opening speech of Iago in the first scene of *Othello*, printed first as it is most often cut for performance and afterward as it appears in the First Folio (with the spelling modernized):

> Three great ones of the city,
> In personal suit to make me his lieutenant,
> Off-capped to him,
> But he, as loving his own pride and purposes,
> Non suits my mediators; for 'Certes,' says he,
> 'I have already chose my officer.'
> And what was he?
> One Michael Cassio, a Florentine
> That never set a squadron in the field,
> Nor the division of a battle knows
> More than a spinster. But he, sir, had th' election;
> And I (of whom his eyes had seen the proof
> At Rhodes, at Cyprus), must be belee'd and calm'd
> By debitor and creditor.
> He must his lieutenant be,
> And I (God bless the mark!) his Moorship's ensign.

And here is the original, uncut:

> Three great ones of the city,
> In personal suit to make me his lieutenant,
> Off-capped to him; and by the faith of man,
> I know my price, I am worth no worse a place.
> But he, as loving his own pride and purposes,
> Evades them with bombast circumstance,
> Horribly stuff'd with epithets of war;
> And, in conclusion,
> Non suits my mediators; for 'Certes,' says he,
> I have already chose my officer.'
> And what was he?
> Forsooth, a great arithmetician,
> One Michael Cassio, a Florentine
> (A fellow almost damn'd in a fair wife),
> That never set a squadron in the field,
> Nor the division of a battle knows
> More than a spinster; unless the bookish theoric,
> Wherein the toged consuls can propose
> As masterly as he. Mere prattle, without practice,
> Is all his soldiership. But he, sir, had the 'election,
> And I (of whom his eyes had seen the proof
> At Rhodes, at Cyprus, and on other grounds
> Christian and heathen), must be belee'd and calm'd
> By debitor and creditor, this counter-caster.
> He (in good time!) must his lieutenant be,
> And I (God bless the mark!) his Moorship's ancient.

The pruning of dialogue requires considerably more care for not only must the rhythm of the verse be maintained but the dialogue must retain its original coherence: one speech must provide an appropriate cue for the one that follows and the link between statement or question and response must be clear. Careless cutting is likely to leave questions without answers, or worse, answers to questions which have not been asked. Here is an example of dialogue from *Othello*, (II–iii–188) in which Othello, roused from his bed by the melee among his officers, demands the cause of the commotion:

Othello: How comes it, Michael, you are thus forgot?

Cassio: I pray you pardon me. I cannot speak.

Othello: Worthy Montano, what's the matter
    That you unlace your reputation thus
    And spend your rich opinion for the name
    Of a night brawler?

Montano: Worthy Othello, I am hurt to danger.
    Your officer, Iago, can inform you,
    While I spare speech.

Othello: Now, by heaven,
    My blood begins my safer guides to rule.
    If once I stir
    Or do but lift this arm, the best of you
    Shall sink in my rebuke. Give me to know
    How this foul rout began. Iago, who began't?

Iago: Touch me not so near.
    I had rather have this tongue cut from my mouth
    Than it should do offense to Michael Cassio.

And here is the same speech in its original form:

Othello: How comes it, Michael, you are thus forgot?

Cassio: I pray you pardon me. I cannot speak.

Othello: Worthy Montano, you were wont to be civil;
    The gravity and stillness of your youth
    The world hath noted, and your name is great
    In mouths of wisest censure. What's the matter
    That you unlace your reputation thus
    And spend your rich opinion for the name
    Of a night-brawler? Give me answer to't.

Montano: Worthy Othello, I am hurt to danger.
    Your officer, Iago, can inform you,
    While I spare speech, which something now offends me,
    Of all that I do know; nor know I aught
    By me that's said or done amiss this night,
    Unless self-charity be sometimes a vice,
    When violence assails us.

Othello: Now, by heaven,

My blood begins my safer guides to rule,
And passion, having my best judgement collied,
Assay to lead the way. If once I stir
Or do but lift this arm, the best of you
Shall sink in the rebuke. Give me to know
How this foul rout began, who set it on;
And he that is approv'd in this offence,
Though he had twinn'd with me, both at a birth,
Shall lose me. What! in a town of war,
Yet wild, the people's hearts brimful of fear,
To manage private and domestic quarrel?
Tis monstrous. Iago, who began't?

Montano: If partially affin'd or leagu'd in office,
Thou dost deliver more or less than truth,
Thou art no soldier.

Iago: Touch me not so near.
I had rather have this tongue cut from my mouth
Than it should do offense to Michael Cassio.

The art of intralinear cutting is not limited to plays of the Elizabethan period. The same method can be applied to plays of any age. Some of the sev-
enteenth- and eighteenth-century English comedies tend to be rather verbose.
These can often gain clarity and force through judicious cutting. Here is an
example from *The Rivals* (I-ii):

Lydia: But you know I lose most of my fortune if I marry without my aunt's consent;
and that is what I have determined to do, ever since I knew the penalty.

Julia: Nay, this is caprice!

Lydia: What, does Julia tax me with caprice? For this long year you have been slave
to the caprice, the whim, the jealousy of this ungrateful Faulkland, who will ever
delay assuming the right of a husband while you suffer him to be equally imperious
as a lover.

Julia: Nay, you are wrong entirely. He is too proud, too noble, to be jealous; if he is
captious, 'tis without dissembling; if fretful, without rudeness. Unused to the fop-
peries of love, he is negligent of the little duties expected of a lover. His affection
is ardent and sincere; as it engrosses his whole soul, he expects every thought and
emotion of his mistress to move in unison with his.

Compare the above with the lines in the standard printed text and see the difference, best tested by reading aloud.

One might expect that the most vehement objections to abridgement would
come from scholars and critics, but this is not usually the case. Those most
familiar with the plays are often the most enthusiastic supporters of any sincere
and reasonably sensitive attempt to stage the plays. Those most likely to object
to cutting are the actors who speak the lines. Actors like roles with plenty of

good long speeches. As far as the average actor is concerned there is no such thing as a part which is too long or too wordy. I am sure no actor who reads this will take offense because no actor ever thinks of himself as average.

In order to forestall the actor's objections to having his lines abridged it is essential that the whole process of preparing the text and timing the results be completed before the play is announced for production. If this is done the performers who are competing for parts will be able to read from the script they are going to be working on, and therefore the shortening is completed before the actor begins to think of the part as his.

There is no guarantee of course that no one will ask to have certain cuts restored or that someone will not want to include lines which he spoke happily in some other production of the same play. It requires a resolute spirit to keep saying no to requests of this kind. Even so, it is not unheard of for lines to be spoken in performance which had not been included in rehearsal. Sometimes this is unavoidable: an actor forgets a phrase and has to repeat half a page in order to get back on the right track; the interesting thing about it is that while lines may be inadvertently added it is rare for lines to be inadvertently omitted.

Cutting, changes, or lines added after the work has begun can be counted on to confuse not only the performers but the prompter and stage crews as well. A firm unequivocal script in which all cuts stay that way and in which everyone knows what lines to expect is certainly one of the most dependable characteristics of a workmanlike production. Only with such a script can one minimize the inevitable misunderstandings regarding light cues, property shifts, and costume changes and emerge with a smooth run, well rehearsed, production.

CHAPTER 3

Typical Problems of Casting Premodern Plays

Choosing the cast for a classic is usually an agreeable chore. Performers take to the material, for there is a thrill in trying out for roles which are widely known and in which great actors of past generations have made theatrical history. The lines, whether in verse or in prose, sound good when read aloud, even the first time, and most of the parts are so contrived as to enable an actor to indicate the main features of a character on his first attempt.

THE PRIMACY OF DICTION

There are many ways in which the casting of a premodern play differs from that of a contemporary work. For one thing, the actor has to have better diction than he generally needs for more recent compositions. Most premodern plays are written in verse, and the speaking of verse requires not only a sensitive feeling for rhythm and melody but also better enunciation than prose. Old plays contain many archaisms which, although charming in themselves, make understanding difficult for the listener unless they are rendered with considerable skill. Furthermore, poetic plays contain many speeches which, while magnificent, are much longer than those in modern works; in order to do them justice the actor needs more lung power and the ability to vary both cadence and pitch. He must be able to sustain and color passages of great length without losing the sense of momentum. With these requirements uppermost in the casting it is not surprising that English actors are so often preferred for the classics. The English educational system seems to put more emphasis on enunciation and correct use of the vocal mechanism than is customary in American schools. English dramatic academies generally insist upon rigorous speech training, in contrast to American ones which tend to give greater value to body training and mime.

When one listens closely to the speech of laymen one discovers that a high proportion have defects which would disqualify them from consideration for any speaking part in premodern drama. A surprisingly large number cannot make a proper "s" sound; instead they substitute "th" or "sh" or simply skip the "s" entirely. Some of these faults afflict actors too. None of those with defective sibillants can be considered for parts in a verse play. When verse or archaic language is spoken from the stage defects of this kind are magnified and they quickly ruin a performance. Can you imagine Marc Antony with a lisp? With determination most of the commoner defects can be corrected, but not usually within the four or five weeks occupied by rehearsals.

The second most common defect, especially among Americans, is the tight jaw. This causes a speaker not only to neglect his enunciation but also to render his vowel sounds with too harsh a gutteral, which in turn makes his voice hard and, in speeches of more than three or four sentences, monotonous; the necessary color and variety in the speaking of verse lies quite out of his reach. An actor with a tight jaw can be quite effective in prose, provided his speeches are short, and in certain roles may even gain forcefulness. But the impression of forcefulness caused by a tight jaw should never betray one into casting such an actor in a speaking part in poetic drama where melody and variety are essential in speeches of some length.

The ability to sustain audience interest throughout a long speech is always the result of assiduous practice; it is not a gift of nature. We listen, fascinated, to the discourse of an accomplished actor and it seems as if it is his personality which is charming us. Actually, we are responding to the art of the playwright who composed the language he speaks and partly to the skill of the actor who by artful inflection and phrasing is making the role clear to us. This level of artistry cannot be attained during the time that most plays are in rehearsal. Consequently one soon learns not to cast any actor, no matter how appealing, in the hope that time will enable him to meet the oral demands of a role by developing skill which he does not possess during casting.

BALANCING THE ORAL ENSEMBLE

Less complicated than the problem of individual diction but equally important to the final result is the contrast between voices. In order to have interesting and colorful dialogue one must have a wide range of voice qualities in the cast. Of course all must have clear enunciation and good rhythm, but no scene should include two speakers whose voices have the same resonance, timbre, or optimum pitch. Furthermore, in scenes involving two or three characters the contrast in voice quality should be as great as possible. If Oedipus has a baritone speaking voice, Creon has to be a bass or a tenor if the quarrel between them is to satisfy; it cannot succeed if both have the same kind of voice. Volpone and Mosca may not under any circumstances have voices of similar quality; they have too many scenes together and these scenes will be dull unless they can provide vocal variety.

APPEARANCE AND BEARING

If ideal conditions prevailed during casting all the contestants would be persons of good bearing, well-proportioned physique, and graceful movement. All would have legs that would look good bare, in tights, or in tight breeches. There would be no flat feet, knobby elbows, short necks, or thick midriffs. As it is, one may expect to see such actors only in the Comédie, the Royal Shakespeare Company, and occasionally in the festival at Stratford, Ontario.

Matters of appearance must necessarily yield priority to matters of diction and voice, yet the parts must be cast in such a way that brilliant delivery not be compromised by unfortunate physique or graceless bearing; what the audience sees must be in harmony with what it hears. Because an actor's appearance produces a stronger first impression in tryouts than his speech, one is tempted to overvalue appearance. To counteract this temptation it is worth remembering that an actor's looks, no matter how good, cannot sustain him in a long and difficult role as well as a good voice properly used. Appearance creates the first impression but it is up to delivery to maintain it.

A clever costumer can do a lot to ameliorate physical flaws such as skinny legs and knock knees through the design of boots, trunk hose, or breeches. Flat feet can be made to look almost normal by means of specially constructed footwear. An exceptionally clever costumer can even overcome that most disturbing flaw, a short neck. But it is best not to depend too much on the costumer for he may not be inclined in every instance to adapt his costume to an actor's shortcomings; he may be more concerned with problems of his own, related to the "feel" of the period or the ensemble effect of his costumes. Or it may be that the costumes, instead of being specially built for the particular play, are being rented, in which case almost nothing can be counted on to help an individual actor's oddities of physique.

SINGING, DANCING, AND FENCING

Many of the roles in premodern drama demand professional competence in singing, dancing, and fencing, as well as the playing of musical instruments. There are to be sure the familiar singing parts such as Ariel in *The Tempest*, Feste in *Twelfth Night*, and Nano in *Volpone*. But there are also many lovely lyrics written into major roles where the actor must build a scene and cap it with a song. These songs are much too lovely to be talked or half sung and much too good to be omitted. Among them are Desdemona's "willow" song (*Othello*, IV–iii), Volpone's "Come, my Celia," (*Volpone*, IV–vii), and Anne Frankford's lute song (*A Woman Killed With Kindness*, scene XIV, line 37).

The freedom with which playwrights call for songs makes it appear that good singing voices must have been plentiful in every acting company. Therefore when producing these plays today, if we are to do them justice we must cast actors of comparable singing ability.

In the plays of ancient Greece and Rome songs are abundant. In the tragedies there are many passages which are quite clearly intended to be chanted or sung or recited to the accompaniment of wood winds. I have not had the opportunity to experiment with this as much as I would have liked, but on the several occasions when I have been blessed with both good singing voices and a gifted musical director the results have been truly electrifying.

The comedies of Greece and Rome contain many more musical numbers than are indicated in contemporary translations. In fact, the comedies of Aristophanes are much more like modern musical shows than the ancient farces we tend to take them for. Some of the songs in Aristophanes' works are really beautiful rather than comical and seem to be introduced to give to the whole an aesthetic quality tempering and balancing the gross obscenity of the gags. One of my favorites is parabasis in *The Birds*, 678–800.

The dances in the plays, although numerous and varied, need not affect the casting very much beyond the necessity for avoiding those who appear to have two left feet. The great majority are capable of mastering any of the steps and figures of the court or country dances during a normal rehearsal period if the dance director is any good at all.

Fencing is a different matter. In any cast there are likely to be a few actors who are incurably "point-shy," who cannot bear to face a pointed weapon and are therefore unable to keep from wincing or blinking when an opponent attacks. To realize late in rehearsals that one has cast an actor with this affliction in any of the parts in the Macduff-Macbeth duel, the Posthumous-Iachimo encounter, or the Hal-Hotspur fight, is to glimpse a catastrophe which only the most expert staging can avert. The other side of this coin is the brilliant and memorable exchange which occurs when both actors in such a scene have real talent for sword play. But the deficiencies and talents which I mention here can be discovered during auditions by putting the contestants through two or three simple passes with the weapons to be used, making sure of course to protect them with masks and gloves. Actors generally enjoy this kind of test during tryouts even when they are not very good with the weapons on first acquaintance.

CASTING THE FEMALE ROLES

Today's producers of premodern drama have one problem that the original producers did not have. This is the problem of casting the feminine roles. Until the seventeenth century men played the women's roles in every country except Spain. The original part of Antigone was composed for a man. The role of Helen of Troy in *Doctor Faustus*, as well as the one in *The Trojan Women*, was written for a man. Juliet's part was written for a man, as was Medea, the Duchess in *The Duchess of Malfi*, Mistress Eyre in *The Shoemakers' Holiday*, and hundreds of others too numerous to name.

In casting a woman in one of these parts the qualities to look for are those which would have helped to make a young man convincing in the role rather than those qualities specifically making a woman effective. Among these would certainly be a light voice, small stature, delicate features, fine complexion, and grace of movement. Big women with hour-glass figures and husky voices need not apply. In fact, a distinctly feminine sexy quality often creates problems. Occasionally a motherly quality is hinted at in the text, as in the role of Lady Macbeth, or Jocasta in *Oedipus the King*, but it is never more than a hint, never more than a young man could suggest without danger of absurdity. On the other hand we have many women such as Juliet, Imogen, Miranda, Rosalind, Dame Pliant, Lady Allworth, and Bel-Imperia, whose most appealing quality is a charming forthrightness that could easily have been rendered by a boy.

Fortunately the draped costumes of antiquity and the puffed hose of Elizabethan England concealed the body so completely as to make masculine and feminine figures indistinguishable except for the feet. If the costumes of some period other than that in which the play was written are to be used, care will have to be taken that blatant femininity, which was not a feature of the original, does not take attention away from more important things.

There are many premodern plays in which heroines disguise themselves as boys, a thing which would have been easy in the dress of the time. In the Spanish theatre, where the feminine roles were played by women, this was considered risqué and several royal edicts forbade it, but as it was popular with audiences the ban seems not to have been very strictly enforced.

In the English theatre, since the girl who assumes the dress of a man is already a male, the situation would have been very different, for the supposed disguise could be expected to make the impersonation more believable. The "heroine" assuming masculine attire could do so with confidence that the imposture would not be betrayed by bosomy curves, a plump thigh, or small feet, so that the hero upon whom the deception was being practiced would not seem to the audience to be either nearsighted or incredibly unobserving.

Today when a woman plays one of these parts the temptation to use the masculine costume to show off a few feminine curves is apparently irresistible. Many theatregoers remember Katherine Hepburn's *As You Like It*; what they remember most vividly is not usually her acting but her shapely legs, cunningly revealed by a very short tunic. That Orlando or any other young man could not possibly have mistaken her for a boy escaped the notice of the most discerning critics. A few of them complained that the evening dragged a bit (after the novelty of the lovely legs had worn off) but none seemed to realize that this was because the courtship lacked plausibility. In the Old Vic touring production of *Twelfth Night* the designer went to some pains to put the play in the apparel of 1630 in which boots, cassock, and roomy breeches made Viola's disguise more acceptable than usual. Barbara Jefford, who played Viola, has very small feet. When her twin brother appeared the difference in the size of their feet was very conspicuous in spite of the similarity in the cut and color of their upper garments.

It is entirely possible, given the fashions of the sixteenth and seventeenth centuries, to make the heroine-as-boy convincing on its own terms, and it has been done. When it succeeds it escapes notice, which is as it should be. For in every instance the disguise pays off in a final scene in which the heroine reveals her true identity as Rosalind does when she appears in the epilogue in her petticoat and stays. The more complete the disguise the more plausible the deception and the more dramatic the ultimate revelation.

CASTING THE CHILDREN'S ROLES

The casting of boy's parts, such as Lucius in *Julius Caesar* and Fleance in *Macbeth*, presents some problems, mainly because boys of this age who can remain interested throughout a long rehearsal are hard to come by. If the parts can be cast convincingly by using adults of slight stature, this is the best solution. One must however resist the temptation to use girls, as was the universal practice in the early days of this century. Very few girls old enough to be cast are shaped in such a way as to be indistinguishable from boys, and once an audience begins to wonder which is which something is bound to be lost from the attention it should be giving the play.

The small children who are introduced to heighten the pathos of certain scenes in the tragedies of both the Greeks and the Elizabethans pose a problem of a different kind. In order to achieve the maximum effect the children have to be very young, for the younger they are the greater their appeal. The two sons of Medea, the little Astyanax in *The Trojan Women*, the daughters of Oedipus clinging to their blind father, Young Macduff, Prince Arthur in *King John*, young Marcius in *Coriolanus*—all serve the same dramatic purpose: to bring tears to the eyes of the spectators. The problem is that children of this age are normally put to bed about the time the curtain is due to go up. To get them to rehearsals, dress rehearsals, and performances requires parents eager to cooperate and to keep on cooperating night after night. Most parents find that this task palls after a week or two and the stage manager is likely to end up transporting the children in addition to all the other things he has to do. Sometimes adult members of the cast have children of their own of the desired age, which may solve the problem because the child can accompany the parent to the theatre and be more or less under his or her eye during rehearsals. Another solution may be to cast two or more children for each part so that they can take turns rehearsing and performing. This way none will have to be kept up past bedtime night after night during a long run and the burden on the parents will also be lightened. An additional virtue of doubling the children is that the inevitable small quick-passing ailments to which small children fall prey need not force recasting of the child's part on short notice.

AVOIDING LOOK-ALIKES

Care must be taken to make sure that no two principals resemble each other closely enough to be confused even for a moment. When similarities of appearance cannot be avoided, contrasts in hair coloring and costume can be invoked. It is surprising how often this basic principle is neglected. In the 1979 BBC production of *Julius Caesar* Titinius looked so much like Cassius that there was a moment in the final sequence when it looked like Cassius had recovered from his suicide attempt and returned to the fray. A similar confusion occurred in the BBC *Duchess of Malfi* when the resemblance between the Cardinal's mistress and the Duchess had us thinking that the Duchess had somehow ended up in bed with her brother, a situation to which the numerous references to incest earlier in the play lent credence. In the 1976 *Midsummer Night's Dream* at Stratford, Ontario, all the court women wore the same style and color of wig, modeled after the same portrait of Queen Elizabeth, and as all were gowned in the same colors, confusion ran rampant. No doubt in the planning stage there had been some purpose in making look-alikes of them, but it made hash of many scenes in the production.

WALK-ONS AND SUPERNUMERARIES

The casting of walk-ons and supernumeraries must subordinate them to the principals so that none, through distinctive appearance, detracts from the center of interest. Soldiers, servants, attendants, and courtiers serve mainly to fill out the scene, populating the street, throne room, or battlefield which would otherwise seem inadequately attended. Supers should not be noticed as individuals at all, and walk-ons only at specific moments, such as Artemidorus in *Julius Caesar* or the Old Soldier in *Antony and Cleopatra*, where a single speech brings the character into the spotlight briefly only to fade again into the background once the speech is over. In order to subordinate these parts they must be cast so that no extremes of height, weight, or physiognomy will cause one to stand out from the group. Idiosyncrasies of movement or posture must likewise be avoided; the soldier who is always out of step has no place except in farce. Supers should be matched as closely as possible in height and physique whenever they are used in a serious play. Only in comedy can the tall and the short, the fat and the thin, the bowlegged and the knockneed march side by side.

As to the number, there is a saying that the eye counts only to five, which can be interpreted as meaning that five soldiers constitute the smallest possible army for the smallest possible stage. For larger stages multiples of five will be needed. In the Merrick production of Anouilh's *Becket* several years ago this principle was ignored and an attempt made to suggest an army with only four supers. The result was that an imaginative and expensive production for which Merrick had gone to great pains to secure Laurence Olivier as star ended up looking poverty-stricken. Most directors prefer odd numbers of supers because odd numbers above five are harder to count. Max Reinhardt, whose crowd scenes were widely admired and imitated, always cast his supers in groups of five with one more experienced actor as captain of each group, the number of groups being determined by the size of the stage and the amount of space to be filled.

CASTING THE "TWIN" COMEDIES

A number of premodern plays exploit mistakes of identity made possible by the existence of twins in the same town at the same time, unknown to each other. The problem of casting is complicated by the fact that, while the twins must plausibly be mistaken by various characters—wives, parents, lovers, magistrates, and money-lenders—the audience must always be able to tell which twin is which in order to enjoy the joke. The best part of the comedy is the anticipation, the pleasure of being able to recognize mistakes of identity which are about to happen. If the spectator is unable to tell which is which much of the comic effect is lost. A friend of mine who once found himself with two pairs of talented twins in his company decided to put on *The Comedy of Errors*. To his surprise the audience was so confused that it hardly knew what was going on, and the response fell far short of what he had hoped for.

Identical wigs and costumes on actors of similar height and physique generally serve well enough to establish the premise of mistaken identity. But the comic effect is better if the resemblance is quite close so that the mistakes are wholly believable. How then can the twins be distinguished so that the spectators can remain always one step ahead of the game? One way, and probably the best and most delightful, is to have the twins alike in appearance but different in behavior, with individual differences of manner, gesture, and stance which are quite pronounced, so that the audience can tell at once which twin they are watching by the way he walks, stands, uses his hands, and behaves in general. By studying each others' mannerisms and developing contrary mime patterns the actors playing the twins can achieve delightful results.

In all twin plays the playwrights have helped with the task of distinguishing the twins by providing for certain properties to be continually carried and associated with one of the pair. In *The Menaechmi*, for example, Menaechmus Syracuse carries through several scenes the dress which Erotium has given him, while Menaechmus Epidamnus, who carries nothing, meets a succession of people demanding from him the dress he does not have. Similarly, in *The Comedy of Errors* Antipholus of Syracuse is continually identified by the chain which the Goldsmith has given him. Also, in most twin plays we find that the different twins consistently enter from opposite sides of the stage.

Only in the *Amphitryon* of Plautus do we have a scene in which a face to face confrontation of twins is played out for comic effect. In all the other twin plays the pairs never meet until the finale. This means that it is often possible for one actor to play both twins. For the final confrontation a second actor in identical costume and makeup can be introduced if the action is blocked out in such a way as to prevent the spectators from seeing him full face. For the actor who doubles into both parts the opportunities to differentiate the two characters are many and varied. Actors delight in the challenge presented by such casting. The advantage to the producer is that if a good pair of "twins" is not available or not skillful enough to carry the parts, one very good actor can be cast to play both twins of the pair. The knowledge that the play has been composed to make this possible also provides insurance against the loss of either one of the actors playing the twins since the play can be continued merely by doubling the remaining actor into both parts.

In passing it is interesting to note how much easier it would have been to establish the plausibility of mistaken identity in the case of Viola and Sebastian in *Twelfth Night* when both characters were played by boys or when one boy played both twins with the aid of a stand-in for the finale.

DOUBLING THE ACTORS IN MINOR PARTS

Premodern plays, more often than not, were composed in such a way that enormous casts could be acted by a comparatively small company of professionals augmented with supers hired for the day. In the Elizabethan theatre it was desirable to have the maximum number of parts played by those who owned the company and divided the profits. If an effect of magnificence could be achieved, if the march of history and the panorama of power politics could be represented by a small group of skilled actors reappearing in various guises as different characters during the course of the performance, all the better.

In *Julius Caesar*, forty different characters are called for, plus half-a-dozen citizens. In addition, a minimum of five nonspeaking supers are needed to attend Caesar, carry his coffin on and off in the Forum scene, and fill the ranks of two armies. Of all these only four or five appear in both halves of the play if we divide it into two parts with the division coming between acts Three and Four. All of those who play senators in the first half are free to play generals in the second. All of those who play citizens in the first half can double as soldiers in the second. By doubling each supporting actor into two or more roles it becomes possible to put on a very creditable production with only twenty energetic actors and six or seven supers.

The Elizabethan theatre had one advantage over us in that the boys who played Portia and Calpurnia could afterward double as citizens and soldiers, making possible an even smaller acting company than is needed today.

In *Doctor Faustus* only two characters, Mephistophilis and Faustus himself, go all the way through the play. Wagner, Faustus' apprentice, appears in five scattered scenes. The Chorus, the Good Angel, the Evil Angel, the two Scholars, and five or six devils, appear each only three times. Twenty-three other characters and the Seven Deadly Sins appear only once. The biggest scene of the play in terms of the number of actors required, the spectacle of the Court of Hell, needs fourteen actors and several supers as minor devils.

Lope de Vega's *Fuente Ovejuna* in which both actors and actresses appeared has thirteen male characters and four female characters who appear throughout the play, five males who appear once or twice each, and an indeterminate number of soldiers, courtiers, and villagers. With a company of twenty, and a half-dozen supers, a fairly handsome production can be mounted, provided a separate group of dancers is available.

In ancient Greece a play was customarily given its first production in a competition featuring works by several poets. The poet himself seems to have functioned as director, teaching the actors the lines he had composed and staging both episodes and choral interludes. One interesting feature was the limitation on the number of actors in speaking parts. For most of the plays which have come down to us the number is limited to three, one principal actor, or protagonist, whose role formed a major part of every episode, and two supporting actors who divided all the other roles between them. No one knows for certain why the cast was limited in this fashion. One supposition is that the limitation bore some relationship to the competitive nature of the event, with the most accomplished actors being distributed as fairly as possible among the contestants in order to give each an equal chance. Thus if you take Sophocles' *Oedipus the King* you find that Oedipus himself appears in the prologue and all five episodes. For the other actors to fill the remaining parts one of them would have to play the Priest, Jocasta, the Herdsman, and the Messenger. The other would have to play Creon, the Corinthian, and probably Tiresias. The rest of the cast consists of the Choral Leader as interlocutor, a chorus of from eight to fourteen men, several soldiers or attendants to fetch and hold the Herdsman, a boy to guide Tiresias, the two small daughters of Oedipus, and what appears from Oedipus' description to be a mixed crowd of Theban citizens in the Prologue.

In *The Trojan Women* of Euripides we find again that the first actor, who plays Hecuba, appears in every episode and the Prologue. The second actor plays Talthybius, who appears in four episodes, plus, in all probability, Poseidon in the Prologue and Menelaus in the confrontation with Helen. The third actor is left to play Cassandra, Andromache, Helen, and Pallas Athene in the Prologue. The chorus of captive Trojan princesses appears in every scene but the Prologue. Four or five soldiers accompany Talthybius, carry in Andromache and the loot from the sack of the palace, take the child Astyanax to his death, bring back the body, set torch to the city, and finally escort the women off to the ships that will bear them away from their homeland.

It is unlikely that anyone would produce an ancient Greek play today with only three principal actors playing all the name parts except as an experiment to find out how it might have worked in actual practice. It is however instructive to study the doubling of roles as a means of understanding the requirements. Knowing that Cassandra and Andromache were conceived by the poet in the certain knowledge that one actor would have to play both often helps us to select more wisely when confronted with difficult choices among equally qualified performers.

I hope no reader of this will take exception to my failure to discuss the important problem of finding performers whose talents and temperaments suit particular roles. The problem has been omitted here because it is not peculiar to premodern drama and is already adequately treated in books readily available on the art of directing. To the extent that the problem relates to specific instances of early drama it is covered under the discussions of individual plays.

PART TWO

The Greeks

CHAPTER 4

Special Problems of Producing Greek Tragedy

Aristotle's definition of tragedy has usually been translated as "the imitation" or "representation of life." It is in fact much more than that; it is a recreation of life, or more specifically, of human activity, and not in particular but in general terms. In its best instances it seems to aim at revealing timeless truths about human kind and it often succeeds in touching feelings and thoughts which are universally shared by all men of all times. Because of this the plays are sometimes mistakenly viewed as being "timely" or "up to date." Actually, the best Greek tragedies transcend time and singularity. The plots are taken, not from life, but from legend and myth. The characters are not individuals but generalized treatments of various aspects of the human condition. Because of this when an actor attempts to develop a role in Greek tragedy according to modern theories of individual character and emotional recall the results are often disastrous. When translators attempt to express the simplicity and directness of Greek poetry in modern English the result often misses the essential grandeur of the original and the poetic quality of beautiful clarity becomes pedestrian and prosaic. When producers modernize costumes and manners they seldom seem able to make the play interesting beyond the first fifteen minutes or until the novelty has worn off, and they end up by emphasizing the strangeness rather than the universality of their material.

CHARACTERISTICS OF GREEK TRAGEDY

Success in the production of Greek tragedy begins with appreciation of the ways in which its art is distinct in its own way and different from subsequent imitations or departures. It is vastly different from our present idea of drama, even of those works which dramatize the same stories. It is much closer to religious ritual than to anything we ordinarily think of as drama and a scrupulous observance of its ritualistic nature is necessary in order to bring it fully to life. Yet it is also different from most modern ritual in that it is less staid and more intensely passionate. The agonized moans and cries of "Ah, me!" and "Woe, woe!" the weeping, the breast-beating, the hair-tearing, and the highly externalized suffering are all embarassingly alien to contemporary culture, especially that of English-speaking people and especially when uttered in a theatre one-tenth the size of those for which the drama was intended.

Greek tragedy is a fully developed form of drama, much more fully developed than most creations of contemporary playwrights. It was intended for audiences to whom oral poetry, whether in lyric, epic, or dramatic form, was a favorite part of a treasured heritage. In order to approximate for moderns the effect which Greek tragedy seems to have had on its original audiences we will need first to recognize the characteristics which mark its substance and form: the fondness for familiar plots, the custom of shaping the characters in such a way as to make the familiar plots plausible, the skillful appeal to the most profound emotions, the habit of balancing the sympathies of the spectators between conflicting points of view, and the extreme definiteness of the form into which the substance of the drama is poured.

Familiar Plots

All the tragedies that remain to us from ancient Greece are dramatizations of stories already widely known as legend or myth, and while these stories appeared in many versions the main outlines were known to most Greeks from childhood. There were no "original" plots. Whatever the story, the outcome would be known to practically everyone in the audience. Most would also know the main turning points, so that suspense and surprise, the two most potent plot effects of modern drama, would scarcely have been possible. In the more popular stories the course of events remains pretty much the same from drama to drama. The dramatist may alter the moral tone of his presentation or introduce a novel interpretation of motives, but he may not deviate very far from the story line of the legend without offending his audience and rendering his play unacceptable. Sophocles could not, for example, have Oedipus discover at the last moment that Jocasta was not his mother after all, or that Laius had died a natural death instead of being slain at that infamous spot where three roads meet. Nor could Euripides have dared to represent the Trojans as victors no matter how much he may have sympathized with them.

When an audience can be counted on to know the outcome of a play and anticipate the turns of the plot it can also be counted on to appreciate ironies not otherwise possible. It enters into the experience of the reenacted myth possessing a tremendous advantage over the characters in the play who do not know what lies ahead of them. Electra's despair when she hears the report of Orestes' death is ironic because we know what she does not, that her brother is alive, near at hand, and soon to rescue her. That is the way the story goes and Sophocles makes sure we do not forget it by showing us Orestes at the beginning of the play and letting us hear his scheme to deliver his sister and destroy her tormentors. There can be no suspense as to whether he will succeed in his effort—the legend makes no provision for failure—but only as to how he will accomplish the dangerous and seemingly impossible feat.

The skill of the dramatist in Greek tragedy is applied primarily not to the invention of plots but to the presentation of a known event in such a way as to show us the how and why of it. The familiar stories are often highly improbable. There is scarcely one of them that does not contain coincidences of the most remarkable sort. But the art of the dramatist either masks the improbabilities or else diverts attention from them, and at the same time manages to present the events to us in a cause and effect sequence which makes it seem that they could not have happened otherwise than as he has shown them. As Sophocles presents Antigone's feeling of duty toward her dead brother, Creon's regard for law and order, and Haemon's insistence upon reason over blind justice, the only possible outcome is the catastrophe as told in the legend. The solitary reader may ask why Creon on his way to release Antigone takes time out to perform burial rites over the dead Polynices when, if he had proceeded directly he would have arrived in time to save her and prevent Haemon's suicide. But no one watching the play unfold in performance ever asks such a question. Sophocles' genius is to make the events plausible as drama regardless of any implausibility the legend might possess.

Making the Character Fit the Plot

This brings us to another aspect of the Greek dramatist's art: his skill in adapting character to the demands of the story. Not only does he arrange the successive phases of the event to give it the feeling of cause and effect, but he also creates the kind of person who would most probably figure in the story. He has already contrived a way of representing a familiar tale in the form of action. Now he shows us what sort of people the action would have involved. The action of Medea in killing her sons in order to revenge herself on their faithless father is certainly strange and horrible, but Euripides in his characterization of Medea gives us exactly the kind of woman who would be most likely to do such a thing. Equally true is the Oedipus whom Sophocles has created in *Oedipus Tyrannus*, a born leader, forthright, quick to act, intolerant of caution, delay, and the warnings of others, in sum a doer rather than a thinker. One cannot help admiring him. Yet his most admirable traits are also his most serious faults, blinding him to the truth which he seeks and leading him ultimately to disaster.

This fitting of character to plot is not unique with Greek tragedy. It can be observed in plays of all periods purporting to dramatize history. Later playwrights however tend to strive for novelty by depicting their principals as different in some striking way from those in the "official" versions, an approach diametrically opposed to that of the Greeks who seem continually to be striving to get closer to the central core of character as described in the legend. A possible exception occurs in the work of Euripides who sometimes gives us characters who seem to be lacking in heroic stature when compared with those of Aeschylus and Sophocles. This has led critics in recent years to praise him for being more "modern" than the other two (as if being up to date were some sort of artistic virtue). It is possible that Euripides was merely less skillful, and the small number of the prizes he won would seem to support this possibility.

Emotionality

So much has been written about the formal aspects of Greek drama that the purpose for which this form was perfected is generally obscured. That purpose is unmistakable: to stir the emotions of the audience, to arouse their deepest sympathies and most profound feelings of awe. Today it is not fashionable for dramatists, except at the lower levels of popular drama —cinema, television, and musical shows—to appeal directly to the sympathies. Theatregoers to the so-called legitimate drama, who are usually more sophisticated, prefer to be flattered into believing that their minds are engaged, so the playwrights load their work with paradoxes and puzzles. If they appeal to the emotions at all their appeal is likely to be indirect or implied.

Early drama, in contrast, goes right to the heart. Thought value there is, more than centuries of commentators have been able to exhaust. But the intellectual effect is not primary. It follows the feelings and increases with reflection long after the performance is over. The primary effect is the emotional one which occurs during the performance. Afterward it exists principally in the memory of how the play looked and sounded when it was at its best. I have heard people who have seen the *Ion* of Euripides call the mother and son reunion in it a "tear-jerker," half in admiration and half in deprecation, as if it were somehow inferior artistically in spite of its patent effectiveness. But that was after the performance was over; while the scene was in progress they wept along with everyone else in the theatre. In performances of *The Trojan Women*, during the scene in which the infant Astyanax is taken from the arms of his mother, I have noticed women in the audience averting their faces, apparently unable to endure the sight. Toward the end of *Oedipus Tyrannus* the blind Oedipus embraces his tiny daughters while they cling to him, weeping, and describes the bleak future which his actions have prepared for them. This scene is by no means essential to the plot. Its obvious purpose is to move the audience to tears and it seldom fails if the children are small enough.

Not only is the play plotted so as to provide scenes of high emotionality such as reunions, partings, quarrels, involving brother and sister (*Electra, Iphigenia in Taurus*), father and son (*Antigone, Oedipus at Colonus, Hippolytus*), mother and son (*Ion, The Trojan Women*), father and daughter (*Oedipus at Colonus, Oedipus Tyrannus*), husband and wife (*Alcestis, The Trojan Women, Helen, Agamemnon*), but also to provide the fullest possible verbal expression of emotion, sometimes in solo passages of considerable length, sometimes in antiphony between principals and chorus. Thus we have Antigone and Ismene grieving over the deaths of their brothers in *Seven Against Thebes*, Hecuba crying out in rage and despair at the murder of Polydorus in *Hecuba*, Admetus and the chorus mourning the death of Alcestis in the play of that name, Xerxes and the chorus lamenting their defeat at the hands of the Greeks in *The Persians*, and dirges, in *The Trojan Women* over the slain Astyanax, and in Sophocles' *Electra* following the report of the death of Orestes. Scenes in which the wounded or dying describe their suffering occur in *Hippolytus, The Trachiniae, Hecuba*, and in *Agamemnon* when Cassandra's prophetic vision prefigures her death. At the other extreme of emotional expression is the joyous exultation of the populace at the end of the *Oresteia*.

Modern commentators have been reluctant to allow full value to the emotional appeal of Greek tragedy, preferring instead to stress the meaning and the artistry of plotting and character revelation. The serious student may thus be made aware of the magnificence of the language, characterization, and plotting, qualities readily discernible in the text, but the powerful assault on the emotions which occurs in performance tends to be downgraded as seeming somehow unworthy of such splendid art. We who have grown up in the English-speaking culture tend to be embarrassed by strong emotional appeals no matter what form they take. Also, it seems rather unlike the other arts of the Greeks as we perceive them: composed, poised, perfectly proportioned, and standing forth in a kind of cool elegance.

The fact remains however that the fundamental aim of Greek tragedy is to move audiences as profoundly as possible. This was understood by the best minds of the time. Aristotle noted it when he described the purpose of tragedy as *catharsis*, a term which everyone accepts in spite of the fact that its exact meaning has been in dispute ever since. Plato recognized the same phenomenon but viewed it as undesirable in a well ordered society. Neither attitude seems to have had the slightest effect on the work of the poet-dramatists.

Balance of Sympathies

Symmetry is one of the characteristics of nearly all Greek art, drama no less than architecture or sculpture, and the balance of opposing elements is the essence of symmetrical composition. This characteristic is especially pronounced in the way in which characters are represented when in direct opposition. It is also one of the characteristics most frequently overlooked, often with unwelcome consequences.

In spite of the sophistication to which modern modes of drama aspire it is still common to believe that in any debate there must be a winner and a loser, in any dramatic opposition a right side and a wrong side, and that when an argument is presented on the stage we should sooner or later learn which side is in the right. There is also among moderns a strong tendency to feel that when two characters are placed in conflict one must be sympathetic and one unsympathetic. This modern view is quite un-Greek, at least in its application to tragedy, for the better the balance between the opposing characters and beliefs the better the play is. The best is when both are convincing to a high degree, when both present points of view with which we are obliged to agree as well as ones to which we cannot subscribe. Thus, when in *Antigone* Haemon pleads with his father to moderate the sentence pronounced upon Antigone, the young man's arguments strike us as sound and we agree with him. But when Creon states his case we are obliged to agree with him also. Both are right and both are sincere as far as they go. We sympathize first with one, then with the other, and when the argument instead of resolving their differences causes an irreparable break we are saddened more than if one of them had been wholly right and the other one wholly wrong. At the same time we are wiser for having understood both sides of the argument.

The emotional power of a confrontation scene such as this is greatly increased when our sympathies are engaged equally by both characters involved in the conflict. As in a quarrel between our parents, friends, or close relatives, we are torn between the two sides and pulled first one way and then the other. This is the emotional effect of many such scenes in many of the plays, and always, when rightly interpreted and performed, it produces a scene of heightened emotionality and insight. I believe that one might profitably begin work on such a scene by looking for ways that each of the contestants can enlist the audience's sympathy in turn.

This is not easy to do. The actors will like this approach because they tend to play for sympathy anyhow and will usually work overtime to develop those aspects of character which attract sympathy. They seldom require much encouragement to proceed in this direction. But other factors may be more difficult to manage. For one thing, it is seldom that one will have in such a scene two actors of equally strong audience appeal. To tone down the appeal of one while increasing that of another requires superhuman tact. And then, although at the beginning of rehearsals it may have looked as if the opponents could be balanced, one often turns out to be stronger in projection or quicker in "study" than the other, causing sympathies to turn, as they practically always do, to the best performer.

Another difficulty arises from the fact that designers of settings and costumes tend to see the basic conflicts in rather simple terms. A good designer will often try, quite naturally, to express the qualities of the play in visual terms, dramatizing the high points in line and color and strengthening contrasts, especially between characters' personalities and points of view. But this visual heightening, while it makes a play exciting to look at, at least in the first few minutes of a scene, also frequently oversimplifies it, obscuring the subtler shadings and making a true balance more difficult for the director to achieve. For example, costuming Haemon in white and Creon in black will make it very difficult for the audience to accept them both as being equally right.

Sometimes it also happens that the author, although aiming for balance, fails to achieve it because of his inability to maintain his objectivity throughout the work. Playwrights in every age have been known to be carried away by the charm of certain characters they have created, by the acting opportunities one of them seems to promise, or by the subconscious leanings toward a point of view which the character embodies. Thus the original intention may be evident to a discerning student of the work while the execution of that intention falls short. The director is then confronted with the necessity of carrying out the author's intention in the face of problems of the author's own making.

Generalized Characters

Greek tragedy has often been compared to a streamlined vehicle in which every detail is subordinated to function and from which everything has been omitted that does not promote efficiency. This streamlining is nowhere more conspicuous than in the characterization. It is so entirely different from any modern approach to the problem of presenting character that it is often very difficult for actor and director to accept. For the principal character in Greek tragedy is a generalized character, not an individualized one. He is true to his kind, whether that kind be ruler, soldier, beggar or prophet, and whether it be pragmatic, visionary, overbearing, humble, or any combination of human qualities. All traits that do not bear directly upon his course of action in the play, all idiosyncrasies, and all mannerisms, are omitted. Reckless leaders, cunning counselors, and cantankerous oldsters there are, but there are no real eccentrics, not in tragedy anyhow.

To the student studying Greek tragedy for the first time the characters tend to seem rather dull, plain, oversimplified, and perhaps even crude, as if, like the early sculptures of Egypt, they represented the efforts of artists not yet in full command of the technique required to recreate human character completely. This first impression however is wrong. The generalized characters of Greek tragedy are deliberately presented that way.

The whole direction of the dramatist's art in characterization goes steadily toward seeking to reveal the *essence* of character, of the qualities of leadership, servitude, loyalty, bravery, recklessness, caution, or whatever else best suits the position of the character in the story being dramatized and the decisions he has to make as the familiar plot unfolds. This persistent effort to capture and recreate essence is characteristic of much of the best of all Greek art. Nothing is more natural than that it should form the basis for the artistry of the dramatist in his presentation of human character in tragedy. Details of character that appear in the legends from which the dramas have been made are often omitted from the dramatization although they might have added color and interest. But unless they heighten the emotional power of the drama they are not included and have no place in it.

Form

One of the most conspicuous characteristics of Greek tragedy is its definiteness of form. The direction of the dramatist's shaping effort is always toward formality, toward compression of plot, regularity and firmness of outline, and balance among the elements of the composition. This is true of all the tragedies that have come down to us, regardless of author, subject, or point of view. Recognition of this is important to the producer because when any formalities are overlooked the result is always the same: a very un-Greek mushiness.

Typically the Prologue introduces the action, tells us where it takes place and when, who figures in it, and what to look for. The Epilogue sums up the significance of the action we have witnessed in a few trenchant lines. Omit or alter either of these and the form is marred. The tragedy loses impressiveness then, as a painting does without its frame or a statue without its pedestal.

This concern for form shows up again in the custom of streamlining and compressing the plot. If the subject is historical the dramatist does not attempt to show the whole history but concentrates his effort on recreating some crucial event of this history. In *The Persians*, for example, Aeschylus makes no attempt to show the course of the Persian war; instead he fixes our attention on that moment when the Persians in their capital first learn of the destruction of their fleet at Salamis. Similarly, of the several plays in which Oedipus appears none shows more than one incident of his long and illustrious career.

The various tragedies are by no means uniform. Different dramatists use different means to attain different effects. But they are all alike in certain formal aspects. All of them tend to alternate choral passages with plot episodes. All tend to equalize the length of speeches between two opposing characters, allowing each the same number of lines. All make impressive use of the *commus*, an antiphonal passage in which one of the principals speaks or sings alternately with the chorus. All construct dialogue in the form of stichomythia, a chain of one-line speeches of equal length and meter, linked by carryovers of thought or phrasing. At its best this stichomythic dialogue stands as the highest development of dramatic discourse. It is one achievement of the Greeks which has never been surpassed. Who can describe the excitement generated by a passage of stichomythic dialogue expertly performed?

Another formality which all the ancient playwrights employ and one which is often the most stirring feature, second only to dialogue, is the "set" speech. This is usually a narrative or descriptive report filled with vivid detail, a virtuoso opportunity for the actor. One such speech is that of the Paedagogus in Sophocles' *Electra*, describing the chariot race in which Orestes is supposed to have lost his life. Another is the Messenger's speech in *Oedipus Tyrannus*. Both examples are from Sophocles' plays but Aeschylus and Euripides have just as many good ones. To the solitary reader these long, highly colored speeches look rather verbose. But audiences listening to such a speech do not know how long it is until it is over; if it is well acted it will seem all too short.

A minor formality, but one which assures understanding and gives to a drama that clarity which is characteristic of Greek art in general and drama in particular, is the naming, early in the play, of the locale of the action and subsequently of each character at the time of his first entrance. This spares us from wondering who the newcomer is and helps to prevent us from confusing one character with another.

THE GREEK CHORUS AND ITS STAGING

Nowhere is the difference between drama as literature and drama as theatre art more strikingly demonstrated than in the ancient Greek chorus; nowhere are the differences between the perceptions of the solitary reader and those of the spectator more pronounced. Anyone reading Greek drama, especially for the first time, is tempted to skip the long seemingly uneventful choral passages in order to get on with the plot. But to the audience in the theatre the performance of the chorus is often the most interesting part of the play, the liveliest, the most colorful, the most awesome or amusing as the case may be, and the most treasured memory after the performance is over.

The Function of the Chorus

The literary function of the chorus is well known. In the main it gives balance and weight to the whole by voicing sentiments—approval, disapproval, doubt, fear, exultation—such as observers, as distinct from the principal characters, might feel. In addition it often serves a structural function by providing exposition in the early part of the play, as well as some sort of summing up at the end. All choral passages whether in tragedy or comedy are couched in poetry possessing an extraordinary variety of imagery and rhythm, giving to the form a power and haunting beauty hardly equalled in any language since.

The aesthetic function is less easily recognized. Yet we know for a certainty that song, mime, and instrumental accompaniment were important parts of the original. We know this from the abundant evidence that exists in the form of contemporary references, fragments of musical scores and songs, and sculptural representations of choral mime and dance.

Many of the terms associated with the choral performance suggest movement. *Strophe* and *antistrophe* suggest movement first in one direction and then in another. But these terms barely hint at the possibilities of patterned movement with a group of performers in files, ranks, circles, and circles within circles, for the choruses of ancient Greece spent far more time in rehearsal than most moderns can. For patterned movement the basic requirement is always the same: plenty of level space for the performers plus a steep seating slope for the audience to look down on the spectacle from above.

Many choruses give powerful indications of the mimetic actions of the chorus as a whole or by sub-choruses of various sizes. The parodos of *Oedipus at Colonus* describes the actions of citizens searching for a culprit who is reported to have defiled the sacred grove with his presence. In *Ion* the attendants of Creusa enter the temple compound at Delphi as sightseers, marveling at the frieze, wall paintings, and statuary. In *Antigone* the description of the Argives' attack on the city and the deadly struggle between the brothers strongly suggests mimetic activity and has in fact been acted out in modern productions with considerable success. *The Bacchae*, with its wild maenads, not only suggests mimetic action but has given to our stage some of the finest dancing choruses of any Greek tragedy. The choruses of comedy provide even more apt instances. Imagine the actions illustrating the women's oath in *Lysistrata* or the delights of being a bird in *The Birds*. This list could be extended indefinitely, for every surviving play contains choral interludes eminently suited to mimetic treatment.

As we know from Aristotle's *Poetics*, music normally accompanied speech and song in the original performances. We know much less, however, about how the music sounded. Only a few fragments of musical notation have been identified. In all of these the melodic line is clear and simple, ideal for the accompaniment of speech or chanted lines. But nothing remains to tell us what varied rhythms might have accompanied the frenzied maenads, solemn mourners, or the fantastic creatures forming the choruses of many of the comedies. There is a rich field of opportunity here for some modern composer.

Summing up the aesthetic functions of the chorus one might say that it is intended to provide not only comment and illustration but also relief and variety for both ear and eye, to separate and set off the dramatic episodes, and overall to enrich the whole experience of the playgoer.

Staging

Staging a chorus always turns out to be more difficult than one has anticipated, even with the finest performers and optimum rehearsal conditions. Early rehearsals always look good and everyone is enthusiastic, but as the performance date comes nearer the potential effect of the chorus seems further and further from realization. Fortunately, this sense of increasing difficulty seems to inspire the performers to greater effort so that the morale of the group undergoes an exhilarating lift. The result is that by performance time the group is usually fused into an entity possessing both purpose and pride. This has been my experience with every chorus I have directed and many of my friends report similar experiences.

In order to know how very good these choruses can be one has to study the work of the Greek companies specializing in the classics, especially the National Theatre and the Piraikon. Their choruses are carefully chosen for quality of voice and uniformity of appearance. Admittedly the Greek language is better suited to choral utterance than English. Making the most of this advantage, the diction of the native chorus is flawless and the voices perfectly modulated and harmonized. So perfect is the group-speaking that it is seldom possible for the listener to know whether three or a dozen are speaking together. Musical accompaniment consists mostly of woodwinds with muted percussion. The choral interludes are choreographed in an infinite variety of movement patterns with the chorus often divided into two or more sub-choruses. Emotions such as fear, grief, anxiety, and sympathy are mimed, sometimes by several performers, sometimes by the whole group in unison. Costumes are usually identical throughout the group so that one is seldom conscious of any particular member as an individual; in fact it is often impossible to tell which ones are speaking. In most of the tragedies I have seen performed by these companies the chorus contained fourteen members.

In productions by other companies the size of the chorus is generally determined by the size of the theatre. For a theatre seating four or five hundred a chorus of fourteen is often too large, it requires more stage space than is usually available and is often too loud when all are speaking in unison. In these theatres the same effect is that produced in a large theatre by fourteen or fifteen voices can easily be attained by seven or eight. The smallest chorus regarded by most directors as practicable contains five persons. In this case the movement and mime would be reduced to a minimum. But reduction of the chorus can be carried too far; then the play is impoverished and its grandeur marred.

In one-third of all the Greek tragedies and all but two of the comedies the title of the play tells us what the chorus represents: maenads, Trojans, Eumenides, Phoenicians, and mourners in tragedy; frogs, birds, wasps, and clouds in comedy. In *Antigone* and *Oedipus Tyrannus* the chorus is composed of elders of Thebes. In *Oedipus at Colonus* it is made up of the townspeople of Colonus. In many instances it consists of the friends or attendants of some noble person.

Casting

In the original productions all of the chorus members were men. Today it is preferable to use men when the chorus is designated as elders or warriors, and women when the text so specifies, but this is not always possible. More important is having a group of harmonious voices and there may not always be enough such voices available from either sex alone, in which case a mixed group may be the only solution. Or, as is often the case, there may be more women available for casting, in which case the "elders of Thebes" named by the dramatist must give way to a chorus of mixed gender.

As to appearance, while good looks are not necessary, it is best to avoid actors who are noticably taller, shorter, or fatter than the rest of the group, for the more nearly the group approaches uniformity in appearance the better the chorus will look. Any member with strikingly different physical features is bound to become a distraction.

The most difficult aspect of casting is finding enough performers with clear diction and melodious voices. Of all those auditioning, one-third on the average will be disqualified by some common defect of speech such a tight jaw, harsh gutterals, poor sibilants, nasality, or excessive regional accent. It is not usually possible to overcome such defects in the course of the four or five weeks' rehearsal period, and since the slightest imperfection of speech even in one member will spoil the work of the whole group the risk is too great to be considered.

Once the elimination of those with speech faults is completed the search begins for voices that complement each other. At first the voices are divided into two groups: "light" and "dark;" the light being the soprano and tenor and the dark being alto, baritone, and bass. With rare exceptions the light voices will speak and sing together and the dark voices will do likewise. If the chorus is to be very large a third group can be cast from those having voices falling between the main classifications. This third group can then be used to speak in unison with either light or dark groups and also on occasion to provide a bridge for the transition from one to the other.

In casting the chorus a great deal of time is spent in the attempt to attain a satisfactory balance between the two main groups, for if they are not well balanced the listening audience will have difficulty adjusting to the successive changes of pitch and volume and will in consequence be unable to understand the lines. Some very fine lines may thus be lost. Audiences accustomed to the rambling dialogue of modern plays, large portions of which can be missed without serious loss, may, if they do not understand what they hear, be unaware of their loss, unaware of the fact that every syllable is indispensable to understanding and enjoyment. For complete audibility the contrasts between the various speaking groups should be contrasts of quality rather than of volume. Variations in volume there may be, but they must be gradual rather than sudden. Since the volume of the sound is multiplied by the number of speakers, the best choral groups use a somewhat muted speech or song with each performer speaking or singing in a rather hushed voice so that four or five or even more voices in unison are no louder than the normal volume of one speaking alone. This relieves the chorus members of concern for projection and allows them to concentrate more completely on perfecting those effects which are possible only in group speech and song.

In order to achieve a workable balance the light voices have to outnumber the dark ones by at least three to two, and if they are very light, by two to one. If the chorus includes both men and women the women's voices of all kinds will have to outnumber the men's because masculine voices come across as heavier and more solid. The different groupings of light and dark also have distinctly different effects on the listeners. For example, dark voices seem as a rule to be more pleasing to the ear and more memorable while the light voices seem more readily capable of arousing the emotions of hearers.

From the turn of the century through the 1930s it was almost universal practice here and in England to present the chorus as a succession of solos, using the whole group in unison only for an occasional song or refrain. In the late 1950s came the annual tours of the Piraikon and the Greek National theatres in which practically all the choral passages were sung or spoken in unison. This made a profound impression on directors of classics in this country so that the use of solos has by now been practically abandoned. There is no question but that true choral speech and song is more theatrical even though it is much harder to perfect than a series of solos.

Rehearsal Techniques

How wonderful it would be if, once the choral performance had crystallized, it could be made to retain its peak spontaneity. It is a sad fact that when people speak or sing in unison they tend to lose spontaneity in the effort to achieve precision. This is particularly troublesome with the more emotional passages such as the one in *Oedipus at Colonus* which describes Theseus' chariots in pursuit of the fleeing Creon, or in the lament at the tomb of Agamemnon in *The Choephori*. There seems to be no easy solution to this problem. Various directors have developed different methods of dealing with the difficulty. Some set their performers to paraphrasing the lines or improvising actions beyond those integral to performance. Others change the speaking groups around, since all members of the chorus already know each others' lines, giving to the light voices lines previously spoken by the dark voices and the other way around. All of these things can usually be done without upsetting the performers, for group performance gives to those involved a kind of stability quite unlike anything experienced by a solo performer. No one method succeeds with all groups or with all plays, so choral experiment must often continue throughout the run of any Greek play.

Once the chorus is free of its books and speaking from memory the absence or tardiness of even one member can seriously damage the entire effort. What happens is that the other members unconsciously alter volume and pitch to compensate for the missing voice so that when the absentee returns the place which he occupied in the pattern no longer exists. If, in the attempt to assimilate him, a new adjustment is made, it is seldom as good as the group effort which preceded his absence and is nearly always unacceptable. The permanent loss of one member, bad as it may be, is usually less harmful to the chorus as a whole than a temporary loss followed by an attempted readjustment. Since it is impossible to replace a lost chorus member and equally impossible to reassimilate one who has missed a rehearsal in any but the very earliest phases of rehearsal, the personal reliability of all those being considered for casting is second in importance only to voice quality. If worst comes to worst it is better to have a chorus of five reliable members than one of fifteen if the fifteen includes any actors whose reliability is uncertain. However, the fact that the group can adjust to the loss of one speaker (even if not to his return) often makes it practicable to cast several more actors than are actually needed. Those who cannot keep up with the grind can then drop out, allowing time for the rest of the group to readjust.

No matter how many rehearsals a chorus has, it is never enough. Most directors quickly discover that the rehearsal of the chorus requires as much time as that of the principals. The earlier plays, such as those by Aeschylus, demand much more. Some of the later ones, such as *Rhesus*, or *Ion*, by Euripides, require only a little bit less.

The vocal aspect of the chorus, whether speech, chant, or song, takes more rehearsal time than the movement or mime. As a rule all the members of the chorus begin by memorizing all of the lines of all the choral passages so that during rehearsals all possible combinations of speech and song, light voices and dark voices, can be tried. Most of the early rehearsals will be spent experimenting in this way. Not until quite late in the rehearsal period does it become necessary to decide which member speaks which lines. In most cases the best combinations reveal themselves bit by bit during the experimental phases of rehearsal.

Musical accompaniment is generally withheld until the latest possible moment. The reason for this is that although the introduction of the music always inspires the chorus and gives its morale a great lift, the pattern of cooperation tends to crystallize, when the music is added, into what it will be in performance, the result is that experiment and change may no longer be profitable.

Choral movement, whether mimetic or choreographed in pattern-making subgroups, presents few difficulties once the speaking and musical accompaniment have been assimilated. For this reason the movement is usually introduced last of all.

Should a chorus speak and move at the same time or should some members do the speaking and singing while others do the dancing and mime? The answer to this seems to depend on the nature of the particular interlude being performed. When both are slow and deliberate, as in the first stasimon of *Antigone*, movement and speech go quite well together. In some of the comedies having fast "patter" songs it usually works out better to have two or three render the lyrics while the rest mime the action, or else to have the chorus leader take center stage to "sell" the song while the rest form a dancing background, picking up the refrain.

Finally, there are the many choruses, especially in the tragedies, which are known so well that they require little beyond clear vocal rendition; these are capable of gaining very little from elaborate added action. Among these are: the summation at the end of *Oedipus Tyrannus*; the ode, "Numberless are the world's wonders," in *Antigone*; the "Who craves to live beyond the normal span?" and "Stranger, seek no other home," in *Oedipus at Colonus*; the dirge, "To all men it is appointed to die," in Sophocles' *Electra*; and "The sacrifice is gone and the song of joy," in *The Trojan Women*.

Grouping

There are many devices, well known to choral directors, for helping the performers achieve a more perfect unison in speech and song. Some directors arrange the choral sub-groups so that those who speak and sing together are always in close proximity, cheek to cheek or side by side, or holding hands, or positioned so that each can see the faces of those with whom he speaks. Having the performers move in unison also helps them to speak in unison. The circular shape of the original Greek acting area is especially helpful whenever it can be incorporated into a modern setting. It is seldom possible to achieve a clear rendition of lines by two or more performers if they are widely separated, as they would be when placed on opposite sides of the stage. Part of this may be due to the acoustical quality of the auditorium which often causes sound waves from widely separated sources to behave differently.

When well cast and carefully rehearsed the theatrical strength of the choral performance is always impressive. The individual stasima, however, vary greatly in the degree to which speech, music, or dance is uppermost. Some choral passages are plainly intended as mimetic interludes, others as choreographic showpieces of striking intricacy, and some—among which are many of those most admired today—as performances in which both movement and musical accompaniment are subordinated to the clear delivery of spoken lines. But no matter which aspect enjoys primacy in the particular instance all elements must be blended so well that the audience is unaware of any one element apart from the whole. When this is done, as I have seen it done many times by different directors, the result is one of the finest experiences one can enjoy in the theatre.

CHAPTER 5

Antigone: A Problem of Balance

Of all the tragedies which have come down to us from ancient Greece, Sophocles' *Antigone* is the one most often performed today. The reasons for this are not hard to find. It has a powerful plot, it provides good acting parts for both men and women, and it contains several of the loveliest choral odes ever composed in any language.

THE NATURE OF THE PLAY

Antigone is often cited as one of the finest pieces of plot construction. When in the nineteenth century the "conflict" theory came into being—the idea that drama represents the struggle between opposing wills—*Antigone* was frequently offered as a prime example. This theory has had its day now, being inapplicable to many of the most successful works of contemporary playwrights as well as a few unaccommodating classics, but *Antigone* still stands as evidence of the fact that the direct collision of strong willed characters makes gripping drama.

The conflict in *Antigone* is however only part of the total effect since it exists only in the first half of the play, for the tragedy develops in consequence of the conflict. The tremendous power of the play in performance derives in part from another factor: the overwhelming momentum with which events progress from the first moment to the last, like the gathering force of some natural disaster which engulfs and destroys all. This has been aptly termed the "steamroller effect" of Sophocles' plotting, conspicuous in a number of his plays, none more so than here.

Several of the finest choruses surviving from classical drama are also in *Antigone*. In any reasonably good production of the play the choruses are likely to prove its most memorable feature. Stuart Sherman in one of his essays on university life describes two professors leaning on a fence watching football practice and one saying to the other, "I got to thinking about one of the odes in *Antigone* last night and the lines kept running through my head and it was so beautiful I couldn't sleep." Everyone who has heard those lines in the theatre knows exactly what he was talking about.

The characterization in *Antigone* is typically Sophoclean and exemplary Greek. Each of the principals is a whole person rendered in three dimensions: passionate, plausible, and unmistakably human. The elements of each personality are in harmony, with virtues and faults inseparably fused. We see each character in its entirety and with perfect clarity of vision. None of them will ever be as close to us as some of Shakespeare's characters perhaps, but we will understand them better because we see them in perspective with our view unclouded by mannerisms or odd quirks of personality. They do not remind us of individuals we know as much as they exemplify certain readily recognizable human qualities. In order to make sure that we understand them Sophocles forces us to keep our distance and see them whole. Thus while we admire their virtues, which are in some instances truly heroic, we see at the same time faults which cause tragic misjudgments and ultimately destroy them.

In spite of the clarity and vividness of the plot, choruses, and characterization, one usually has the feeling, when reading this play in English, that something is interfering with one's perception, as if the work were being seen through a smudged glass. This feeling is due to the difficulties of translating this particular play. *Antigone* has always been popular and there are more translations of it than almost any other Greek tragedy, but the fact is that there is as yet no translation that can be used in toto for production. The original Greek, while brilliant, is exceptionally difficult. Translators who render the choruses well seem unable to make the dialogue lifelike, while those who provide the actor with good lines to speak seldom achieve the right poetic quality in the choruses.

Because of the many lines comparing and contrasting the two brothers and the two sisters, in *Antigone* we encounter, in its severest form, one of the desperate tangles of what the translator, struggling to turn ancient Greek into modern English, calls the "pronoun problem." In English we have only one pronoun relationship. If we say "he" we have to be sure that the reader or hearer knows to whom that "he" refers. In order to do this we must place the proper name close enough to the pronoun to prevent confusion. If we are speaking of two persons we have to be careful that whatever pronouns we use are clear as to which of the two they refer. The only way we can do this is by repeating rather frequently the names of the two characters of whom we are speaking. In Greek this cumbersome practice is obviated by the fact that pronouns can be used to refer to several different persons simultaneously without confusion. Thus, in Greek the following sentence can be given without parenthetical proper names and still be clear to an audience:

There were two daughters, Antigone and Ismene, and two brothers, Polynices and Eteocles. Of these, he [Polynices] went forth to Argos while he [Eteocles] remained in Thebes.

When he [Polynices] returned they killed each other, so that she [Antigone] was forced to bury him [Polynice] while she [Ismene] refused to help.

It is sometimes assumed that because the play is titled *Antigone* it is about Antigone, that the tragedy is her tragedy, and that the principal role is hers. If this is permitted to influence the staging, the play is certain to suffer in performance. Antigone only appears in two scenes and the prologue. She is gone from the stage by the time the play is a little more than half over, before the turning point has been reached, and long before the end.

Of the four characters only Creon appears in every scene throughout the play from the first episode to the Exodos. When the play was originally performed with three actors playing all the parts the principal actor would have had to play Creon. The actor playing Antigone would have had to double in one of the three parts in the Exodos.

If we apply to the principal characters the test of Aristotle's definition of a tragic hero as a man of eminence to whom catastrophe occurs as a result of some well meant but erroneous judgement, Creon fits the description. None of the others does. Although he is newly ascended to the throne, Creon's eminence as ruler of Thebes is unquestioned. It is his decision to leave the body of Polynices unburied which sets in motion the whole terrible train of consequences. And in the end it is he who suffers the most as he finds himself deprived of all that he held most dear.

I have heard Creon described as a tyrant, an egocentric dictator, and even as a species of "stuffed shirt." I have even heard the Sentry's part discussed in terms of comic relief. It is conceivable that these contemporary labels might be employed to stimulate argument among undergraduates in a literature course, but they have no place in the work of an actor endeavoring to bring one of the characters to life.

I doubt that Sophocles intended us to take sides in the conflict between Antigone and Creon. I do not believe we are intended to see one character as right and another as wrong; one as sympathetic and another as unsympathetic. Each character is both right *and* wrong; right in principle and wrong in application of those principles. We are obliged to agree when Creon asserts that a strong government is essential to a stable and secure society because we know the statement to be true, but we are repelled by the barbarity of his decree concerning the dead Polynices. Antigone's appeal to the unwritten law wins our approval because it is humane, but her rudeness to Creon shocks us. In the scene between Creon and Haemon we feel for both and are torn between them as we would be torn by a quarrel between two friends whom we like equally well.

This balance of sympathy is more moving than if we were encouraged to favor one character and abhor his adversary. Furthermore, we enjoy greater insight into the situation because we hear each side with sympathetic attention. This is more truly tragic because it involves our emotions more deeply than if we were allowed to take sides.

Today's audiences in America can be expected to sympathize with Antigone's point of view from the first. Our respect for authority is not as strong as our habitual admiration of the rebel against authority. Antigone, no matter how she plays the role, is going to have the wind at her back. Creon therefore will have to work overtime to compensate for the handicap he suffers as the voice of authority. It is imperative that he succeed in the attempt so that his final great scene in the Exodos will move us as deeply as the author obviously intended; for if Creon fails to do so the play cannot achieve the catharsis which is the purpose of this tragedy.

In comparison with Sophocles' other plays the writing in *Antigone* seems curiously uneven, as if the different parts had been written at different times and then put together without the reworking that might have given the play that unity of style we admire in his *Electra* and *Oedipus Tyrannus*. The Sentry, for example, seems nearly colloquial in his diction and his part seems overwritten in relation to his function in the plot. In contrast, Creon's part in the Exodos seems terribly under-written. The actor struggles to convey his deep grief with only a bare minimum of lines. The difficulty confronting him is readily apparent when we compare the material the author has provided him with what he has provided Electra for the expression of similar emotions. The Commos, in which Antigone laments the fortune that sends her to her death without having allowed her opportunity to experience the love, marriage, and motherhood which most women enjoy, seems somewhat out of character in the girl who has defied the law fully aware of the published penalty.

Before we move on to the discussion of the characters there are several interesting things still to be considered. One of these is the irony of the first episode, in particular the irony of Creon's announcement of the decree prohibiting the burial of Polynices right after we have seen Antigone set forth to perform the very rite he is now forbidding. By the time he has finished his announcement Polynices is already buried.

A second thing worth noting is the powerful effect of the silent character as seen in three places: Antigone in Episode Two listening and saying nothing for sixty-eight lines after she is brought in under guard and accused of defying the law; Haemon in Episode Three, silent for forty-three lines while his father speaks; and Eurydice in the Exodos, who listens wordless for fifty-two lines to the Messenger's account of the death of her son. In each of these the listening character is the one which the audience watches. The longer it is before he speaks, the more dramatic it becomes.

Third are the lapses of time between Episodes One and Two and between Episode Four and the Exodos. Episode One begins in the morning, apparently soon after daybreak, and ends with the Sentry dispatched to guard the corpse again. When he returns with Antigone it is by his account well past noon, so four or five hours must have elapsed between the end of the previous episode and his re-entrance with his captive. Similarly, after Creon hurries out at the end of Episode Four, several hours will have passed before the Messenger's entrance with the account of Creon's journey to the tomb. Altogether, with the two time lapses, the action of the play extends over a full day from the Prologue just before dawn to the final exit of Creon late in the afternoon.

The plays of ancient Greece are sometimes described as occupying just as much time, dramatically speaking, as their performance required; actually this is not true of very many of them. Most of them have one or more time lapses that are filled in by the chorus. Many of them embody changes of locale, as from a public place to a council chamber, or from a temple to a town square. It is best not to be too dogmatic about the time or place patterns nor try to make the plays fit one's own idea of unity of time or place.

One thing about Antigone puzzles me, and the puzzle has not been diminished over the years by the productions I have seen or worked on. It is the way the play seems to change its nature according to the size of the theatre in which it is performed. The emotional impact is not lessened or altered by the size of the audience, but the play itself changes. In an intimate theatre with an apron stage and no more than three or four hundred spectators the closeness of the actors and the many shadings of thought and feeling which they are able to communicate makes the play seem almost as realistic as a work by Ibsen or O'Neill. But in a large theatre seating a thousand or more the play is like a monument, majestic, awesome, and terrifying—but not in any sense realistic. In the formality of its structure, the balance of its elements, and the beauty of its language it emerges as an impressive and moving ritual.

This is something to remember when preparing Antigone for production. The place of performance is going to have a profound effect on the way the play appears to the audience. To rehearse it in a small room and perform it in an amphitheatre is one way to court disaster.

CHARACTERS AND CASTING

Antigone requires an acting company of from twenty-two to thirty people: eight principals; a chorus of from eight to sixteen depending on the size of the theatre; at least four nonspeaking soldiers to act as guards and carry bodies; the leader of the chorus; and a small boy to guide the blind Tiresias.

The Chorus

The chorus is described as being made up of Theban elders or noblemen and we might expect to see a group of men of about Creon's age and general appearance. The more alike they are in height, weight, and general bearing the better the visual effect. All must have good voices and exceptionally clear speech without faults or regional accents. The group must include both light and dark voices, or, to use the musical terms, tenor, baritone, and bass speaking voices. The light voices should predominate in a ratio of about three to two over the darker ones.

It is possible to produce the play with a mixed chorus of men and women, and even with a chorus composed entirely of women, but a chorus of substantial middle-aged males is better, as the women give to the Commus and to Stasimon Three, ("Ode to the Power of Love,") a different character than the men and one quite different from what the original must have been when spoken entirely by men.

The so-called "Leader" of the chorus is really a character without a name who acts as interlocutor, speaking for the group when questions or comments are addressed to the principals. Sometimes he is costumed as a councilor or attendant of the king and sometimes he remains with the choral group throughout. It is possible to do without him and have the questions asked by various individuals in the chorus. It is possible, but it is extremely difficult and I have never seen it done successfully.

Antigone

There is no particular way that Antigone has to look, although a small girl always looks better in contrast to the bigger and taller men with whom she has to appear. There is however a way she ought to *sound* if her scenes are to attain their maximum effectiveness. It is always best when the actress playing Antigone has a definitely emotional quality of voice. It is best when her mention of love conveys the impression of a person with a great capacity for affection. It is best when her mention of Polynices brings her to the verge of tears. And her lament in the Commus is certainly best when charged with emotion.

It is easy to forget that people who hold most firmly to principles are often highly emotional about it and react emotionally rather than rationally when their beliefs are challenged. Too often the character of Antigone, because she seems so sure of convictions, is played too firmly. This gives her a hardness which is quite out of character for the pitiable creature we see in the Commus. This is one of the high points of the performance and it is certainly the highest point of Antigone's role; her other scenes must harmonize with it.

To the reader Antigone does not seem very feminine, but this is different from the impression she usually creates in performance. Part of the way she seems to the reader derives from the language Sophocles gives her. In her replies to Creon she is unmistakably rude, her manner is brusque, and her whole air is at odds with what any ruler would have a right to expect from a subject half his age. This is what strikes us as unfeminine. But we are obliged to note that she uses this manner only in her exchanges with Creon whom she plainly loathes. It is not evident in her relationship with Ismene. In several instances in her dialogue first with Ismene in the Prologue and later in her exchange with Creon she is sarcastic, but one can scarcely call sarcasm unfeminine.

Creon

An important factor in the motivation of Creon is his intense hatred of Polynices and determination to punish him for the death of his son, but this is omitted from the exposition and mentioned only in the final scene. Those who know the Theban legend will remember that Megareus, Creon's youngest son, had been killed the day before in one of the first actions of the war. Thus in the quarrel between Polynices and Eteocles, Creon, originally the arbiter between them, has suffered the first and bitterest loss. Knowing this, one hardly wonders at the rage with which he strikes back at the traitor Polynices.

But Sophocles lets no one mention any of this until the play is almost over. Why? Certainly not because he could have expected every member of his audience to remember this detail of the story. Audiences at a play live in the present; what they know is what they are told or shown. I can only surmise that Sophocles saved the mention of Megareus' death until the Exodos because it is then that he builds sympathy for Creon and that he avoids it earlier in the play for fear that it might unbalance the conflict between Creon and Antigone by giving him too much sympathy too early.

The actor who plays Creon cannot help knowing about Megareus and the knowledge can help him in making his hatred of Polynices more understandably human than mere malice.

Most of the qualities evident in Creon's speech and actions are admirable: his love of order, in the state as in the home; his belief in discipline, especially self-discipline; his belief in man's duty to society; and his determination to do right and rule firmly. Less admirable are his devotion to blind justice, his fear of bribery (always the curse of an authoritarian system), and his sarcasm. Shocking to all is his facetiousness in moments when nothing could be more out of place, as in his comment on Antigone's lament at the end of the Commus: "If 'last words' could postpone death men would go on talking forever."

Creon's character undergoes no change during the play. He is the same person at the end as he was at the beginning. But our sympathy for him increases, beginning with his failure to win Haemon. From the moment in the Exodos when he enters preceded by the corpse of Haemon our sympathy for him is complete.

Haemon

In performance Haemon is always one of the audience's favorites and the actor who plays him is sure to receive much praise. This is curious because when one is merely reading the play he seems rather colorless. His argument is so good, his language so well chosen, and his demeanor so mature that he seems too well controlled for a youth. One would expect such a very young man to be more impulsive and certainly much less articulate. But in performance the clarity of his logic and the patience with which he presses his plea are admirable, all the more so because of his youth.

Not much is made of his love for Antigone, which becomes apparent only after the fact in the Messenger's description of his suicide. This may be due to the Greek idea of youthful love, which was very different from ours. Love, in their eyes, instead of being a divine fire guiding young folks into each others' arms to live happily ever after, was viewed as a kind of madness which unbalanced people, making them reckless and setting them at odds with their parents and causing all kinds of havoc in human relationships.

Haemon's role turns out best when played by an actor who looks youthful. He need not be handsome but he should be attractive in appearance. This youthful appearance when combined with maturity of manner is most effective.

Ismene

Compared to Antigone, Ismene at first reading seems timid. The part succeeds however if she is played for strength, stressing her dominent characteristics of unselfishness, pity, and understanding sympathy for her sister. In Episode Two she stands up for Antigone against Creon and is taken into custody expecting to die alongside her sister.

If the actress has a voice slightly darker and deeper in pitch than Antigone's and is able to convey to the audience the impression of a personality of some warmth and sympathetic understanding of others, she is certain to be successful in the part and the scenes in which she appears will gain power.

The Sentry

The soldier who brings the news of Polynices' burial is sometimes called "comic." It is true that his speech borders on the colloquial and that his manner is without dignity, but he is definitely no comic. The event he reports is shocking to all who hear him and he soon finds himself in peril of his life. Laughter at this point would ruin the tone of the scene. Yet some commentators have identified the sentry's scene as an early example of comic relief. Relief from what? The play has hardly begun. Relief at this point is the last thing an audience needs.

The Sentry's scenes come off best when he is made up, not as a youth, but as a middle-aged man of serious mein. One might think of him as a professional soldier trained to obedience, accustomed to carrying out orders that seldom make sense to him, and philosophical about the whims of his superiors. An attractive trait is his respect for Antigone and the obvious reluctance with which he brings her before Creon.

Tiresias

This part, both in *Oedipus Tyrannus* and *Antigone*, needs one of the strongest and most accomplished actors one can find. His warning to Creon must be terrifying to all who hear it, including the audience, in order to provide adequate motivation for Creon's change when he rescinds the decree and hurries to undo the wrongs he has done Polynices and Antigone.

The part does not require any particular mimetic ability since Tiresias, being blind, moves very little. But it does require an impressive stage presence, a fine voice, and a feeling for the worth of the lines.

The Messenger

The role of the Messenger in Greek tragedy is always one of the best in the play and is usually given to an actor with exceptional vocal range and delivery. The part is composed as a sort of show piece, like an aria in opera, which permits an actor of extraordinary vocal artistry and highly developed mimetic ability to display his accomplishments. He may be one of the choral group, one of Creon's attendants, or the Leader of the chorus. It is always best if he is one who has been on stage in some capacity long enough for the audience to recognize him when he enters for his big speech in the Exodos, for if he seems familiar his scene comes across much better than if it had been spoken by a newcomer.

SETTING, PROPERTIES AND COSTUMING

The Setting

The action of the play requires entrances for the principals from two directions and a separate entrance for the chorus. Creon's palace, or whatever indicates it, is usually best when placed upstage left so that those coming from this direction move diagonally to the right when coming into the acting area, this line of movement being easier as a rule for right-handed actors. Both entrances and subsequent movements are easier to manage when the palace is at one side rather than dead center. There is no real need for any doorway or arch for this entrance and the movement flows easily without it. It does help however to have several steps and a low platform on the palace side to give greater importance to the entrances from that direction. Entrance and steps need to be designed so that a body on a bier can be carried out by four men without difficulty. There also needs to be a shallow approach step and space enough off stage to set the bier down without turning.

On the opposite side of the stage is the exit which leads to the plain where the body of Polynices is lying. No steps or platforming are necessary on this side; in fact, the action flows better here when nothing impedes it. From this direction comes the Sentry, the Messenger, and Creon with the body of his son in the Exodos. Antigone exits in this direction when she goes to her tomb and Creon goes out here when he hurries off to release her and bury Polynices.

In order to keep the lines of movement clear it is best to have the chorus enter and leave through some neutral opening on the audience side of the acting area. If the theatre has vomitories in the auditorium these are ideal. Tiresias can use the same entranceway since he comes neither from the palace nor the plain.

A pair of benches, one on each side of the acting area, is useful. One can be used for the scene between Antigone and Ismene in the Prologue since the intimate nature of the scene makes seating more natural for the sisters than if they were standing. The other bench can be used by Haemon when, after failing to convince his father of Antigone's innocence, his despair requires something for him to sink down on for a moment or two before he makes his exit.

Properties

The text mentions no properties, but several are necessary, and as is usually the case when the properties are few, those that are there are important. The soldiers need weapons, Creon needs some symbol of his authority, and there usually is needed some sort of bier to make the bringing in of the bodies effective.

Shields and throwing spears are appropriate for the soldiers. Round shields look best, between thirty and thirty-six inches in diameter, painted with symbolic devices such as we see in the vase paintings. The characteristic Theban shield is more accurate and more practical in combat but it is never as attractive as the round one. The spears look best when the eight-foot throwing spears are used rather than the longer and heavier *sarissa*. The throwing spears are lighter and more graceful in appearance, and are carried in pairs lashed together.

Creon needs some sort of scepter or staff of office, a gilded and ornamented symbol of power passed down from ruler to ruler. Tiresias also carries a staff but of a different kind. Sometimes this is a rustic staff forked in the upper quarter, the conventional signification of the seer.

Biers are often used to bring in the bodies of Haemon and Eurydice for several reasons. One is that with a bier a body can be positioned so that all members of the audience can see it without effort. Another is that it can be made to fit the action of a character who has to play a scene of mourning on his knees over it. Sometimes Creon enters carrying Haemon in his arms, which makes an effective entrance but has the disadvantage of reminding us of the entrance of Lear with Cordelia in his arms. When both Haemon and Eurydice are carried in on biers Creon can play his last scene between them, turning first to one then to the other. If biers are used they should be provided with draperies so that the bodies can be partly covered, and the cloths should be of similar color as this always looks better. If the covercloth is large enough to trail a bit when the bier is carried the effect is enhanced. Ordinarily a bier is carried by four men, and it is always more impressive when it is carried on their shoulders.

Sometimes Antigone on her way to her death enters wearing heavy chains on her wrists and ankles. This is very effective in bringing home to the spectators the idea that she is being executed as a criminal, thus strengthening the sympathy for her and increasing the emotional impact of the Commus.

Costumes

In recent years it has been fashionable to costume the classics in some other period from that associated with ancient Greece. There are however few historical styles as well suited to the dignity of Greek tragedy as the draped garments of the period in which the plays were composed. These garments are extremely difficult to wear and require weeks of practice before actors can wear them comfortably, but they can be very handsome, and when worn well by all members of the company they are impressively appropriate.

In planning the color scheme the designer faces two problems: how to indicate the relationships of the members of the royal family and how to subordinate the chorus, soldiers, and attendants. The best treatment of the family members I have seen was one that gave to each person a garment of the same shade of red. This set them off from the other characters and was especially effective in the Exodos when Creon knelt between the two biers holding his son and wife.

Antigone is most effective in the Commus when she appears all in white with her himation worn in such a way as to form a covering for her head—the conventional Greek indication of mourning. Worn in this way the himation should be of some very fine thin material, the "fine linen veil" with which she is described as hanging herself.

Tiresias is sometimes garbed in black and sometimes in white with a black himation. It is best not to consider putting him all in white because then he would repeat the effect of the scene immediately preceding in which Antigone was in white. One all-white or all-black character is usually enough for a play.

It is important that the costumes of the soldiers be conceived as background for Creon and Antigone and therefore not be strong in color. Gray, gray-green, or some other dull, neutral tone is best, with leather rather than metal for belts, gorgets, and greaves. This is important because they must under no circumstances distract the eye from the central action. Too often soldiers are decked out in red with metallic trimmings and unless there is lively action on the part of the principals the scene always suffers.

The costumes of the chorus are less critical because they are not seen within the same frame of vision as the principals. In Greece the choruses of the tragedies are dressed in costumes of identical cut and color. One may follow this custom or one may vary the costumes slightly but it is always best to keep the colors subdued and the lines of the draperies similar even if they are not exactly alike, for the less the chorus is perceived as individuals the better the effect of the whole.

NOTES ON STAGING

A problem arises from the fact that *Antigone*, unlike most tragedies, begins and ends rather abruptly. Moreover, the opening scenes make little allowance for audience ignorance of the legend. The director must exert superhuman ingenuity if the spectators are not to go halfway through the first episode before they begin to feel that they really understand what is going on.

The scenes with the Sentry work best if Creon assumes, right up to the moment that Antigone speaks, that some stupid mistake has been made which will be cleared up as soon as she speaks. These scenes are tricky; if the Sentry is too ill-at-ease the audience tends to be amused and if they snicker the whole tone of the scene will be ruined.

A long pause after Creon's sentencing of Antigone (line 760), before Haemon makes any attempt to reply, generally makes the boy's final speech very moving.

The Commus is capable of attaining an emotional power hardly to be suspected from a study of the lines in printed form. Supporting music and an impressive spectacle of Antigone, looking pathetically small alongside her burly guards, being led to death, will guarantee a catch in the throat of even the most blasé theatregoer.

At what point in Tiresias' final speech does Creon recognize his mistake? This must be immediately clear to the audience. One way of making it clear is to darken the stage slightly, beginning at about line 1069, to reach an acceptable gloom before Tiresias exits. A low, muttering roll of thunder accompanying his reference to the Furies at line 1076 will make Creon's transition much easier to play.

The Messenger's speech plays best if Eurydice remains motionless throughout. All eyes will be on her in any case. The actress often wants to make some appropriate gesture of grief, but any movement is likely to lessen the tension. About the only move that can be made without weakening the grip of the scene is a slight turning away and even this should be experimented with before incorporating it into the performance.

The staging of the final scene ought to endow the conclusion with a feeling of magnitude. This is no petty calamity we are witnessing in *Antigone* but a cataclysm claiming the lives of three noble beings and destroying the will to live in another. Such suffering must seem admirable, not merely pathetic. The proper effect of the performed play is thus quite different from that which the solitary *reader* is likely to experience. To him the play seems to diminish toward the end as characters die off and Creon is left alone, mourning among the dead, but this diminuendo is aesthetically unsatisfying to the *audience* of a tragedy in which universal questions of justice and duty are debated. The sweep and scale of the finale of this tragedy may be enhanced by a variety of means: by artful lighting such as might, for example, invoke the splendor of a fiery sunset; by appropriate music to accompany Creon's agony; by surrounding him at the end with sympathetic supers and chorus; and, most of all, by building the scene to his final exit. Such is the art of staging. Carried out with sensitivity and taste it goes far toward giving the play its full value as tragedy.

CHAPTER 6

The *Electra* of Sophocles: A Problem of Proportion

Sophocles' *Electra* has not, in recent years, received as much attention from critics as the other treatments of the same story by either Aeschylus or Euripides. Yet Sophocles' version is much more dramatic than either of the others when performed. Several of its scenes are among the most moving ever contrived by any dramatist of any period. Sophocles has not simplified the characters but he has subordinated them to the plot, and it is his skillful plotting which above all other considerations makes his work effective in the theatre.

GRANDEUR AND MOMENTUM

Sophocles' concentrated on dramatizing the legend in such a way as to make the most of the opportunities for irony and emotional appeal. The force that propels Clytemnestra and Aegisthus toward their doom is not only Orestes' and Electra's thirst for revenge, or yet the mandate of Apollo; as presented by Sophocles it is more than both together. The force is the relentless operation of that law of nature which decrees that the fittest shall survive and that the unfit—the old, the ill, the weak, and the worn out of the species—shall fall prey either to the hazards of their environment or be overtaken by their successors. The fate of the King and Queen is the ultimate fate of all living things. Through the art of Sophocles the events of the play unfold in a majestic progression that seems to relate them to the inexorable momentum of universal nature.

The result is a work of impressive grandeur, awesome and powerfully dramatic in its climactic moments, a work which possesses to an extraordinary degree that quality called sublime. It is the same quality that is unmistakably present in masterpieces such as Dante's *Inferno*, Michelangelo's *Last Judgement*, and many of Beethoven's symphonies.

Grandeur is only the first of the impressions one receives from the performance of this splendid work. After beginning slowly, (at first it scarcely seems
to move at all) the progression gathers momentum. The play is almost a third
of the way along before the first signifcant action occurs with the Old Man's
report of Orestes' death in the chariot race at Crisa. It is two-thirds over before
Orestes himself appears with the urn. But from then on it gains speed, hurtling
into the climactic trapping of Aegisthus only forty-odd lines before the finale.

This acceleration of action in the final third of the play sweeps the spectator
along from one intensely dramatic scene to another still more exciting, with
the headlong movement heightened by the suspense generated by the immi-
nence of Aegisthus' return. For the producer the pattern of acceleration poses
several problems. Not only do the big scenes come quite far along in the progression but they come so fast and so close together that it becomes difficult to
develop them to maximum effect. On the other hand, in its earlier moments
the play moves at such a glacial pace it is difficult to convince an audience that
it is moving at all. The main problem in the first part seems to be keeping the
audience reminded of the fact that Orestes is already in Argos and will soon to
reappear. Of course they will have seen him in the Prologue, and, if they stop
to reflect will realize that his reappearance is imminent, but audiences live in
the present and it is easy for them to forget, with all the talk of his being far
away or dead, that he is actually nearby. The more convincingly Electra com-
municates her despair the easier it is for them to forget. Thus we have a problem of proportion in tempo between the slow-moving beginning and the breath-
taking rush of the denouement. Aegisthus' confrontation with Orestes at the
end always seems too brief. Yet we cannot escape the fact that the ponderous
movement of the preparatory first half adds weight to the final third, giving it
that overwhelming downhill "steamroller" momentum for which Sophocles' plays
are famous.

I have often wondered whether Episode Three, Chrysothemis' return from
the tomb, is really necessary in performance and whether the progression might
not be improved if this episode were omitted, but I have never had the courage
to leave it out. Then too, I have been intrigued by the problems this espisode
presents. For the same reason I have never been able to encourage any of my
friends to produce the play without it.

I should also note that the problem of proportioning the progression is much
more acute in an English-language production than it is in the original Greek.
The Greek language is more fluent than English so that the play flows along
more smoothly. When performed in Greek it is only about two-thirds as long
so that the first signs of forward motion come much earlier.

The producer of *Electra* in English would do well to consider upon what
varied resources he might draw in the effort to enliven the earlier scenes: music, choral activity, evolving light changes, elaborate settings, and eye-filling
costumes. In the Greek theatre today these choral performances are so beautifully done that the chorus utterly absorbs our interest; even the longest chorus

passages seem far too short. Perhaps by following the example of the Greeks an English producer might go far to overcome the problem of the first third, assuming of course that he has at his disposal the time and talent which the Greeks possess in such abundance.

CHARACTERS AND CASTING

If in the original production three actors played all the principal parts, the first actor could have undertaken only the role of Electra since she appears in every scene and in fact never leaves the stage after her first entrance. Of the other two, the second actor would have played both the Old man and Aegisthus, while the third would have doubled between the parts of Orestes and Clytemnestra. Either of them could have managed the role of Chrysothemis in addition, but it seems likely that it would have fallen to the one playing the Old Man and Aegisthus because it is he who would have to be the more skillful, both of his parts being technically more difficult than those of Orestes and Clytemnestra.

All of the characters are generalized, each being refined and streamlined in terms of his function in relation to the unfolding plot. Electra, for example, expresses the aching injustice of a situation that cries out for redress. Clytemnestra reveals to us the bitterness of a life of fear from which death is almost a welcome release. Aegisthus shows us the ruthless and self-centered tyrant whose death is a blessing to Argos. And Orestes is the rightful heir who brings a deserved retribution.

Electra

The actress who plays Electra does not need to be nearly as stage-wise as one might think. The technical demands of the role are much simpler than those of most other heroines in Greek tragedy. Her most difficult scenes come early in the play while the audience is still fresh and receptive. As the play progresses her part becomes smaller and less difficult. But because of the number of fairly long speeches and the length and variety of the antiphonal passages which she shares with the chorus the role demands an actress with a rich musical voice and exceptionally good diction. Intelligent casting of this part should therefore put vocal range and quality ahead of all other considerations. To the extent that appearance figures, it helps if she can be made up to bear a noticable resemblance first to her mother Clytemnestra and after that to her brother Orestes.

The character of Electra has received a great deal of attention from students of the legend, especially as treated by Aeschylus and Euripides. It is not unusual for critics to confuse the different Electras or for actresses to attempt to explain the motives of Sophocles' Electra by reference to the others. I think this is a mistake. The other Electras are presented as women victimized by their passions. Sophocles' Electra is the master of hers.

Freud coined the term "Electra complex" to identify the aberration characterized by a woman's excessive attachment to her father coupled with comparable hatred for her mother. This idea is not much use in understanding the character of the Electra which Sophocles created, for in his characterization he strives consistently to present characters who are typical rather than abnormal. As a general rule he shows no interest in aberrations. The characters he creates are heroic in the intensity of their feelings but except for this intensity they do not deviate from normality. Their emotions are not strange to us; they are the same as ours, only larger. Abnormal characters interest us today because of their strangeness. Sophocles' characters are fascinating for the opposite reason: because they are familiar. Thus to think of his Electra in terms of the Freudian complex is to allow oneself to be misled into conceiving of her as a warped personality. Electra's grief for her father and hatred for her mother are fully motivated not only by the adultery of her mother, the murder of her father, and the usurpation of the throne by Aegisthus but also by their brutal treatment of her.

David Grene, who has given us one of the finest translations of the play, professes to see no justification for this Electra and declares himself puzzled by her ruthlessness, wondering why Sophocles expended so much creative effort on such an unpleasant character. I do not know whether Grene is giving us an impression drawn from any performance of the play or only from his study of the text, but it seems to me that the obvious answer to his puzzlement is that Sophocles is not particularly interested in whether his characters strike us as pleasant or unpleasant. Nor does he strive for antipathy. He simply presents them as they are, but with understanding. Sympathy comes from the actor's management of the part. Sophocles' aim is clearly in the direction of creating a character that can plausibly perform the actions which the treatment of the legend requires. For *Electra* is not primarily a play of character but of plot, character is secondary to the course of the action. The character of Electra which he created in this instance is exactly the kind of person that the story demands. This is the justification for her existence. She does not have to have an attractive personality. He nature and her behavior ring true and this truth is the core of Sophocles' creation.

Orestes

Orestes has often been compared to Hamlet because both are principals in a play of revenge. The plays of Aeschylus and Euripides offer further points of comparison but in the *Electra* of Sophocles the resemblance ends where it begins, in the fact that each revenges a father's murder.

This Orestes is very young, clearheaded, fearless, and purposeful. He has appraised the risks in his enterprise and he recognizes the dangers confronting him, but he never hesitates. In his talk with Electra he is cautious until he knows who she is and soft-spoken afterward lest their exchange be overheard. Emotional expression in the reunion is voiced almost entirely by Electra. Orestes is less outspoken in his responses because his mind is on the task ahead of him. He seems unmoved by Aegisthus' predicament once the trap has been sprung and he proceeds to carry out the bidding of the Pythian oracle.

Because he has to describe to us the plan of action in the first minutes of the play while our ears are still becoming accustomed to the acoustics and the quality of the voices, the actor who plays Orestes must have very clear speech. A very youthful appearance is also desirable since he is at least ten years younger than his sister. Otherwise a tall good looking fellow would be nice to have, especially if he can be given a family resemblance to his mother and sister.

The Old Man

The man seems to be elderly but he is certainly not decrepit. His most conspicuous qualities are dignity, sympathy, and a strong sense of mission. He practices upon Clytemnestra a successful deception when he renders the false report of Orestes' death, but he must not seem devious. In fact, the more straightforward he seems the more successful he will be. His description of the chariot race is a gem of a speech and an actor is needed who can do it justice. He hurries the action, interrupting Orestes and Electra in order to urge them on to the task before them. He has nothing to say in response to Electra's joy at finding him still alive; his mind, like that of Orestes, is fixed on the work he has to do.

He appears in Argos as a royal amabassador. It is important that he look and carry himself like an ambassador. Electra does not recognize him at first, nor he her.

Chrysothemis

Chrysothemis is mainly a foil to Electra, to set her off in grief and determination. She seems intended to appear to be the sensible, down-to-earth sister, by comparison to Electra not quite admirable, but practical. As a foil she should have a voice which will afford some contrast to that of Electra.

As to appearance, her age would be nearer that of Electra than Orestes. Somehow we tend to think of her as a younger sister, just as we tend to think of Ismene in *Antigone* as an older sister. She should not be too pretty or the prematurely aged Electra will seem too old alongside her. It would be good if the resemblance between her and Electra and Orestes could be emphasized, as well as that between her and Clytemnestra.

Clytemnestra

In one scene of only 290 lines Sophocles gives us an extraordinarily complete portrait of the woman whose actions, more than those of anyone else, have created the situation in Argos which Orestes' action must remedy.

Finding Electra with her friends outside the palace where Aegisthus had placed her, Clytemnestra, mindful of the presence of the women surrounding Electra, launches immediately into a defense of her killing of Agamemnon many years earlier. The defense is not very convincing, for while she makes a pretty good case for herself on the grounds that Agamemnon deserved to pay for the life of her daughter, Iphigenia, whom he sacrificed at Aulis, she omits mention of the fact that she herself had been unfaithful to him during his absence in Troy. Electra of course is quick to make sure that this fact is exposed. Thus we see through the Queen's motives at once. Presently, when she offers her prayer to Apollo we see a glimpse of the insecurity and fear which form the dark undercurrent of her existence. For though she has succeeded in ridding herself of the husband she hated, and joining in sovereignty over Argos with the man whom she loved, the knowledge that she is loathed by Electra, and in continual danger of losing her life if Orestes returns, poisons her days and fills her nights with terrifying dreams. As she implores the god to deliver her we realize that we are watching a woman whose joy in life has been destroyed by fear and to whom death would be a deliverance. Before this happens Sophocles gives us a glimpse into her inner being through her reaction to the Old Man's description of Orestes' accident and funeral. Conflicting emotions rack her when she experiences at one and the same time unexpected grief at the loss of her son and joyous relief at the news of his demise.

There is a tendency to cast in the role of Clytemnestra an actress of conspicuously physical charm on the supposition that an adulteress should also seem sexy. This seems to me rather juvenile. Clytemnestra's passionate youth is many years in the past and certainly nothing inhibits sexual desire more severely than fear.

Aegisthus

In Greek productions Aegisthus is customarily shown as an unmistakable villain and when I first saw him played in this way I was taken aback. But the effectiveness of such a representation, especially in a large theatre, can scarcely be faulted. His scene is short, his lines are few, and he must register definitely if the climax is to succeed. Those speeches which Sophocles has given him reveal only a harsh, impatient, overbearing personality. His exclamation upon discovering Clytemnestra dead shows no grief or anything else so much as self concern. His last line is a sarcasm in reference to the manner in which Agamemnon died.

Such broad simple strokes are probably necessary for a briefly seen character to be effective in the vast outdoor theatres of antiquity. But in a modern theatre one-tenth as large a character can be represented in greater detail. His scene is much more dramatic when it can be made to show more than one side of his nature. For this reason many directors capitalize on the revelation in such a way as to allow him to seem devastated by grief. This yields a more moving and lifelike scene, leaving us with the impression that his attachment to Clytemnestra was more than a matter of lust and ambition and adding to his final moments a touch of pathos which enriches the play.

Because of the brevity of his one great scene the role of Aegisthus requires an actor of considerable skill and impressive appearance. If Orestes is tall, Aegisthus should be tall also, for he must dominate the stage up to the moment of his exit.

SETTING AND PROPERTIES

The setting should not be one of stark simplicity. This is not a tragedy which can be played against a few pylons and drapes. There must be enough to engage the eye during the slow-moving early scenes.

If credence is given to the Old Man's description of the scene in his opening speech one would have to show the palace of the Pelopidae and give some indication of the directions in which lie the Agora and the Temple of Hera. His mention of "Mycenae rich in gold" might provide some clue as to the nature of the ornamentation. Schliemann's diggings at Mycenae uncovered a massive fortess-like structure that today causes all who see it to marvel at the energy and ingenuity of its builders. It is built of gigantic stones, situated on a steep hill and approachable only through a great tunnel-like entrance, the famous "Lion Gate." After passing through the gate one comes upon a vast stronghold encompassing palatial dwellings, stables, barracks, watch towers, tombs, and spacious terraces from which one can scan the countryside for miles around. The old city, now partially excavated, lies spread out at the foot of the hill. Beyond it the rolling terrain, covered with olive groves and clusters of oleanders, recedes into the haze which ultimately blends sky, sea, and land into one continuous band of purplish blue. In this landscape there are only two routes by which Aegisthus could return to his palace and on either of them he could be seen from the terrace of the palace while still half an hour away.

How much of this we would want in a modern setting is something which the judgment and taste of the designer must decide. The effect of the high platform in front of the palace from which the approach of Aegisthus can be marked is certainly one of the more desirable features. The main entrance into the house seems to be central to the scene because of the number of grand entrances by Electra, Clytemnestra, and the bearers of Clytemnestra's body. Some designers have recreated an approximation of the Lion Gate for this entrance but it has never worked out very well because of the differences in function and style between the gate to the citadel and the front entrance to the palace. The huge door that Gordon Craig designed for Eleanora Duse in 1905 has appeared in so many publications since then that it is as difficult to ignore as it is to replicate; it seems the perfect background for the play. If such a portal is used, however, it must be wide enough when both doors are open for the bier to be carried in easily on the shoulders of Orestes' men. Designers habitually underestimate the width of openings, through which such large properties must be carried, so perhaps it would be best not to settle the exact dimensions until the bier has been built, hoisted on the shoulders of the performers and the whole ensemble carefully measured.

In Mycenae the tomb (called "Agamemnon's tomb" although no one is sure which royal person was actually interred there) is quite near the palace on a lower level just below one of the terraces. One can without much effort see the tomb from the terrace. Chrysothemis therefore does not have far to go to perform her rites although she would have a rather steep climb hurrying back to report her finding of the strange offerings left there.

Which brings us to the question of the direction from which the various entrances should be made. It seems logical that Aegisthus and Orestes, being in a sense antagonists, should enter from opposite directions. The only question is which of them should be given the better entrance from stage left, the preferred side for most right-handed actors. My own inclination is to give this entrance to Aegisthus because his scene is climactic and his long-awaited arrival provides the most dramatic entrance in the play with the sole exception of Clytemnestra's bier. Orestes' entrances and those of the Old Man would then be made from stage right. Since neither of these needs to be especially dramatic the fact that it is left-handed need not handicap the performers.

In ancient times the theatre had an altar in the center of the orchestra circle which seems to have functioned as the focal point for the many sacrifices which are offered up in the plays. Clytemnestra's offering is probably intended to be made at such an altar and it would certainly facilitate the action if an altar were included in the setting. This would serve several purposes: its presence would reinforce the religious nature of Orestes' mission, reminding us that he is acting upon the bidding of Apollo; and after Clytemnestra's sacrifice the remains of her offering, continuing visible, heighten the irony of her thinking herself secure at the very time that her danger is greatest.

In a modern theatre it would be possible for this particular setting to have more levels than are usually desirable in a Greek tragedy. In most a fairly large flat area is needed for the activities of the chorus but in this one most of the choruses, and especially the parodos and first antiphony, can be choreographed as well on varied levels as on the flat floor. None of the choruses here requires fast movements of the kind indispensable to the performance of *The Bacchae* or *Oedipus at Colonus*.

Among the hand properties the most significant item is the urn which supposedly contains the ashes of Orestes and over which Electra grieves. This urn must be graceful of outline and handsomely ornamented as befits the repository of royal remains. It must be of a color which will be easily visible against Electra's costume. And it must be of a size, shape, and weight that the actress can manage to best effect. It is sometimes necessary to try half a dozen different urns before settling on one which meets all requirements, so one should make sure that the property man knows in advance that he is going to have to continue making or finding urns until the right one is secured.

After the urn the most important property is the bier upon which Clytemnestra's body is carried in. The bier needs to be made so that it can be carried gracefully by four or five men—for the slightest awkwardness will destroy the solemnity of the entrance—and carried off again by the women of the chorus, since the men will have been occupied with Aegisthus. Those portions of the bier that are visible to the audience should be elegantly finished. There is a danger that the bier may turn out to be too high for Aegisthus to embrace the corpse easily while kneeling upstage of it. The best way to avoid this is to have the actor who plays Aegisthus experiment with benches of various heights until the right height is found; the bier can then be built to these dimensions.

The text of the play does not make much of the fact that Orestes and his men are armed to the teeth and ready to fight any minions of Aegisthus who come between them and the execution of their mission. Most of the time their weapons are concealed under their cloaks, but when they prepare to enter the palace we should see that they are prepared for their task. After they have slain Clytemnestra they show themselves briefly with blood on their hands and weapons. When they reenter carrying the corpse of Clytemnestra their weapons would of course be hidden again, but after Orestes reveals himself the weapons should be displayed so that Aegisthus finds himself surrounded by armed men who leave him no avenue of escape. The circle of bloody swords escorting him into the palace then makes a memorable picture.

Since Aegisthus is not armed he should at first be accompanied by a number of archers or spearmen so that for a moment it will appear that Orestes' enterprise hangs in the balance. But when, after hearing that the corpse is within, he dismisses his guard, the way is open for Orestes' surprise.

The only remaining properties required by the action are the offerings brought in by Chrysothemis and Clytemnestra. Those of Chrysothemis are described as "funeral libations" by some translators and "burnt offerings" by others. They might be carried on trays by one or more attendants as it would be difficult for Chrysothemis to play her scene while holding them. Electra seizes them from her, dashes them to the ground, then gives her instead her own girdle and a lock of her hair while the attendants gather up the scattered fragments of the original offering.

Clytemnestra's offering is of a different kind. It is carried in by her hand-maiden and, after being held high during the supplication, is placed reverently on the central altar where it remains for the rest of the play. The offering consists of "fruits of the earth" which one might expect to be a handsome tray of fruit and flowers. The bright colors enhance their visibility and strengthen their dramatic function of keeping us reminded of the irony of the Queen praying for deliverance to the very god who has decreed her destruction.

COSTUMING

Electra's repeated references to the manner in which she has been abused by her mother demand that she be costumed in garments which by comparison with those of the other women will seem shabby and threadbare. On the stage this effect is attained by the use of coarse fabrics, uneven hems, and liberal smudging. Her poor rags would not of course be very bright in color but because she must dominate the stage through nearly half the play they cannot be very dark either. She is sometimes costumed in black but this is a mistake because it makes her recede into the background. Black is not only hard to light but it also tends to endow the character who wears it with a certain elegance, an effect which is opposite of the one we need here. A costume lighter in value than those of the surrounding chorus would set her off to advantage, and a light costume is easier to make soiled and ragged. The girdle which she removes to give to Chrysothemis should not be too elegant; if she had been oppressed for as many years as she says she would not have anything handsome about her.

Her rags should cover her completely. A glimpse of shapely arms or legs has no place here. We should not be able to sense an attractive figure under the clothes that we see. Any suggestion of sex appeal is at odds with the character of the tragic heroine originally played by a man.

However her hair is arranged it will need to include a detachable switch in order to facilitate the business where she tears out a handful of hair to give to Chrysothemis as an offering on the tomb of their father.

Chrysothemis' costume should be entirely different since she has enjoyed all the amenities of palace life, with handmaidens to bathe her, dress her, and do her hair. Her clothing ought to be of the finest materials gracefully draped and she should wear a modicum of tasteful jewelry. With all this it is better if she is not made to appear too attractive for she must not attract our sympathy or attention away from Electra. Her physical coloring—hair, eye makeup, and complexion—can be made less vivid than that of Electra. Perhaps the costume designer can contrive some combination of colors which will make her seem rather cold and remote. The greater the contrast between her and Electra the better their scene together will be.

Clytemnestra should appear haggard and at the same time be richly gowned, crowned, and bejewelled. She is older than any of the others; perhaps this could be indicated in the pallid tone of her body makeup, in her complexion, and in her hair coloring. Her principal garment will need to be bold of color so that when her corpse is uncovered recognition is instantaneous. Red is the best hue for this purpose. If it is used on her no one else in the cast should be dressed in any remotely similar shade. The most effective color I have seen her in was a sort of faded crimson in what appeared to be linen or wool. The designer was apparently trying for the true tone of the ancient Tyrian purple which we know to have been a dull crimson. In this instance the effect was brilliantly right for the play.

Aegisthus' entrance is awaited throughout most of the play. When he finally enters his time on the stage is brief so we can afford to costume him in something very striking. A good deal of gold about him in the form of jewelled crown, enamelled pectoral, embossed girdle, gilded sandals, and so on, would enhance his appearance. Since he is an older man, well past middle age, an ankle-length chiton with an overdrape would be appropriate. He carries no weapon so we are not encouraged to wonder why he makes no attempt to defend himself. Nor can he carry a staff or scepter since these would interfere with his business of uncovering the corpse. In Greek drama the older men are conventionally bearded, so he should be.

The Old Man is much older than Aegisthus, equally bearded, and somewhat more grizzled. His costume should be rich, as becomes a royal ambassador, but he should not be nearly as rich in appearance as Aegisthus. He can carry a staff, perhaps a symbolic staff of office, as this in no way hinders his action or his big speech describing the chariot race.

Orestes, being a youth of no more than twenty years, might properly appear in a short chiton, especially if he is played by an actor with good physique. Over this he needs a voluminous cloak of some dark color under which he can conceal his weapons. This cloak often has a hood with which he covers his head and hides his face when he enters with Clytemnestra's corpse. He wears a signet ring which belonged to his father and which he shows to Electra to prove his identity.

Orestes' attendants are dressed as he is, but in less brilliant colors. The dramatic effect of their appearance with bloody hands and weapons after Clytemnestra's execution will be greatly enhanced if their garments are also splattered with blood, although this will require a second set of chitons, which will have to be donned while they are offstage during the supposed killing, but the effect is worth the extra work. The effect is repeated when they throw open their cloaks after trapping Aegisthus.

Since the chorus is composed of Mycenean women they might appropriately be gowned in rich fabrics and ornaments so as to afford the greatest possible contrast with the impoverished Electra, but in costumes nearly identical. When they are different we tend to become conscious of individuals in the group and this impairs the total effect.

NOTES ON STAGING

In the opening scene it is important that the behavior of Orestes and his men convey the acute danger of their mission. His description of his plan of attack works best if played as far from the palace and as close to the audience as possible, in something of a conspiratorial tone.

If the Old Man's entrance as ambassador (line 660) can be managed so as to surprise the audience by appearing to be an almost miraculous response to Clytemnestra's prayer the scene is greatly enhanced.

The three-sided passage in which Electra and Clytemnestra react to the Old Man's false report of the death of Orestes (line 673) is too brief for the amount of emotion it must convey. Because of this it makes extraordinary demands upon the skills of the two actresses.

The description of the fatal chariot race (lines 680 to 761) should not be too glib. Remember, the Old Man is making it up as he goes along, watching the effect of his words on the Queen. He has no way of knowing that Lew Wallace is going to borrow his description for the similar race in *Ben-Hur*.

The succeeding antiphony between Electra and the Chorus (lines 823–70) is one of the finest in all Greek drama, especially if set to music and sung.

The "urn scene" (line 1120 and following) and the subsequent reunion of brother and sister combines one of the most moving with one of the most thrilling scenes ever contrived by any playwright in any language. It is certain to inspire the actors to their finest achievement. The Greek companies I have seen play this passage at an incredibly high emotional pitch, higher than is usually possible in the less fluent English language.

The only real problem with the "revelation scene" (line 1458 and following) is to keep the actor from letting his excitement trick him into playing it too fast. In my experience it scarcely seems possible to play the scene slowly enough to develop its full value.

It is best to have the corpse carried in on a bier and placed well forward on the stage in a position where every member of the audience will be able to see all the details of Aegisthus' reaction. To place it upstage in the palace doorway, as I have sometimes seen it done, not only makes it hard for the spectators to see it but also forces Aegisthus to play his uncovering while turned away from the audience.

CHAPTER 7

The Trojan Women: A Problem of Emotional Tone

At its best *The Trojan Women* is a grand, rich dirge of vast dimensions, presenting characters of heroic stature dignified by grief and suffering. The language is some of the finest of a great poetic age, giving full expression to the emotions and lingering long afterward in the mind like the cadences of some great symphony.

Structurally the work is exceptionally strong and clear, giving us, not a plot in the usual sense of the word, but a progression of clear-cut virtuoso scenes for accomplished actors, separated by brilliant choral passages, and enframed in irony by means of a prophetic prologue.

AESTHETICS OF THE DIRGE

The powerful pathos of certain scenes has led some commentators to question Euripides' aesthetic judgment; perhaps the play is so harrowing that it exceeds the limits of art. My own belief is that this question could come only from one who has never experienced a really first-rate production of the play, for there is nothing maudlin about its appeal, its poetry is magnificent, and its total effect profound and satisfying. I have seen it staged many times, often well done and sometimes splendidly done, and while not all the actors have been equally effective, none of them, even the most skillful, has reduced the inherent stature of any character very much. But really good actors can make it an inspiring experience for the audience. At the same time those of lesser genius seldom seem to spoil it.

Those who provide us with introductions to the various translations invariably mention the brutalities of the Peloponnesian war which might have been in Euripides' mind when he composed the play. This is possible, but we do not know exactly when he wrote *The Trojan Women* and we must also remember that the ugly side of warfare, the way in which it brutalizes its participants, destroys cities, and wastes life, is no new discovery, and was not then. The four horsemen were never far from the Athenians of the fifth century, and the physical horrors of the Peloponnesian war which they lost were for most of them not very much different from those of the Persian war which they won. The ability to discern the finer qualities of human character in the midst of humiliation and defeat is an achievement of genius; the ability to give full voice to these qualities is the genius of the poet.

CHARACTERS AND CASTING

If three actors played all the parts, the first actor would have played Hecuba who appears in all scenes. The second actor would have played all the other women, each of whom appears but once. The third actor would then have played the men: Poseidon, Talthybius, and Menelaus, and would have had ample time to change costumes between his appearances in the different roles.

Hecuba

The contrast between the Greek view of life and that of the Judeo-Christian is nowhere more vividly exemplified than in the character of Hecuba. We tend to think of adversity, grief, and suffering as purifying and ennobling. The person who suffers greatly, especially if he suffers unjustly, becomes in our eyes a kind of martyr, like Job, superior in fortitude and strength of character to those who have not endured comparable trials. The Greeks saw the effects of suffering upon human character in a different light. As in certain Mediterranean cultures today, the person who suffers extremes of pain, injustice, or grief, although accorded sympathy, is thought of as temporarily unbalanced and deserving of special consideration because, for the time being, he is not himself and therefore not entirely responsible for what he says and does. Not until he regains his balance can he again be considered a whole man. Suffering, therefore, does not ennoble a person, rather it unbalances him. The effect of repeated adversity may be to permanently dehumanize the sufferer. The ability to survive is admirable but the cost of survival under great adversity may be such a hardening of character as to make a person unfit for human society. This is what the Greeks mean when they speak of a character as being made "unclean" by grief, an idea strange to our way of thinking. We see evidence of the Greek view in the characters of Oedipus, of Jason, of the Electra of Sophocles, and most vividly of all in that of Hecuba as presented by Euripides.

Hecuba appears in two plays of his, in *The Trojan Women* and in *Hecuba* which is believed to have been composed about ten years earlier. The two representations are entirely consistent. The character we see in *The Trojan Women* is the same woman, but at the beginning of her *via dolorosa*. *Hecuba* shows us the same poor creature near the end of her life when, upon discovering that the last of her sons, Polydorus, has been murdered by the king to whom she had sent him for safe-keeping, she executes upon his slayer a horrible revenge. According to the prophecy made by her victim and also according to the legend the bitterness of her grief rendered her unfit for human form and she turned into a bitch. Thereafter when she attempted to curse she could only bark. Finally she threw herself into the sea, and on the coast of Thrace near the spot where she perished a monument was erected to her memory.

The Trojan Women has often been called plotless by those who believe that tragedy should conform to the description given by Aristotle. But if we use the term plot to designate the progression of events the plot of this play is the progression of Hecuba from grief to despair, to the attempt to destroy herself by leaping into the flames of her burning city, and finally, after being frustrated in this attempt, to a bitter determination not to be broken, come what may. Her suffering here seems to harden and toughen her spirit and although at the outset she is certainly every inch a queen at the end she seems still more heroic. She does not resign herself to the grim future and she does not submit. She simply survives. It is not a pretty picture, but it has a convincing truth.

Hecuba's attempt at suicide is the climax of the play. This is the point toward which the progression builds and from which it recedes to the finale. The enshrouding of little Astyanax, the grandson upon whom she had pinned her hopes for posterity, is the last straw. As she finishes laying out the tiny corpse she turns to her women and cries out that the gods offer nothing but affliction and hatred; man is what he is only through his own actions. Soon afterward she sees the fire spring up as the city is put to the torch and her suicide attempt follows.

The basic problem of the actress playing Hecuba is to proportion her emotional attack in such a way that she can continue to intensify as she builds to the climax and to avoid hitting too high a level too soon. If she goes all out at the beginning she may become tiresome before the peak is reached. The greater the performer's emotional and vocal range, the more successful she is likely to be, provided she can manage the proportioning. The essential qualities of authority and dominence are probably less difficult to attain, having been built into the role by the playwright.

The best Hecubas I have seen have always been given by actresses who conceived Hecuba as a strong queen, a born leader accustomed to respect and obedience. Against this firmness was set the occasional giving way to tears and the glimpses of her suffering. Not until the second half of her scene with the dead child did she break down completely. Other Hecubas, playing for pathos earlier in the progression, have been less moving and less meaningful and have not held their audiences as well.

How old should Hecuba be? This is the invariable question of the young actress. She calls herself "old" but this is not necessarily an indication of actual age as much as an expression of how she feels relative to her lost home and loved ones. References to her in Homer, as well as in Euripides generally, indicate a woman of maturity, dignity, and impressive bearing, no longer young and certainly past middle age, but not what we today think of as actually elderly—not bent nor haggard nor crack-voiced. In other words, old enough to be older than any of the others but not old enough to suffer any limitations upon her vocal range or grace of movement. If played this way her final scene when, after being stopped in her suicide attempt, she can hardly drag herself to her feet for her final exit, can be extremely moving.

Poseidon

Poseidon's part contains some of Euripides' finest poetry. The speeches with which he opens and closes the Prologue are especially splendid. The principal problem confronting the actor comes from the fact that he must speak these lines at the very beginning of the play while the ears of the audience are still adjusting to the acoustics of the theatre and the quality of an unfamiliar language. This argues for an actor with a good voice, a wide musical range, and extremely clear speech. If in addition he can exert a commanding presence in spite of the dim light in which he appears, he should do very well.

Athena

Athena's part is not especially difficult except for the fact that, like Poseidon, she must make herself heard early in the play under difficult conditions. For the most part she is merely a foil for Poseidon. Her longest speech is only ten lines. As for appearance, a tall girl does very well in this part.

Cassandra

Hecuba speaks of Cassandra as if she were hardly more than a child and this is usually the best way to play her. In the *Iliad* Cassandra's curse was that, while she foresaw the future and described it to all, no one believed her. In this play the incredulity of her hearers is not stressed; her prophecies are. Well played, the somber passage in which she glimpses the manner of her own death is spine-chilling, all the more so because it occurs in the midst of her rejoicing at being, as she supposes, the bride of the great Agamemnon.

A fragile ethereal quality is appropriate for her and harmonizes well with her joyous song. From what Hecuba tells us we know that she is out of her mind, driven mad by the violence done her during the sack of the city. In the sharing out of the spoils Cassandra has been allotted to Agamemnon. Now, fancying herself a bride instead of the captive she really is, she decks herself in bridal raiment and enters carrying a hymeneal torch. The more innocent and helpless she seems the more effective her scene becomes.

She has one song and two rather long speeches which can be partly sung. An actress with a good singing voice who can also manage the contrast between the tone of the happy rejoicing and the dark prophecy is what the part requires, almost like two characters in one.

Talthybius

Except for Menelaus and five or six supernumerary soldiers, Talthybius is the only one of the Greeks we see. He appears four times, each time upon some errand for the conquerors. He plays better as a civilian than as a soldier. Euripides has chosen to represent him as sympathetic to the plight of the women. He says several times that his task is odious to him and he apologizes for the orders he has to give. He is gentle in his treatment of the mad Cassandra and tender in his handling of the child Astyanax. For this part we need an actor who can convey warmth and sympathy, a strong man but one also reverent, grave, and never brusque or harsh.

Andromache

In all the accounts of the Trojan war, Andromache, wife of the heroic Hector, is represented as the model of wife and mother. Euripides here follows the conventional view but ennobles her further by giving her one splendid scene where she is forcibly parted from her infant son when the Greeks come to take him away to the execution decreed for all surviving Trojan males. An actress of strong emotional appeal can make this scene all but unbearably poignant and at the same time a thing of great beauty.

Menelaus

As the only one of the Greek captains whom we actually see, Menalaus should seem the personification of the proud overbearing conqueror. He boasts about the vengeance he is about to wreak on his unfaithful wife and he lords it over the poor captured princesses of Troy.

Euripides shows him not only as a cruel man but also a hollow one, for he soon meets his match coming face to face with Helen. When this scene is over his boasts lie unfulfilled and the wife he swore to slay goes blithely back to Sparta with him to resume her place at his side as if nothing had happened.

In order to avoid the possibility of laughter Menalaus must be impressive in appearance. This is no part for a man of below average height. If he is tall and big-voiced he is less likely to appear ridiculous. His emptiness will become apparent in any case because Euripides has made sure it would.

Helen

After being named repeatedly as the cause of the war and all the ensuing misery and cursed with horrible oaths by the women of Troy, Helen finally appears. It is not clear how Euripides intends the character to seem to us and as a result the role has provided actresses with an almost unlimited range of options. All make her as beautiful as possible but some endeavor to make her as hateful as the Trojans say she is while others attempt to give us some insight into the nature of irresistible beauty. Still others show us a creature who, while fickle, vain, and cowardly, thrives nevertheless on her ability to manage men to her own advantage.

Helen seldom seems as beautiful as the legend describes her because every member of the audience has his own idea of beauty and all are different. Yet at the same time because she is Helen and because in the play all pay tribute to her beauty, she does bring with her onto the stage an aura of beauty that always favors her performance.

The character Euripides has given us is notable for her self-assured poise, her cunning appeal to Menelaus's vanity and superstition, and for her cringing in fear when she pleads for her life. The last words she utters are: "Remember all, and slay me not!" After that she accompanies the soldiers to the galley without even looking back at the Troy she brought to ruin. All in all it is a remarkably plausible recreation of the Helen of the legend.

Actresses sometimes mar her exit by letting the audience see a sort of smirk of triumph on her face as she turns away from the others to make her exit. This is quite unnecessary; it is obvious enough that she has won without her having to mark it in any way.

The actress who plays Helen does not have to be genuinely beautiful. All she needs in the way of appearance is a face and figure that the costumer can do something with; one, in other words, without noticable flaws. What she does need and cannot do without is a beautiful speaking voice and naturally graceful movement.

SETTING, LIGHTING, AND PROPERTIES

The locale of the play lies somewhere near the city of Troy on the day after it has been overcome and sacked by the Greeks. Some noblewomen of Troy, survivors of the holocaust, are gathered together to await transportation to the various lands of the Greek captains who have claimed them as slaves. Except for the break in the wall through which the wooden horse was brought, Troy still stands, with its "crested walls" and "shining towers." The tents of the Greeks, Helen's chamber, and the palace of Priam seem to be nearby. Frequent reference is made to the waiting ships although none need be visible to the audience.

The last act of the victors is to set fire to the city. The spectacle of the burning, with the spreading smoke and the crash of falling towers, supplies an awesome climax of sound and spectacle after which the women leave to embark on the ships which will carry them into slavery.

The setting requires the usual flat space for the movements of the chorus, plus some platform or position of eminence from which the god Poseidon and the goddess Athena can speak the Prologue. Some producers have positioned them in the auditorium on either side of the stage, an arrangement which has the advantage of separating them from the main action as well as putting them close to the spectators. Others have had them materialize vision-like behind scrim sections of the setting. The central promontory however is still the simplest arrangement and the one most often used.

Also necessary, and possibly at the same place, is an elevation from which Hecuba can attempt to throw herself into the flames of the burning city.

Beyond this the only physical requirement of the setting consists of the entrances, three different ones coming from three different directions, one for the women, one for Helen who has been kept apart from the others, and one for the Greeks who come and go from the camp and ships.

Reference is made to the breaking of day at the beginning of the play and to the approach of night at the end. This seems to indicate the familiar dawn-to-dusk cycle found in so many of the tragedies. Poseidon and Athena seem to meet just before sun-up when there is just enough light to see the desecrated temples. Hecuba awakes as the sun comes up.

It would be out of keeping with the tone of the play to light it as if there were bright sunlight, or to use very colorful filters on the lights except for the conflagration at the end. More appropriate would be lighting suggesting a gray overcast sky and a chilly day. Against such lighting the torch of Cassandra would furnish a welcome contrast and the spectacle of the burning city at the end of the play would provide visual relief.

The burning of Troy is one of the more memorable "effects" in Greek tragedy and it should therefore be made as impressive as the ingenuity of the lighting designer can make it, with great leaping flames, and not, as is too often seen, a mere glow of ruby light on the sky-drop. There should be enough smoke to turn the stage into a seeming inferno until the fire begins to die down and the women prepare to depart.

The required stage properties consist of the symbols carried by Poseidon and Athena, Cassandra's torch, the cart piled high with the treasure looted from Priam's palace, the weapon with which Menelaus threatens to kill Helen, the "great orb" of Hector's shield upon which the body of the infant is placed, the burial shroud and materials needed in preparing him for interrment, the torches with which the soldiers set fire to the city, and whatever weapons the soldiers carry when they accompany Talthybius and Menelaus.

Cassandra's torch seems to be a brand she has snatched from the campfire. About a third of the way through her scene Hecuba takes it from her and, since Hecuba herself cannot work with a torch in her hand, gives it to one of the women who carries it off stage so that the flame will not create a distraction. The torch is much more dramatic in an outdoor theatre where actual flame can be used. For indoor productions a clever property man can make a torch that is almost as good if he cares to take the time and trouble.

The loot from the palace is described as being brought in on a cart with Andromache and her little son. Hector's bronze armor is specifically mentioned, along with gold ornaments, silverware, and pilfered fabrics. Only in a very large theatre can this spectacle be made as impressive as it might have been in its original form, with several mule-drawn carts and a large train of attendants. In an indoor theatre of average size it is better to let Andromache walk, following the spoils which can either be heaped on carts or carried on the shoulders of supers. If the idea that Euripides presents—of the victors hauling away huge quantities of treasure from the homes of their victims—is to register, the spoils must be abundant and their richness of texture and color impressive. A good many glittering golden things should be arranged to catch the light, interspersed with richly colored fringed and embroidered fabrics. The armor of Hector would include his embossed cuirass and at least one helmet with a horsehair crest. If properly staged, the passage across the stage of the carts or bearers should bring a gasp of awe at the elegance of the loot. As the amount of treasure from any noble house of the time would have filled not one but many carts, the display should be as lavish as the property man can make it.

The shield of Hector, which is used as a bier for the murdered child, is the most important property in the play and should accordingly be given the utmost artistry. The finest shield I have seen was the one used in Eva Le Gallienne's National Repertory production in 1966. It was circular and appeared to be about forty-two inches in diameter with an embossed face and concave back about six inches deep, just deep enough for the child's body to fit into snugly in the foetal position.

The burial cloths are best when of white material. White helps visibility, which is always a problem in a scene as closely confined as Hecuba's lament over Astyanax, especially when the center of interest, in this case the corpse of the infant, is small.

The weapon that Menelaus carries when he comes to kill Helen is most often a sword, but the scene plays better if it is something more barbaric, such as a club or axe. These look murderous and provide a more striking change when Helen's pleas cause Menelaus to relinquish his intention of killing her on the spot.

As to the soldiers' weapons, the war is over now, no combat threatens, and the corralling of the female slaves would hardly require battle implements such as spears and shields. For the management of slaves clubs or whips would be more appropriate and also make the soldiers appear more brutal.

COSTUMING

Today it is fashionable to costume an old play either in modern dress or in some period other than that in which it is placed by the author. As a result I have seen The Trojan Women in almost every kind of dress imaginable. One production had the Greeks in German uniforms, zooming in and out on motorcycles. This was novel and attracted much interest. But all it really added was novelty, which wears thin after the first twenty minutes and cannot carry an otherwise weak production. The truth is that novelty, which is great for comedy, is not really valuable in tragedy. The Trojan Women, because of its harrowing scenes, needs aesthetic distance rather than immediacy. Such distance the dress and architecture of antiquity provides. The draped costumes of fifth-century Greece already possess the dignity cum grace which is the visual quality most needed in tragedy.

The chorus should not be in rags. These are all women of high rank and birth. Their garments, although now stained and torn by the events of the previous night, are of the finest materials. They would not be in mourning for they would have had no time to don mourning. Most likely they would now be wearing whatever they put on when surprised in their homes by their captors. None should be wearing any ornaments since their captors stripped them of their jewelry. As a group they should be subordinated in color and tone to Hecuba, Andromache, and Cassandra; since they remain on stage all the time they must not divert attention from the principals. If they have scarves with which they can cover their heads during the dirge over Astyanax' body, this helps the tenor of the scene.

Hecuba, who is on stage every minute from beginning to end, needs the most carefully designed costume, with ample drapery to enhance graceful movement, rich coloring, and enough detailing of borders to engage the eye during the long scenes. All references to Hecuba suggest a woman of great dignity and power, impressive in bearing, and graceful in movement.

Talthybius the herald is not a warrior and should not be dressed as one. Since he is a man of at least middle age an ankle length chiton in some subdued color would be appropriate.

Menelaus, in contrast, should be showy, in handsome armor, with greaves and bright colored embroidered chiton. By the time he makes his entrance the play is beginning to need visual relief so that an elegant costume for him would provide a needed lift for the scene. Should he wear a helmet? Only if one can be provided which will enhance his appearance and which he can wear comfortably throughout the scene.

Helen needs every resource of the costume designer to make her convincing as the most beautiful woman the world has ever seen. Soft fabrics, subtle warm colors, well-placed waist and neck lines, and carefully arranged draperies are called for. Jewelry of gold and enamelware, bracelets, rings, earrings, and a fillet for her hair, are all desirable. Helen, being the wife of Menelaus, has not been treated as roughly as the Trojans. Her coiffure or wig should be designed so as to flatter her features from every angle. Most people think of Helen as blonde, probably because of the "fair Helen" of many English translations, so hair of a blonde or red-gold color generally works well.

There remain only the soldiers who are in and out of the scene so often, carrying spoils, accompanying Talthybius and Menelaus, taking little Astyanax from his mother and bringing him back as a corpse, setting fire to the city, and finally herding the women off to the waiting ships. Soldiers in ancient times did not wear uniforms, but for our purpose they look best when costumed alike, and, because we are accustomed to seeing soldiers in uniform, they will also look less individual and more soldierly. Since they must remain on stage throughout several of the longer scenes their coloration will have to be dull—gray, gray-green, or brown—with a minimum of ornament. They can wear breastplates of bronze or cuirasses of leather. Helmets are good, especially the kind that conceal the face, for these give them an impersonal inhuman look appropriate to their function in the play. Greaves or calf-high boots, along with chitons coming down to just above the knee, will make casting less difficult by easing the problem of finding men with equally good legs. The soldiers should be as nearly as possible the same height and weight, and if all can be bigger than the average man this will help to make their captives look smaller and more helpless. Any discrepancies in height should be avoided. Such discrepancies are for comedy, not tragedy.

The costumes of Poseidon and Athena can follow the conventional representations of these deities as they appear in sculptures and vase paintings. In these Athena is gowned in a long chiton, wearing a helmet of the Corinthian style pushed back to reveal her face. Poseidon is usually shown with a curly chest-length beard and a crown of sea-weed, in a long chiton, sometimes festooned with seaweed. Fabric of some unearthly color and texture helps to set them off from the humans. Various substances have been tried by different designers, such as oil-cloth, rubber sheeting, or plastic-faced fabric, all of which fall in rather stiff statue-like folds. Since neither deity needs to move around much, the unyielding materials need not hamper them seriously. Gray, gray-blue or gray-green have been the most successful colors. In the rather cold light of pre-dawn morning these colors provide an appropriately ethereal look. Some designers have also put them into half-masks either of silver or of some hue similar to that of the costumes and this often helps to set them off and seem more god-like.

NOTES ON STAGING

The power of Cassandra's scene depends on the strength of the contrast between her generally happy mood and the sudden glimpse of her dark future. Her torch is an effective property up to the moment Hecuba relieves her of it; thereafter it cannot be allowed to remain on the stage as its light is distracting.

Stasimon One, describing the raising of the siege, the wooden horse, and the sack of the city, lends itself superbly to choreography.

The smaller the child and the bigger the soldiers (line 786), the more effective the exit as he walks off between them. Some directors have had him turn back and attempt to comfort his mother or to retrieve some toy but this can be too harrowing, especially if Andromache's scene has gone well.

On Menelaus' line, "I come to kill," (905) he sometimes seizes an axe or club from one of his soldiers and starts to strike Helen with it, only to be checked by Hecuba on the line, "No, Menelaus, listen to her." Hecuba's line is sarcastic but Menelaus subconsciously welcomes the check.

If Helen's appeal to Menelaus (line 1040) gets too sexy the audience will snicker, but many an actress cannot resist giving Menelaus a fairly good going-over during this speech.

Any difficulty about getting the child to lie absolutely quiet during this long scene (line 1207) can be safely solved by substituting a dummy.

Hecuba's speech of despair (lines 1272–83) builds to her attempt to throw herself into the flames. The business of the soldiers stopping her in time is always difficult and requires much extra rehearsal.

It takes a great deal of rehearsal with all hands on deck to coordinate the spectacle and the noise of the burning city with the lines so that the splendid poetry of the women's lament and farewell is not lost.

Sometimes the gods reappear briefly in the dusk after the women have left the stage, with a roll of thunder to remind us of their vengeance awaiting the victors. Their reappearance is not part of the original play but it improves the production in the same way that an epilogue provides a satisfying sense of completeness.

PART THREE

History: Tragical and Romantic

CHAPTER 8

The Tragical History of Doctor Faustus: A Problem of Impact

The story of the man who sells his soul to the devil is a perennial favorite throughout the western world. In most versions he makes a contract (signed with his blood) for a term of years (usually twenty-four) during which he is to enjoy unlimited power and have every wish fulfilled. At the end of the term devils come to claim him and carry him off to eternal hell-fire. His motives in the transaction differ according to the teller. Sometimes he is impelled by greed, as in *The Devil and Daniel Webster*, sometimes by the yearning to recapture his youth, as in the *Faust* of Goethe and Gounod, and sometimes by a combination of scepticism and curiosity, as in *Doctor Faustus*. Marlowe's hero questions the existence of heaven and hell; not until he approaches the end of his contract does he discover their reality. But by then it is too late for him to escape the consequences of his twenty-four-year association with the powers of evil.

The story is basically narrative rather than dramatic, unfolding in many episodes over a long period of time. As a narrative it exhibits excellent form. It has an attention-arresting beginning and a conclusion whose sense of finality cannot be faulted. As a drama however it lacks most of the elements of what we are accustomed to call dramatic plotting: suspense, surprise, conflict, and confrontation. It has some ironies, but not as many as most dramas of comparable magnitude.

What then is the source of its fascination as tragedy? For fascinating it certainly is. In any reasonably good production there is hardly a dull moment, and there are practically no passages during which one can enjoy one of those restful little naps which to some people are the chief pleasure of theatre-going. Perhaps the fact that we know the story so well keeps us alert for those developments we know lie just ahead. Probably the universality of the story holds us, for who has not felt as Faustus does the yearning to know all, experience all, to have unlimited power, and limitless wealth, and also felt at times as if no price were too great to pay for these things. Certainly the magnitude of the story compels our attention, for it deals with issues of vast significance: the duality of man's nature wherein good and evil contest perpetually for his soul, and the mystery of higher learning in which are revealed the secrets of the ancients and the orbits of celestial bodies. This sense of magnitude is intensified by Marlowe's noble language, splendid verse and imaginative expression.

Some plays possess primacy of plot, like *Oedipus Tyrannus*, some primacy of character, like *The Cherry Orchard*, and some primacy of language. In *Doctor Faustus* the primary element of its peculiar power is language. Marlowe's language has all the qualities of greatness. It is supple, eloquent, and embraces a scope and largeness capable of expressing the visions and reflections of the loftiest imagination. In *Doctor Faustus* its imagery, of the sky, the stars, constellations and meteors, seems to surround the action with the vastest reaches of the universe.

But although its greatness as a play comes mainly from the magnificence of its language, the lines do not stand alone, nor does the play in performance reach its fullest effect without the action and spectacle which Marlowe has prescribed. Especially the spectacle. In a play about a man who sells his soul the devils are bound to be prominent. But here we have not only devils but Mephistophilis and his black magic, Lucifer, Belzebub, and the whole hierarchy of hell; we see the Seven Deadly Sins, the Pope of Rome, the Emperor of the Holy Roman Empire, Alexander the Great honorably attended, Helen of Troy, and many others who enable us to "see away our shilling" grandly, giving us much to think about and talk about for a long time to come.

A LESSON FOR PLAYWRIGHTS: HOW TO MASK A MISSING MIDDLE

The dramatization of the Faustus legend has always presented an author with a difficult problem of organization. The story has three parts: Faustus' making of the contract with the devil, his activities during the twenty-four years of his contract, and his ultimate damnation. The first part of the story is always the best part. Faustus' yearning to escape the bondage of poverty, age, or conventional morality, as the case may be, can always be made to appeal to the imagination of reader or spectator. The manner in which he makes contact with the powers of darkness is always fascinating. The materialization of Mephistophilis to seal the contract and implement Faustus' desires is inevitably gripping. The conclusion, with Faustus' futile struggle to escape his fate, followed by the big moment in which the devils appear to claim his soul is also certain to be thrilling. It is the middle part of the story that is troublesome. After Faustus' imagination has pictured the possibilities of a life unrestrained by any of the ordinary limits of human activity it is very difficult to contrive a series of episodes which will live up to expectations. But the twenty-four years must be filled somehow or other or we will end up with a drama which is too brief. Tragedy demands a dramatization that is long enough for the size of its subject. If it is too short it cannot attain the grandeur which we expect in a plot dealing with eternal verities.

Different authors have solved the problem in different ways. Stephen Vincent Benet in *The Devil and Daniel Webster* simply skipped over the middle part and settled for a serio-comic elaborated conclusion. Goethe filled in the middle with philosophy and romance to the admiration and approval of most of his readers, and the same course was followed by Gounod in the opera. Marlowe took an easier path. He filled in the middle with episodes from the old German folk tale from which he had taken the plot in the first place. Except for the Court of Hell, the Seven Deadly Sins, and the vivification of Alexander the Great, the middle episodes consist entirely of buffoonery and legerdemain. These scenes, mainly horseplay and visual trickery, do not read well and by any standard of taste fall far below the aesthetic level of the first and last parts. This, Marlowe's proverbial lack of humor, and some entries in Henslowe's money-book of payments to other writers for "additions" to the play, lead us to believe that the middle third of the play includes the work of hands other than Marlowe's.

Be that as it may, the middle episodes are much more effective on the stage than one would imagine from even the closest study of the printed play. They were written for comedians and magicians. They provide a wide range of varied opportunities for the comic artists of the company and in performance they are often entertaining far beyond expectation.

At first glance the arrangement of events in the middle section seems to follow no plan. In comedies a playwright normally places his funniest scenes last and arranges the other scenes sequentially according to comic effect so that the play beomes funnier as it goes along. But this play is different. The funniest scene, the one in which Faustus plays tricks on the Pope, comes first. The one least hilarious, the scene at the court of the Duke of Vanholt, comes last. Why is this? Why would a playwright sacrifice the dramatically potent "build" of a comic progression? The best reason I can think of is that Marlowe wants the middle portion to run, as it were, down hill in order to show the decline of Faustus' imagination. His power corrupts him and indulgence weakens both will and imagination. At the outset of the twenty-four years his imagination knows no bounds; at the end the best he can do is to conjure up some fruit in midwinter for the pregnant Duchess of Vanholt. In between the episodes the Chorus appears three times to point this lesson.

CHARACTERS, CASTING, AND COSTUMING

Named in the text are thirty-three speaking characters plus a minimum of fifteen supernumeraries and three "apparitions" (Helen of Troy, Alexander the

Great, and Alexander's "paramour"). Only four characters go all the way through the play: Faustus, Mephistophilis, Wagner, and the Chorus. Only eight have more than one entrance. All of the remaining characters appear but once. The largest number on stage at any one time is nineteen, in the Court of Hell; of these seven are the Deadly Sins and five are what might be called "utility devils." It is thus apparent that one could do justice to the play with an acting company of about twenty if the same actors could play both men and women. This is the same number as is required for most of the plays of Shakespeare.

The fact that so many of the characters appear only once opens the casting process to almost unlimited doubling. I have seen productions in which I could spot three or four individual performers in as many as four parts apiece, and this was probably only the tip of the iceberg. If the costuming and makeup are carefully planned most of the doubling could probably escape detection from even the most inquisitive eye.

Doctor Faustus has been called a one-man show because of the prominence of Faustus' part. It is certainly true that the quality of the performance given in the titular role goes a long way toward elevating the work to those heights which we glimpse in reading the text, but an actor who is less than brilliant, if he is competent and well spoken, can still be quite satisfactory, so strong are the elements of language, thought, plot, and spectacle supporting his performance. I have seen some fairly good productions in which rather pedestrian actors were taking the part of Faustus and yet the play was by no means dull. So I cannot agree with the designation "one-man." The role of Faustus is in any case far less difficult for the leading performer than that of Oedipus, Macbeth, Lear, Tartuffe, or a hundred others I could think of.

Faustus

The most indispensable quality for an actor who plays this part is a melodic voice of exceptional range coupled with crystal clear diction. After this one might hope for an actor of attractive appearance and definite audience appeal. Because of the length of the part and the ordeal of rehearsing with a large company of multirole performers, many costume changes, and complicated stage machinery requiring innumerable run-throughs, any actor essaying the role needs steady nerves and physical stamina above the average.

The character of Faustus as Marlowe has conceived him is extremely interesting. Imaginative people are always interesting on the stage. This one has an imagination that knows no bounds. At the same time his curiosity about everything is intense and quite undisciplined. Marlowe's thought seems to be that there are things in life that must be taken on faith; things about which one is just as well off not knowing too much. This is different from the modern way of looking at life, but it is sincere with the author. Along with Faustus' curiosity goes a leavening scepticism. He does not believe in many of the things to which belief is usually given; he is determined to see for himself. Along with this he is often witty and sometimes mischievous. He plays with his supernatural power with a sort of juvenile exuberance using it for practical jokes on persons who by reason of reputation, position, or occupation are always unpopular with audiences.

During the course of the play Faustus' character undergoes profound changes. At first he does not believe in damnation and he doubts the existence of heaven and hell. He is willing to acknowledge the supremacy of Lucifer if by doing so he can gain the power he wants, but he does not seriously believe in Lucifer either. Not until he has seen him. Then he realizes that the forces of evil are real. Earlier, his expressions of doubt had prompted Mephistophilis' only display of emotion and it may be that this unusual phenomenon eventually penetrates Faustus' thinking even though he seemed to ignore it at the time. In the beginning Faustus wonders whether he has done well in calling on Lucifer, but he conquers this doubt. When Mephistophilis comes for the contract Faustus is unable to write because his blood rebels. Once he has seen Lucifer and the Court of Hell he knows that Mephistophilis' warning was justified. From then on, at intervals, his thoughts turn back to the salvation he has sacrificed but Mephistophilis repeatedly distracts him with legerdemain and spectacle.

During the twenty-four years of the contract term Faustus' imagination that once knew no limits becomes gradually more feeble. His lust for learning is soon surfeited and his curiosity slackens. The desires that led him to sell his soul are no longer anything more than a dim flicker. A sense of waste and frustration overcomes him and he seeks forgetfulness in the arms of Helen of Troy.

Finally, when his last hour arrives he is unable to repent his bargain or seek salvation in prayer in spite of his fear of what lies in store for him. Up to now every wish has been fulfilled. Now when his only wish is to escape the consequence of his actions this is the one wish which Lucifer will not grant. Faustus is now a very different person from the audacious sorcerer who at the beginning of the play set out to conjure up a devil to serve him.

Since the action spans twenty-four years it might be appropriate to show Faustus aging and it might, in the next-to-last scene when he asks for Helen of Troy to help him forget, be quite effective to show him as an elderly man trying to find some of the love he seems to have missed. We do not know how old he is at the beginning, but if he were to be shown as about forty or forty-five this would make him an old man by the time he is finally carried off by the demons.

The play is usually costumed in the general style of the sixteenth century although it could be placed a century earlier or later. Because of the strong medieval flavor evinced in the use of allegorical characters and references to Reformation theology it seems unlikely that the play would thrive in modern dress or in the costumes of any period later than a hundred years from that in which it was written.

In the first scene Faustus looks good in the sixteen-century flat cap and long gown seen in Holbein's portrait of Erasmus. Black or any very dark color should be avoided because of the difficulty of making him visible in the dimly lit conjuring scene. Some gray material, light enough to stand out among the dark surroundings, would be better.

After Faustus has signed his pact with Lucifer the devils bring him rich apparel which he puts on at once, discarding his scholar's gown. The purpose of the rich apparel is to make him easier to see during the scenes that follow, for he is going to appear alongside first a Pope and then an Emperor and he will have to be able to hold his own there, catching the eye of the audience when necessary, something which would be difficult in a drab scholar's gown. The rich apparel therefore should be made of some sturdy eye-catching stuff light enough in color to be seen against any background and easily picked out from any group of colorful courtiers.

Mephistophilis

It takes a great deal of directorial skill to keep the actor who plays this role from stealing the show. This is partly because evil is always interesting on the stage, especially when it hints, as this does, at the existence of things beyond common knowledge and impossible of description. Part of Mephistophilis' strength and appeal is certainly that Marlowe has created a distinctive character of impressive dimensionality. The result is that we tend unconsciously to watch this creature whenever he is on stage, as if to catch him off guard in order to discern some clue to his thoughts and feelings.

Mephistophilis at Faustus' urging tells us just enough about himself for us to see him as a soul in perpetual torment, one who from centuries of suffering with no escape and no relief in prospect is forced to adopt a mask of stoic endurance. The damnation of Faustus over which he presides is not his but Faustus' doing; Mephistophilis merely assists by providing the means. All this he does efficiently and effortlessly as if it were something he has done a thousand times before and which he knows he is going to have to do a thousand times more.

He has surprisingly little to say. Most of his lines are rather laconic replies to Faustus' questions. In answer to Faustus' first summons he has a speech of nine lines, then later in the same scene another of seven lines in which he tries to dissuade Faustus from his course. After that, beyond his brief dialogue responses, he has only two speeches of sixteen lines each and one of six lines. After calling up Helen of Troy to help Faustus through his last night on earth he disappears until he returns to carry Faustus down to hell.

When Mephistophilis first appears in response to Faustus' conjuring he is so hideous that Faustus cannot bear the sight of him. What kind of costume can achieve this effect? The old woodcut on the title page of the 1620 edition of the play depicts a small dark dragon-like creature about the size of a bloodhound. One might reasonably expect Mephistophilis to be bigger than this but the idea of a creature not wholly human is appealing. By combining elements of human, animal, and reptilian life a very interesting and acceptably horrible costume might be attainable. This has the virtue of agreeing with the ideas prevailing in Marlowe's time regarding the way devils ought to look. In the popular sixteenth-century books on demonology there are vivid illustrations to aid us in visualizing all the different kinds of devils.

Before Mephistophilis can speak, Faustus orders him to change his shape to something less repulsive. He then disappears and returns in the robes of a Franciscan friar which he wears until the very last scene. This change requires two actors, one in the guise of the ugly devil and another, the one who will play the speaking part, waiting already made up as the friar. For the finale the first hideous Mephistophilis might reappear to supervise the demons carrying Faustus to hell.

The specification of the friar's garb is not haphazard. Mephistophilis' role has all the attributes of a scene-stealer. To overcome this he is put into an outfit which will make it easy to subordinate him when necessary to various other characters. The Franciscan habit is brown, with a hood which covers the head and shadows the face. Alongside the more brightly costumed Faustus, Pope, and Emperor he can be made to fade into the background so that the others can claim their rightful share of attention, something which would not be possible if he remained thoughout in a bizarre costume.

The Chorus

This part requires an actor with a commanding presence and an exceptionally good voice. He appears four times, once to deliver the Prologue, twice during the progression to make sure we know what is going on, and finally to speak the Epilogue, "Cut is the branch that might have grown full straight. . . ." His lines are some of the best and most memorable in the play, so they must not be wasted on a mediocre performer.

In Marlowe's day the costume of the Chorus was conventionalized so that at his entrance the audience would quiet down, knowing that the performance was about to begin. As a rule he was handsomely gowned in black, with a neat beard, a laurel crown, and carrying a staff with sometimes a scroll or book. Dressed thus, it seems that his function would have been immediately recognized.

Wagner and the Two Scholars

Wagner and the two scholars would ordinarily be dressed more or less alike in flat caps and long gowns, similar in appearance to that of Faustus himself before the signing of the contract. The two scholars who pay him a visit in the second scene seem to be students or apprentices of about the same rank as Wagner. Later, when they reappear in scene fourteen, they are twenty-four years older and nearer to Faustus in dignity and bearing. With so long a time between entrances, care must be taken to make sure that when they reappear we know who they are. Their first scene is somewhat light in vein and has some almost comical banter with Wagner. Their second appearance is much more serious as Faustus discloses to them his commitment to Lucifer, bids them farewell, and they repair to the next room to pray for his soul.

Wagner seems to fill the functions of both apprentice and servant. He has one brief explanatory speech prefacing the finale and one of ten lines between scenes six and seven which appears to have been assigned to him by mistake as it is much more in the vein of the Chorus. Wagner appears in five scenes but the actor who plays him can still double in several other parts.

The Good and the Evil Angels

In the first half of the play these two angels appear three times, the one angel to warn Faustus of the danger of his course and the other to encourage him. In their second and third appearances the Good Angel seems to come first in response to Faustus' misgivings about the dilemma in which he finds himself. The Evil Angel always speaks following the Good Angel, which might indicate that he materializes afterward to counteract the persuasion of his heavenly counterpart.

The angels are usually contrasted in color and style, the Good Angel being blonde, fair complexioned, and garbed in white or light blue; the Evil Angel is brunette and dressed in black or dark red. In the old UFA cinema the materialization of the angels was highly dramatic. They came into being some distance above the floor, where they stood, high and brightly lighted, with huge wings half again as long as their bodies. In T. W. Stevens' Century-of-Progress production they appeared on balconies at either side of the acting area. I have also seen them materialize, the one above head height at one side of the stage and the other rising from the orchestra pit on the opposite side as if coming up from hell.

Valdes and Cornelius

Valdes and Cornelius are famous sorcerers to whom Faustus turns for the secrets of necromancy which make it possible for him to summon spirits from the nether regions. Cornelius is meant to represent Cornelius Agrippa, a well known magician. Valdes has not been identified, as far as I know, but he may represent someone known to the original audience. They take turns boasting of their magical powers and there is not much to choose between them. From the actor's viewpoint Valdes has the better lines to speak. One character could easily serve the function of both of these. The main reason, I imagine, that there are two necromancers instead of one is that three characters always make a better scene than two and the scene is thus more impressive than if it had involved only Faustus and one other person.

As to their appearance, it should tell us at once that they are magic-makers and no ordinary folk. Their robes can be embroidered with all the symbols of their art—moons, stars, and magical symbols—they should appear prosperous. One of them might be a turbaned oriental. If manpower is available they should each have several bizarrely dressed servants.

The Comedians

There are at least six comic parts, not counting the friars in the Vatican scene. The first one appears in scene four as the butt of Wagner's foolery and is simply called "Clown." He seems to be a pauper in filthy rags whom Wagner hires. A good actor can make him very funny, but the part is too small to attract many good actors. If lesser performers cannot make it work, the scene can be cut without great loss.

Robin, Rafe, and the Vintner, who fill in the space between Faustus' Vatican adventure and his audience with the Emperor, are more comical than the Clown. Robin is a stable-boy who has purloined one of Faustus' books with the idea of raising a few devils of his own. Rafe is a horse-handler who works in the same stable. As their occupation is one of the lowliest in sixteenth-century society they must be rude of manner and rough of dress. The Vintner (barkeep) whose goblet they steal should be much better dressed as he belongs to a higher occupational level although he might be wearing an apron. The transformation of Robin and Rafe into an ape and a dog is easily accomplished by means of rubber animal heads and a little sleight of hand, or even by mime if the actors are good enough to bring it off. Their antics after they are transformed can be hilarious.

The monks who wait on the Pope are supposed to be ridiculous and they will appear so if they are widely disparate in size and shape. Their robes should not be brown like Mephistophilis' nor black because we already have more than enough dark tones among the devils. So white, possibly white with black scapulars, usually works best. The comic part of their behavior is the ridiculous way they carry on when tormented by Faustus.

The knight who scoffs at Faustus in the Emperor's court should be comical in appearance as well as in manner. This is mostly a matter of costuming although it will help if an actor is cast who is several inches shorter than the average and bowlegged. The horns are usually made as part of a wig which is slipped on his head while he is masked from the audience by other performers.

The horse-courser is a cocky flamboyant creature and his garish dress should show it. He is a horse-trader, a sharper of a kind that everyone in the audience has been bested by at least once. His best comic bit comes with his surprise when he pulls on Faustus' leg and it comes off in his hands. He will need a second costume for when he comes in soaking wet, the same gag that Shakespeare uses in *The Tempest* with the fool Trinculo.

Lucifer, Belzebub, and the Other Devils

Lucifer, being the Lord of Darkness and supreme ruler of the underworld, should be as majestic as imaginative design and ingenious costume-craft can make him. He usually wears an imperial crown and carries a scepter of some bizarre design, and to give him dignity he wears a wide cape with a great train. Most designers put him into dark red and black, combining satins and gauzes with metallics and sequins to catch the light. His facial makeup should be as hideous as it is possible to make him without entirely abandoning human configuration. A tall actor with a deep resonant voice is needed to make his physique and diction live up to expectations.

Belzebub stands next to Lucifer in the hierarchy of hell and would be similarly costumed but with not quite as long a train or as many sequins. Instead of a scepter he sometimes carries a bull-whip with which he summons and herds the lesser devils who impersonate the Seven Deadly Sins.

The other devils who appear when needed to assist Mephistophilis, assume the shapes of various worthies as required, and finally carry Faustus to hell, are dark animal-like shapes derived from medieval wood-cuts. They are best costumed when no one can detect individual or human qualities in their manner or appearance. Recently, costume and novelty shops have been stocking an increasing variety of rubber masks that cover face and head and some of these are ugly enough to be used for the devils. One virtue of masks is that the devils can then double in other characters without having to change makeup. It is best if the "utility devils" are not seen too clearly so that spectators are aware of them only as dark shapes on the periphery of the action. Imagination can supply the rest. In no case should these minor devils be red or any bright color which would draw attention away from the principals.

One of the devils appears to be feminine, to judge from the Clown's lines, the later scene in which Mephistophilis at Faustus' request brings him a "devil-wife," and the lines of Lechery in the Court of Hell scene. In the original production we know that these parts were played by men and this knowledge may give us an inkling as to how the female devils might have been portrayed, for when men represent women of this sort they tend to exaggerate busts, hips, and coy feminine manner.

The Apparitions

Since devils can assume any form it is possible for Mephistophilis to call up historical or allegorical figures merely by ordering his subservient devils to assume the required shapes. Thus the Seven Deadly Sins, Alexander and his Paramour, and Helen of Troy are actually only devils who for the time being take the shape of the person summoned. If one could contrive some means whereby Faustus could see the apparitions while we, the audience, could see the same apparition and could also glimpse the devil behind the illusion, this would heighten the scene by introducing an irony always present but not usually visualized.

The show of the Seven Deadly Sins is certainly the big production number of the play, and the costumes here are the best of the show. The representation of these sins was a favorite with sixteenth-century artists so we have many drawings to let us know what they looked like. Four of the sins are elegantly gowned and three are in drab garments; they alternate so as to give variety to the progression. Pride is usually in bright colors and rich fabrics, Covetousness a miser in rags, Wrath a gaudy warrior, Envy a gray pinched creature, Gluttony an enormous rich fat man, Sloth a snail-slow pauper, and Lechery a garish bejewelled prostitute.

Neither Alexander nor his Paramour speak, fortunately. They merely appear, with several attendants if possible. The nearer we can come to making Alexander resemble the image on coins and portrait statuary the better the scene will be. His Paramour can be done up like an eastern princess, with ornaments of gold and precious stones, silk veil, and so on. With attendants carrying their trains and waving fans over their heads this pair can make an impressive appearance. If they parade across the front edge of the stage the whole retinue will show up to best advantage.

Helen of Troy is another of Mephistophilis' apparitions and, like Alexander, without a word to say. If the actress playing Helen possesses a moderate degree of natural grace she might make an effective entrance crossing the stage. Otherwise it might be better to play safe and reveal her reclining on a couch *a la* Recamier, with a mirror in her hand. Some producers have dodged the problem by staging her entrance from aisle or vomitory so that the spectators see only a silhouetted figure with trailing draperies and gain the rest of their impression from Faustus' reaction to her.

The Pope and Cardinal of Lorraine

Both the Pope and the Cardinal should appear in full regalia: The Pope in white with his triple crown and the Cardinal in his red full-dress outfit. The more embroidery and jewelry that can be loaded upon them the better the total effect.

Since this is a comic scene, the shorter the Pope the more absurd he will appear under his voluminous robes and tall crown. The Cardinal, for contrast, should be as tall as possible and as thin as the Pope is fat.

The Emperor

Whether the Emperor is Charles V or Maximilian II is not material to the scene. What we do have is what in Marlowe's day was the most powerful monarch in Europe and he should look the part, with crown, scepter, and ermine-trimmed mantle. We have many fine portraits to guide us in planning his costume. Alongside is his Empress, equally handsome, a half dozen dignitaries and richly costumed attendants, along with the knight who scoffs at Faustus.

The Duke and Duchess of Vanholt

This pair is best played for comic effect by making the Duchess a six-foot giantess with a coy lisp and very very pregnant. Alongside is the Duke, a diminutive octogenarian with splindly legs, a skimpy goat beard, and a cracked voice.

The Old Man

The role of the Old Man is best given to one of the more accomplished actors in the company as the role is an important one but not endowed with the best lines. In a good company the better actors ought to expect to play not just the juicy roles but also occasionally small parts important to the success of the production but for one reason or another too difficult for the average performer. This is such a role.

The Old Man should be impressive in appearance, like the Michelangelo Moses, dignified and serious, but not much older than Faustus himself at this point. By the sheer power of his performance he has to triumph over the demons who come for him. This shows us what Faustus might have done if he had not been weakened and corrupted by his association with Mephistophilis.

SETTING AND SPECIAL EFFECTS

Marlowe's spacious verse demands a spacious acting area uncluttered with trivia. The astronomical imagery which fills the play seems to call for a stage surrounded by sky and filled with stars. This is where the modern producer enjoys his greatest advantage over those who performed the play originally on an outdoor stage in broad daylight, for the effect of sky and stars is easily obtainable with today's lighting equipment.

On the practical side the production needs ample means by which characters can make swift entrances and exits, and on occasion give the illusion of materializing from nowhere. This requires scrims, traps, vomitories, or flying rigs. The theatre that lacks one or more of these usually has some of the others. For example, thrust-state theatres—like the one at Stratford, Ontario—often lack fly lofts but they usually have traps and vomitory entrances; while proscenium theatres lack entrances from the auditorium they usually have traps and rigging systems. The Vatican scene gains greatly from the use of a puppet bridge from which the floating dishes in the banquet can be manipulated, but if this is not possible a magician's fishing-line hoist is a possible alternative. At the end of the play a great many people are going to be disappointed if the devils do not take Faustus down to hell through a yawning hole in the stage floor. And by way of contrast, the Old Man ought to fly upward to his reward in heaven.

Backstage there will have to be booths for the many fast changes of costume, protected space for the musicians, and a smoke machine for the conjuration, the Court of Hell, and the final damnation.

Faustus will need some furniture for his study: books, a table to put the books on, and a chair to sit in as he soliloquizes. This set is required four different times and probably also in the finale. The retorts and astrolabes used in the operatic version are hardly needed here, and the scenes are so short that unnecessary properties merely slow the scene-changes. Thrones are desirable for the Emperor and the Duke of Vanholt. A ridiculously long banquet table loaded with appetizing dishes is essential for the Vatican scene.

For the Court of Hell, the Vatican, the Emperor's Court, and the Duke of Vanholt's, something will be needed to localize the scene: coats of arms, banners, crosses, or similar distinctive drops or set pieces. Sometimes these are projected images, sometimes pieces rolled in, and sometimes things let down from the flies. I have seen all of these used in various productions. Whichever is used depends more on the facilities available in the particular theatre than anything else.

THE MUSIC

There are eight scenes in the play that need musical accompaniment. Interestingly, this is so natural a part of the atmosphere of human aspiration, necromancy, imperial majesty, and emotional torment that although music has been a part of every Faustus I have seen I am hard put to recall any of the tunes. Good music makes a scene memorable even though it may itself be forgotten.

The music of Marlowe's own time is not usually effective today. Modern audiences have become accustomed to much more sophisticated music, especially in support of scenes of this kind. Among the vast libraries of recorded music available today there is much excellent material, provided only that it not be too readily recognizable. Recently an increasing amount of music from movie sound tracks has appeared on the market and portions of these might be employed for accompaniment. Beyond this, there is always the possibility that one might have special music composed for the occasion.

NOTES ON STAGING

Mephistophilis' first appearance works best when he comes in view slowly, materializing from behind a rock or dead tree or rising from a trap. Once visible, he needs to be seen clearly by the whole audience so that his hideous appearance can be appreciated. Upon being ordered to change to a friar he returns to the place from which he came and a second actor (the one who will play the speaking role) enters in the friar's robes. The author has allowed no time for a costume change here, so two actors are needed.

The stabbing of the arm to get blood with which to sign the devil's contract is an old trick, but when the bright blood runs down across the actor's white forearm the audience invariably gasps.

If there is to be one intermission it usually comes after the Court of Hell. If for any reason there are to be two, the first one usually comes at the end of Scene Five while the second comes after the Duke of Vanholt scene.

For the Court of Hell the entrance of Lucifer and his minions is usually preceded by strange music and accompanied by thunder, lightning, and clouds of smoke. The Seven Deadly Sins need to be seen clearly, herded in by devils with pitchforks and dominated by Belzebub with his fiery whip. Lucifer, his court, the devils, and the Seven Deadly Sins, all on stage at once, make a magnificent spectacle.

The Pope's banquet, with the Pope and Cardinal trying to eat from delectable dishes floating around the room, is hilarious. Faustus' tormenting of the psalm-singing friars is childish but delightful.

The finale must not disappoint. On the stroke of twelve o'clock there is thunder and lightning and a red glow. Mephistophilis appears in his original ugly form accompanied by a troop of devils who drag Faustus screaming into Hell, preferably into a trap belching flames and clouds of smoke.

CHAPTER 9

The Spanish Theatre and Lope de Vega

During the very same years that the theatre of Shakespeare flourished in England a similar development was taking place in Spain and enjoying comparable popularity. Spanish drama of the period resembles English in many ways. Spanish plays, like the English, are almost entirely in verse or poetic prose, and in both countries the popular drama as a rule pays little heed to the so-called "unities" of time and place. Instead there are many scenes arranged episodically or chronologically in such a way as to secure the greatest contrast from scene to scene. The locale of the action is mentioned only when significant; the rest of the time the scene is either unlocalized or inferred from the presence of certain characters: the presence of royalty indicating the court, that of peasants the field or village, that of soldiers the battlefield or camp, and so on.

When so much of the play is unlocalized there is little need for scenery and no need for scene-changing to interrupt the continuity. Hardly any set properties are required, for the action allows few opportunities for actors to sit down, and the eloquent set speeches are always delivered standing.

Spanish theatre buildings of the Golden Age bear a striking resemblance to those of Elizabethan England in that both evolved from inn yards to enclosures open to the sky with galleries on three sides and a platform stage jutting out into the yard. In Almagro one may still see a seventeenth-century theatre, the *Corral de Comedias*, perfectly preserved, and if one is there at the right time of the year one may even see the plays of Lope de Vega and Calderón performed.

The audiences that attended Spanish plays were very like those that filled Elizabethan theatres such as the Globe and Fortune. In the public theatres of both London and Madrid one could have seen noblemen, merchants, apprentices, and members of both sexes along with a sprinkling of hucksters and street people.

But the differences between the English and the Spanish theatres of the period are as interesting as their similarities. The most interesting difference is in their respective attitudes toward politics on the one hand and their decorum of language and manner on the other. Elizabethan dramatists repeatedly fell afoul of the law in their treatment of political matters. Any representation of regicide or rebellion was viewed by authorities with a suspicious eye. No play could be printed or performed until it had passed the scrutiny of the Master of the Revels who was free to delete or alter any lines that struck him as politically injudicious. Bawdry, however, never bothered him. There were no limits to the obscenity of language and gesture that could be put on the stage, and for most Elizabethans, whether courtier or countyman, titled lady or fishwife, the coarse jokes, lewd puns, and sexual suggestiveness were an acceptable and expected part of the entertainment. Only the Puritans objected to what they regarded as the immorality of the stage, railing against it in pulpit and pamphlet. But Puritans were too few in number for anyone to pay them much attention except in fun.

In Spain it was quite the other way around. Decorous language was the rule, in comedy as well as tragedy. The manners of the characters, regardless of rank, were generally good. The peasant in a play is as courteous as a king. The level of sentiment between lovers is always high no matter what their social station may be. Low comedy never descends to obscenity or that level of chamber-pot humor which seems to have delighted Elizabethans of every class of society.

It is interesting to wonder whether the Spanish concern for decorum was related to the fact that the acting companies, unlike those of England, included women. The ancient custom of having all parts performed by men had never been adopted in Spain.

Conspicuously absent in Spain is that fear of rebellion which colors the royal view of the public theatre in England. The Spanish court seems never to have made any connection between its own activities and those of nobility as shown on the stage. Representations of revolt such as *Fuente Ovejuna* could never have been presented on an English stage but in Spain they aroused no noticeable anxiety on the part of government officials in charge.

Spanish playwrights dramatize many of the same stories as their Elizabethan contemporaries, but their plays are generally shorter and less complex. Occasionally we see a triple-plotted work, as in *Fuente Ovejuna*, but the fondness for multiple plots that marks the work of Shakespeare and his fellows is nowhere nearly as evident in Spain. Nor is the collaboration of playwrights as common in Spain as in England. Most Spanish plays are composed by one poet only. There are no writing teams such as kept Henslowe's theatres in London supplied with crowd-pleasing novelties.

Lope de Vega is to the Spanish theatre what Shakespeare is to the English—the most popular writer of his time as well as the most widely appreciated by his own and also by later generations. He is credited with the creation of some fifteen hundred plays. Only about one-third of these survive but that one-third is nearly equal to the entire extant corpus of Elizabethan drama. Like most Spanish poets, Lope concentrated all his energies on his writing. He took no acting parts and he did not share in the management of playhouses. But he could deliver to the actors a completed act every day so that they could begin rehearsals on the first act before the finale was written.

The appetite of Spanish audiences for new material was as insatiable as that of modern audiences for movies and television. The result was that poets such as Lope de Vega, whose work was in great demand, mastered the art of quickly putting together plays with neat and coherent—if not often original—plots, vivid life-like characters, and lines possessing both the elegance and the eloquence which popular taste demanded.

Lope de Vega's plays impress one first of all with their expertness. One has the feeling immediately that he knows where he is going and how he is going to get there. He loses no time at the outset in getting the plot into motion and from then on it moves steadily, each scene carrying it further along. The set speeches, although rich in imagery, do not hold up the plot movement because in practically every instance they describe action which is relevant but not visible to the audience.

The plot often develops in the direction of some dilemma or seemingly insolvable problem up to the final moments when the solution is suddenly produced and the play brought quickly to its conclusion for, as Lope himself says in his essay, "The New Art of Writing Plays" (*Arte nuevo de hacer comedias en este tiempo*), "Do not permit the untying of the plot until the last scene; for the crowd, knowing what the end is, will turn its face to the door and its shoulder to what it has awaited three hours."

Lope shares with all Spanish authors of his time an appreciation of the power of music and dance and never misses an opportunity to provide for them in his plays. Occasionally he includes the lyrics for songs, but more often he merely indicates places where a song would be appropriate and leaves the rest to the actors who, being equally aware of the dramatic effect of music, are not likely to neglect the opportunity. Dances he seldom indicates, nor does he need to. Dance was an indispensable feature of entertainment in Spain from earliest times. Indeed, dance is to Spain what music is to Italy, a form of expression practiced by everyone from the King down and one in which professional entertainers were naturally expected to excel.

Spanish music, with its stirring rhythms and striking blends of major and minor keys, is extremely theatrical. It provides for a dramatization of emotion in song to a far greater degree than does the music of Elizabethan England. Dancing, however, takes first place always. Instrumental music supplies a support and song supplies a background for dance more often than either is employed alone.

In one very important respect Lope de Vega resembles Shakespeare. It is not a way that is always immediately apparent to a reader but one which is wonderfully helpful to the actor, providing him with a wealth of opportunities for the enrichment of his performance. It has to do with the imagery of language. The imagery of most poets is mainly visual, augmented by that of hearing and touch; those of taste and smell as a rule scarcely figure. The poet whose language appeals to all five senses is rare. Shakespeare is one such. Lope de Vega is another. Lope's language in general and his longer speeches in particular make us taste, smell, and feel as well as see and hear. The set speeches may at first glance appear to be more wordy than their function in relation to the plot would seem to require. It is not until one has read these speeches aloud to an audience that one realizes what marvels they are. Their language is the kind one loves to speak. With it one discovers the power to make people listen and not only that but to make them hungry or thirsty, proud, fearful, or angry. This gives one a wonderful feeling when one is on stage with an audience all around.

The set speeches are splendid, but the dialogue is not. It is, in fact, extremely difficult. This is not the fault of Lope de Vega, nor of the Spanish language. It is due to differences in conversational interchange between the two languages. Dialogue in English is entirely different from dialogue in Spanish.

Formality of manner and speech with a variety of indirections and grace notes is natural to Spanish conversation (as any visitor to Spain knows who has ever ordered a beer without adding "por favor"). Translated into English this produces dialogue that seems to us stiff and artificial, with little resemblance to what we are willing to accept as lifelike discourse. English-speaking actors are hard put to deliver such dialogue in a way that will make it sound natural. The colorful imagery is still there but the same imagery that makes the set speeches delightful is offset by the awkwardness of the dialogue. The net result is that the dialogue of most translations speaks English with a strange Spanish accent.

English is a wordy language with a certain looseness that comes in part from its enormous vocabulary. Those who speak it tend to use more words than they need. The best stage speech in English however often impresses its listeners with a kind of bogus directness. I say "bogus" because the impression of directness is often more a matter of sound than of sense.

Spoken Spanish, like Italian and French, is a mellifluous language which is at the same time more compact than English. When translated into English it tends to emerge with too many cognates and Latin derivatives to sound very English. In order to make it sound right the Latin-derived terms have to be replaced by Anglo-Saxon ones. This is difficult for the translator, and for the director and actor too, because as rehearsals progress and they become more familiar with the lines the translation gradually loses its strangeness. One becomes accustomed to lines like the Master of Calatrava's in *Fuente Ovejuna*: "This soothes my anger," which is absurd English, or Esteban's exclamation, "My heart told me so," which would be better expressed as, "That's what I was afraid of."

The only solution to this sort of problem is to borrow the ear of some friend with a good feeling for our language if he can be persuaded to spend some hours listening to rehearsals in order to catch such awkward expressions and suggest alternative phrasings. This might well be the most difficult part of the director's task, for few outsiders have the stamina to sit through hours of rehearsal. The repetition wears them out after about half an hour. Staunch friends are therefore a necessity for the producer of Spanish drama. Fortunately, because of the strength of the elements other than language, in the public performances an enthusiastic and responsive audience can always be counted on.

CHAPTER 10

Fuente Ovejuna:
A Problem of Language

The play takes its title from the name of a village in Andalusia. *Fuente* means a source or flow of water such as one would find in a spring, fountain, well, watering trough, or mountain brook. We see it as a prefix to the names of many towns in Spain, somewhat in the way that we have towns with names like Palm Springs or Sadler's Wells. *Ovejuna* relates to sheep, or the gathering of sheep. So the title *Fuente Ovejuna* literally translates as "watering place of sheep." This does not make a very good title in English, so one must either retain the Spanish title or coin one that conveys the idea without being literal. Sometimes, therefore, the play is billed as *The Sheep Well*, which is pathetically undramatic. One of my friends called it *The Revolt of the Sheep*, which is close to the sense of the original, but has the disadvantage of reminding people of George Orwell's satire, *The Animal Farm*.

The town of *Fuente Ovejuna* is famous in Spanish history as the locus of an insurrection in 1476 in which the arrogant lord of a province, an officer with the rank of Commander in the knightly order of Calatrava, after inflicting unspeakable indignities upon his meek and sheep-like subjects, finally goes too far and is overcome and slain by them. The village was then masterless, and it fell to the sovereigns, Ferdinand and Isabella, to reestablish order. At first they sent a magistrate to seek out and punish those responsible for the death of the lord, but wherever he inquired he was met with the same answer, "Fuente Ovejuna lo hizo," that is, "Fuente Ovejuna killed him." Finally, faced with the dilemma of either punishing the whole population or pardoning everyone, the rulers pardoned them and made the village a royal domain. Today the saying, "Fuente Ovejuna lo hizo," is still heard occasionally, a sort of fifth amendment response to unwelcome questions.

Lope de Vega develops his story with characteristic skill. First of all, King

Ferdinand and Queen Isabella are idealized as the perfect rulers—infallible, just, and paternal. Also, being Spanish, they are represented as remote and formal. Next, the peasants are shown as simple happy folk, pious, polite, and obedient, abused beyond endurance by their cruel and ruthless overlord. Finally, the lord himself, Commander Fernando Gómez de Guzmán, is depicted as a power-greedy vassal of doubtful loyalty to his king whose punishment is long overdue. Most attractive are the peasants: the youth Frondoso, the maid Laurencia to whom he is betrothed, and Laurencia's father, Esteban, the mayor, or head man, of the village. When the Commander seizes Laurencia on her wedding day and carries her off to his citadel, the pent-up resentment of his long-suffering subjects gives way to the fury of outright revolt.

This sounds like dramatized history, doesn't it? Well, it isn't. Actually it is a romance built around a historical incident. History provides a very effective villain in the lord whose actions threaten the happiness of our peasant hero and heroine. History makes it possible to introduce the popular rulers, Ferdinand and Isabella, as deus ex machina. The use of historical incident and several characters who really existed allows the author to employ melodramatic devices without cheapening the romance. The arrogance and ruthlessness of the Commander is almost beyond credibility, but it is accepted because we know that he existed and that he perpetrated the crimes which Lope shows us. Ferdinand and Isabella are understanding and fair beyond all probability, but Spanish history idealizes them as Lope does, and since their pardon of the villagers is an historical fact we accept them as presented.

One would expect a play about a revolt to be dark, violent, and passionate. Some violence there is in the scenes of insurrection and in the exultation immediately following, but the most violent actions, such as the assault on Ciudad Real, the rape of Jacinta, and the torture of Mengo, occur offstage and are reported without emphasis on the violence or suffering. There is plenty of emotion but the most vivid and memorable scenes are the lighter, tenderer, and more delicate ones. The songs and dances are bright and lively. There are no sad songs and there are no mournful dances. The result of all this is that the play in performance strikes one as extraordinarily open-hearted and sunny. The world of *Fuente Ovejuna* is a world of sunshine, laughter, and light-hearted banter. The tyranny of Fernando Gómez de Guzmán casts a shadow over the town but it is like the shadow of a passing cloud on a sunlit landscape and when it is gone all is bright again.

THE PLOTTING

The plot is composed of three lines of action, separate at first but then gradually interrelated and finally brought together in a grand finale. The principal line of action concerns the villagers and their relationship to their ruler, the Commander, the courtship and marriage of Frondoso and Laurencia, plus the comic relief provided by Mengo and Pascuala. The second line of action involves the youthful Master of the Order of Calatrava who, at the urging of the

Commander, attempts to seize the fortress of Ciudad Real only to fall a foul of Ferdinand and Isabella. He is defeated and forced into obeisance to them. The third line of action introduces the King and Queen, brings them to the defense of Ciudad Real against the knights of Calatrava, then involves them as judges and patrons of the villagers who have revolted against their lord, the commander of Calatrava.

The villagers occupy the foreground of our interest. Their actions and feelings are given more complete expression than those of the nobility. All the lighthearted, comic, and sentimental scenes are theirs. On a different level, more remote and elevated above everyday things, is the royal court; it is viewed as it were from a distance, like figures of a frieze or tapestry, with strong outlines, but without dimension. In between are the knights of Calatrava, represented in high relief, vivid, but without depth or subtlety.

The use of three lines of action in three different perspectives gives to the progression contrast and variety. It provides a rough alternation between the village scenes and those of the court and battlefield.

The fifteen scenes that make up the progression are constructed as an accelerating sequence, with the more leisurely and longer scenes coming early in the piece and then the scenes decreasing in average length as the action develops, with the shortest scenes toward the end. Of the fifteen scenes, there are four in the first act, five in the second, and seven in the third.

Each scene is a distinct unit contributing to the forward flow of the action. But the sequence is not articulated. Characters do not continue from one scene to the next. One set of characters leaves the stage, another comes in, and the play continues, but in a new scene. Curiously, no provision is made for either beginning or ending scenes in any very dramatic way. Most scenes simply begin with two characters entering in conversation and end when the last of them leaves the stage. When they leave they seldom say where they are going. There are no tag lines or rhyming couplets to mark the scene endings and no provision made for overlapping or joining scenes in the Elizabethan fashion. The nearest thing to articulation is found in the fact that the continuity proceeds unbroken by pauses between scenes so that one may not permit blackouts or scene changes to interrupt the flow. To Lope de Vega continuity means progression without pause or interruption. As he said in *The New Art of Writing Plays*, "The stage should seldom remain without someone speaking, because the crowd grows restless in such intervals and the story is attenuated. Extended action without speech is inartistic."

CHARACTERS AND CASTING

In order to give the play a reasonably good production some forty performers are going to be needed. Fewer than this would leave the court and fiesta scenes looking skimpy while the military scenes with only a handful of soldiers would hardly seem important enough to warrant royal intervention. About half the company will be musicians, dancers, and supers whose principal function will be to fill out the stage, giving life and color to the crowd scenes. The play contains twenty-four speaking parts—twenty men and four women. Some of the men who appear in only one scene can be doubled, making possible an acceptable production with eighteen actors and four actresses. Unfortunately, the possibilities of doubling between villagers and soldiery or courtiers are limited by the short time for costume changes.

There are three groups of characters: the villagers, the court, and the soldiery. The villagers include four young men, three girls, and three middle-aged men, plus the dancers and musicians. The Calatravans include the Master of the Order, the Knight Commander, three officers who are not knights, and two or three attendants and soldiers. The court of Aragón-Castile-León embraces the King and Queen, a general, a judge, and some courtiers and pages. In addition to all these there are two men who come from Ciudad Real to the court. These appear to be men of some rank and substance but since they are apparently neither knightly nor noble their appearance would resemble that of the villagers.

The Villagers

The biggest and best role belongs to Laurencia, the heroine. She has the longest and most varied part, covering a wide range of emotion and acting opportunities. It helps for her to have a good singing voice and she ought to be able to do the Spanish country dances with distinction and style.

The ideal actress for this would be a twenty-year-old petite beauty with many years' experience in classical leads who could play the light bantering courtship scenes and the passionate denunciation of the town council with equal aplomb. The only physical requirements are that she have the face and figure of youth and be shorter than the hero, Frondoso. To find such a person, who has the skill and experience and can still pass for a girl of twenty is the heart of the problem.

There are only two other female villagers with speaking parts and both of them are about the same age as Laurencia. Lope mentions no mothers, nurses, or old women, so there seems to be no reason why any should be cast. This is not a realistic play in which every mob must show a cross-section of the population in the manner of Belasco or Cecil de Mille.

The part of Pascuala is a foil to that of Laurencia and should be cast with possible contrasts in mind. She need not be pretty, but she should be vivacious, witty, and personable. In the revolt she reveals herself to be rather bloodthirsty. She will not need to sing but she ought to be able to join in the dances.

Jacinta, the third peasant girl, does not have a large enough role to show any very definite character traits. She is the one whom the Commander takes away and presumably rapes but she reappears later in the play seemingly none the worse for it. It is probably better not to make her too pretty as sympathy for her would take away from the interest in more important aspects of the plot. The "rape" of a plain girl is not likely to arouse our resentment as much as that of the heroine whose abduction stirs the village to revolt and destroys the Commander.

Esteban is the head-man of the village and also the father of Laurencia. His is a character of considerable charm, combining wisdom, dignity, and a sense of humor. Since he carries an important burden of dialogue he must have a good voice and clear diction. His age can be anywhere between forty and sixty. Specifics of appearance are unimportant but it will help the character if he is attractive in manner and upright in bearing.

Juan Rojo and Alonso are councillors, similar in age and bearing to Esteban. Alonso appears only twice and can therefore double in other parts such as that of the Judge.

We see more of Frondoso, the hero, than of any other male villager. He is about the same age as Laurencia, as attractive as possible, and he must be taller than she is. He does not have to cover as wide a range of emotions as Laurencia, but he does need to have the skill to give variety to his many scenes. He ought also to have a good singing voice and be able to dance a creditable *pasa doble* with his bride. Since he challenges the Commander in one scene and suffers torture in another he should have a virile quality that will make these actions convincing. If he is too slender or "poetic" he will be less effective. He should have a good physique, at least from the waist up, so that he will show up well when he is partially stripped in the torture scene.

Mengo, Frondoso's friend and counterpart, is about the same age. He is something of a comedian too, a sort of Sancho Panza, and the best humorous lines in the play are uttered by him. He can be quite homely, shorter than average, and fairly chubby. A good natural comedian always does well in this part. Since he has to endure two beatings, neither of which is comic, he must also be able not only to amuse an audience but also to gain their sympathy.

Barrildo and Leonelo are young men of the same age as Frondoso and Mengo. Leonelo is supposed to be something of a scholar, perhaps home on a holiday from school, and since he appears only once the part can be doubled.

The Calatravans

Fernando Gómez de Guzmán, Knight Commander of the Order of Calatrava, is a vivid character, drawn by Lope in bold outline and strong color with very little detail or shading. He is arrogant; he can be eloquent when needed, as his persuasion of the young Master shows, but ordinarily rather short spoken. He is especially blunt in the manner in which he addresses the villagers. Lope has given him no soliloquies to tell us what he feels or thinks.

When one is reading the play the character of the Commander is vivid but not nearly as clear as some others. As prime mover of the plot his function is evident and his character is well fitted to his function, but in performance he comes alive in an entirely different way than the reader might expect. He seems stronger, more vigorous, larger than life, and fascinating. It is obvious that the author intended us to hate him, fear him, and rejoice in his overthrow, but because he dominates every scene he appears in, and because we see him in adversity as well as in triumph, it becomes difficult to keep an audience from developing sympathy for him. This sympathy runs counter to the Commander's purpose since we are intended to rejoice along with the villagers when his head is carried in on a pike. Some means must be found therefore to reinforce in the scenes preceding his death the hatred and fear the villagers have for him. We must be glad to see the peasants destroy him and rejoice with them in his overthrow. Fortunately he gives no sign of having any sense of humor or feelings of tenderness.

As to appearance, the Commander is always more effective when played by a big man with a harsh voice. He should be made up as a hard-featured man. He is older than the others but not gray-haired. We tend to associate gray hair with virtues of age which do not exist in the Commander's character.

Rodrigo Tellez Girón, hereditary Master of the Order of Calatrava, is a very young man, possibly no more than eighteen or nineteen. His manner toward the Commander is assured and courteous, as if nobility comes naturally to him. We see him in only four scenes, each time in a different situation and mood. His youthfulness does not appear in his manner nor in his lines, therefore it must be unmistakable in his appearance.

Of the three officers—Flores, Ortuño, and Cimbranos—Flores has by far the largest and most demanding part. It is Flores who describes the spectacle of the forces of Calatrava setting forth to Ciudad Real, and it is Flores who at the end reports the revolt to the King and Queen. In order to do justice to his two magnificent set speeches Flores must have a good voice and good speech.

The part of Ortuño requires a good deal of activity but contains no lines that would tax the ability of an average actor. Nothing in the play gives us any idea of his age, but there is no reason to think of him as very old.

Cimbranos is the least of the three officers. He has one speech in which he reports to Fernando Goméz the siege of Ciudad Real, and there is another, later, which might be his, when "a soldier" describes to Rodrigo Tellez Girón the revolt of the villagers at Fuente Ovejuna.

The Court

There is not much to be said about these characters, none of whom is more than a two-dimensional portrait figure. Ferdinand and Isabella, "Los Reyes Católicos," should look the part and their courtiers should support the image. This is more a matter of costume, setting, lighting, and makeup than of casting. All the director needs to do is to cast the characters so that the designers have good-looking people to work their magic on.

COSTUMING

When in Scene Eight we see the knights of Calatrava retreating from Ciudad

Real we know exactly how they should look because Flores has described their appearance in detail in Scene Two. White-plumed helmets, elegant armor, surcoats bearing the crimson Cross of Calatrava on a green ground, boots, spurs, and cut-and-thrust rapiers mark the warriors and their retainers. The effectiveness of Scene Eight would of course be enhanced if we could supply them with two sets of costumes, one for when they are victorious and another, torn, bloody, and smoke-stained, for their retreat and their reappearance in Fuente Ovejuna in the midst of the wedding.

Fernando Gomez will need a hunting costume for his deer-hunting scene, and something equally appropriate for the scene in which he is relaxing in his castle when surprised by the rebellion. The Master of Calatrava needs an especially elegant costume for the scene in which he presents himself at court to beg forgiveness from Ferdinand and Isabella, but he should be more informally dressed when he receives Fernando Gómez in Almagro.

The other soldiers can wear helmets, breastplates, and boots most of the time. When the revolt breaks out they are all surprised without their weapons, so they might look better if they are then without helmets and breastplates. When Flores appears before the King and Queen he should be without armor, and bandaged to show that he has been injured in the revolt. Sometimes he also limps and carries a crutch.

The villagers can be colorfully costumed in Andalusian peasant dress with appropriate modifications to suit the period in which the play is set. For the fiesta that greets the return of the victorious Calatravans, the wedding of Laurencia and Frondoso, and the final audience with the King and Queen, the basic costumes should be "dressed up" with additional ribbons and perhaps more formal headgear.

Laurencia and Frondoso wear special costumes for their wedding, light in color (for visibility during the confusion of the revolt which follows) and with many trimmings. Each also has a second costume, like the first only soiled and torn, since after being dragged off by the Commander they reappear disheveled. Both costumes have to be designed for quick changing. Laurencia, for example, has only twenty-seven lines between her abduction and her reentrance, all torn and bedraggled, in the council meeting.

For the fiesta and also for the climactic council meeting it is probable that the council members such as Esteban, Juan Rojo, and Alonso would wear some sort of robes of office with appropriate symbols such as chains or staves. If these are dark in color the sudden appearance of the disheveled Laurencia in her white wedding gown will be most dramatic.

The dancers and musicians are usually costumed like the villagers so that they can double to increase the size of the mob in the revolt. The dancers however need certain things that the villagers do not, such as special shoes, extra petticoats for the women, and scarves for the men. One very Spanish item is the knee-length pantalette worn by the female dancer. The Spanish country dances, unlike the modern Flamenco, limit the women to showing the slightest suggestion of calf, and then, just in case, the pantalettes are regarded as essential for decency. It would be very un-Spanish to allow the women to dance without the pantalettes.

The costumes of the royal court can be the same for each scene in which it appears. The King and Queen wear crowns, chains of office, and carry scepters. A photograph of the tomb of Ferdinand and Isabella in the cathedral in Granada will show exactly how they ought to look. The other members of the court are similarly costumed, but not quite as bright in color nor as heavily bejeweled. Don Manrique, the general in command of the King's forces, might be wearing half-armor and boots since he sets out directly to retake Ciudad Real. The Judge who reports back from Fuente Ovejuna might wear a judicial robe and cap. The soldiers of the King are usually more elegantly uniformed than those of Calatrava in order to emphasize the difference between the royal and provincial retinues.

In the fifteenth century certain fabrics such as satin and brocade were restricted to members of the royal family so one has to be careful not to put the Calatravans in materials that were forbidden to them by the sumptuary laws of the time. Costumers are often impatient of such restrictions but ignoring them does not usually improve the character of the production.

SETTING

The practical requirements of the setting are quite clear, for without certain specifics of space and movement the play cannot be given an acceptable presentation.

First of all, the dances and crowd scenes demand a large flat floor area. If twelve dancers are used the minimum flat space will need to be about eighteen by twenty-four feet. The exact area needed can be determined early in rehearsals by marking out a space on the floor of the rehearsal room to see what area the dances can be fitted into. If the theatre has a thrust stage the area might be square. Sometimes it is possible to accommodate the dances in a smaller area when they are viewed from three sides, but this should be tested before the floor plan for the setting is finalized. Too often designers tend to see the play in static visual terms and provide floor plans with steps or ramps that limit movement and pinch the action.

The second requirement is some provision for swift and easy entrances and exits of large numbers of performers. The crowds and the dancers appear quickly and disperse readily. This means at least four exits with sufficient off-stage space to avoid bottle-necking. A couple of vomitories on the audience side of the apron, although they seem not to have been used in the original Spanish theatres, are very useful for this kind of movement.

The third requirement is some means by which dramatic entrances can be made by Laurencia in the Council scene, the Commander in the Wedding scene, and Frondoso in his reunion with Laurencia. None of these entrances can be effective if the character has to cross any very great open space before making contact. One of the disadvantages of the average thrust stage is that its shape seldom provides well for this kind of entrance. So some means will have to be developed especially for this production.

The court scenes are better if the setting is designed so that the monarchs can be "revealed," for there are too many people in the court for more than one walking entrance of the group. Lope has one scene in which the two appear to be meeting as if coming from opposite directions, but while such cross-apron parades are quite effective, they cannot be repeated without becoming tedious. It works better therefore for the court to be discovered in most instances by means of a draw curtain or turntable.

If the stage is large enough to allow it, an upstage transverse platform about two feet high is helpful for separating the action of the court from that of the commoners.

Whenever there are dances in a play there is the problem of footing. The floor must be smooth, but it must also have enough texture so that the dancers will not slip. Ballet companies have their own floors that travel with them, and such a floor might be used to advantage here. Otherwise it might be sprinkled with water as ballet rehearsal floors are, being dampened just enough to provide a grip for the feet. Floor cloths and carpets are undesirable when dances are featured.

For Spanish dances, which feature stamping and heel beats, the floor has to be extra solid. If in addition it can also be made somewhat reverberant, this will enhance the effect. In Spain the dance floors are constructed of carefully selected woods with a wearing surface about the thickness of porch decking, resulting in a floor which is both reverberant and solid.

The presence of musicians should receive more attention than it usually gets. Musicians have to be somewhere out of the way, where they can play without being jostled, or, when offstage, where they can see the main action, be heard by the audience, and not be in the way of actors or stage hands.

Spanish actors, like the Elizabethans, played practically all their scenes standing or walking. Very few provisions for seating are needed. For *Fuente Ovejuna* two moveable benches capable of holding two persons each, on either side of the apron, will accommodate any seating that seems appropriate. These benches can easily be moved to various positions or put completely out of the way. Thrones for the King and Queen are sometimes used for their decorative value but they are not really necessary, the court scenes being brief enough in every instance to be played standing.

Decor

The Cross of Calatrava is an important symbol which might be incorporated into the decorative scheme in various ways. I have seen it used very effectively on a backdrop or drapery behind the scenes in which the Calatravans appeared. The cross itself is crimson, of a distinctive shape, somewhat like the cross of the Knights of Malta but with back-curving ends instead of flat ones. It is usually gilt edged and displayed against a green background. On a cloak or surcoat it is worn over the left breast, a fact that is mentioned several times in the play, notably when Frondoso makes it the target of his cross-bow in rescuing Laurencia from the Commander.

The scenes involving Ferdinand and Isabella might be identified similarly by some elements of scenery featuring the familiar red and gold arms of the united kingdoms of Castile-León and Aragón.

To most English-speaking audiences the geography of Spain and the relationship between Ciudad Real, Almagro, and Fuente Ovejuna will be meaningless without a map. It has therefore become a tradition to have a show curtain or backdrop on which these places are identified on a map of the Iberian peninsula. Ciudad Real was an important stronghold dominating the main route between central and southern Spain in somewhat the same way as Monte Cassino controls the route between Rome and Naples. Only a map can make this clear to an audience; then the audacity of the Knights of Calatrava in seizing this important point and the vigorous reaction of the Catholic Kings becomes immediately apparent.

There is another kind of decorative opportunity here, for showing, perhaps through scenery projected or painted, something of the picturesque countryside around Fuente Ovejuna. Something attractive and characteristically Spanish might be developed here.

Properties

Practically all of the properties are carried on and off by the performers. There are weapons for the soldiery, such as glaives for the Calatravans and halberds for the guards at court, banners and standards for both, and scepters for the sovereigns.

Esteban, being Alcalde, or head man of the village, needs a staff of office which in one scene the soldiers use to beat him. It is probable that each man who comes to court from Ciudad Real will also carry a staff of office to mark him as an ambassador of the city they represent.

For the fiesta which greets the return of the victorious Calatravans there are heaps of fruit and flowers in baskets and carts, flowers to throw, and floral circolets for the folk dancers. Later, for the wedding scene there are more flowers, wedding presents, and appropriate decorations to brighten the scene.

Laurencia needs a wicker basket for her laundry in the scene by the river bank where she encounters the Commander. The Commander will need a cross-bow with a dart in it, along with the sword, probably the same cut-and-thrust rapier which he carries in earlier scenes. This he unbuckles and lays aside before he approaches the girl. These cut-and-thrust rapiers were often over four feet long; it would be awkward to make love while wearing one, as the Commander has probably learned from experience.

For the revolt the villagers are armed with weapons such as they might take from their regular work: pruning hooks, sickles, clubs, cleavers, and sheath knives. Laurencia speaks of unsheathing her sword, but since peasants could not possess swords it must be that she has taken the weapon from one of the soldiers. In the fifteenth century, military arms were forbidden to all but nobility and their hired retainers.

After the revolt, during the celebration, the head of the Commander is carried in on a pike and all dance around it. The staging of this is going to take considerable artistry and the head will have to be carefully made in order to achieve just the right effect and not create either revulsion or nervous laughter. Audiences today are accustomed to all sorts of gruesome effects as a result of their television and movie experience but severed heads on pikes are still somewhat strange and can precipitate laughter if not expertly managed.

When Mengo is brought in after his successful resistance to the inquisition by the Judge the villagers crowd around and ply him with food and wine. The wine is in Spanish wine skins, not bottles. The food ought to be colorful fruit and sweetmeats in baskets arranged so that the audience can see and appreciate them.

MUSIC AND DANCE

The simpler country dances of Spain, unlike the modern Flamenco, are easily within the reach of actors of average ability so that within the four or five weeks ordinarily allotted to rehearsal a group can master all the dances and songs called for by Lope. The more intricate rhythms of castanets and heel beats may be unattainable but the simpler basic ones certainly are not. Most dancers can master the fundamental patterns in two or three weeks and perform all the simpler castanet rolls without difficulty. In order to achieve this a good teacher is needed, a dance director thoroughly familiar with Spanish folk dances and with a large repertory from which dances can be chosen to fit the talent at hand.

The music is easier. Two or three guitars will do nicely as accompaniment and although the fingering is different from that which most Americans know, the difference is usually overcome without difficulty.

For the songs it is best to adapt the style to the voices available using a simpler rendition familiar to American ears and avoiding the ornamentation and falsettos that characterize the original.

The first musical number is the welcoming of the victorious Calatravans returning from the conquest of Ciudad Real. Of the many possible numbers for this occasion, a *bal de circolets* begun with a spirited roll of castanets followed by the entrance of the dancers with semicircular floral wreaths which end up forming an arch for the victors to pass under, does very nicely.

Next comes the big wedding scene, beginning with a romantic song by Barrildo and Leonelo, followed by a country dance such as the *Ave*, a round dance for twelve. After this Mengo chimes in with a comical song of his own invention. When the speech making is over the bride and groom take the floor with a lively *pasa doble*, such as the *Ole de la Curra*. A good dance number here can always be counted on to bring down the house with bravos and cries of "More!" and an encore may be added. This sets the stage for the sinister entrance of the defeated Commander and the abduction of Laurencia.

In the exultation following the overthrow of the Calatravans there are songs composed for the occasion by Frondoso, Barrildo, and Mengo. Then the head of the Commander is carried in on a pike while the villagers celebrate with a dance for which a *Seguidilla* usually goes well, a simple staccato square dance for twelve to sixteen with castanets and heel beats.

One of the liveliest moments in the play comes in the reunion of Laurencia and Frondoso, beginning with her soliloquy expressing her yearning for him which turns into a duet when he comes out of hiding to join her.

The last scene builds to the moment when the King decides to pardon the whole village and take it under his protection. At this the guitars and castanets burst forth, the singers give voice to a ballad of thanksgiving and all the rest join in a joyous dance. For this rousing finale a round dance such as *A lo Alto y a lo Bajo* goes well. This could be topped by another *pasa doble* by Laurencia and Frondoso and blended into a curtain call supported by music. The audience often begins to applaud before the dance is concluded, so one might consider a second curtain call in which the dance director and music director can take bows.

REHEARSAL AND PERFORMANCE

Before beginning to cast the play a number of things must be settled. Both the dance director and the music director will have to be on hand to help with the casting. The dance director will have to select the dancers and test the dance talent of those trying out for the parts of Laurencia and Frondoso. The music director will have to choose the music and the instrumentalists, arrange the scores, and test the singing voices of those trying out for the leading roles. Depending on the quality of talent available, the dance director will determine the specific dances to be used according to the demands of the play and the abilities of the dancers; if the dancers are inexperienced in this kind of dance some concessions will have to be made to their limitations.

Provisions will have to be made for several rooms, one for reading auditions and others for singing and dancing, with pianos and accompanists.

Except for Laurencia and Frondoso the dancers do not double in speaking parts. Rehearsals for the dance group will often be scheduled at the same time as the others, so to use performers, except for the two principals, who appear in both would make rehearsal impossibly difficult. It is good however to have rehearsal rooms for the different groups close enough together so that the directors can get from one to another easily and confer together when necessary. The rehearsal rooms, while close, still have to be far enough apart so that the sounds from the music and dance will not interfere with the quieter scene rehearsals.

The actual rehearsing of *Fuente Ovejuna*, most directors agree, is exceptionally enjoyable. The main outline of each scene is clear and easy to grasp so that the actors take hold of their characters early and firmly. The lines are readily memorized and not as easily forgotten as those of many modern plays. This is fortunate, because many lines are going to have to be rewritten as the rehearsals progress. One of the charms of Lope's play is that the actor is always able to see his progress. This makes satisfying work for him. In many ways the material reminds one of Shakespeare's; it is eminently playable, easy to understand, and extremely responsive to the actor's art. It has, however, one fault that Shakespeare's does not have: it does not hold its shape. Fine points of characterization and stage business are as easily lost as they are achieved. A particularly telling inflection, a significant pause, or an effective gesture may, after it has been rehearsed to perfection, simply fade away during successive performances until the quality attained during rehearsals at the cost of so much effort is completely lost. In order to keep the play in top shape through a run of more than a few performances repeated brush-up rehearsals have to be scheduled.

Once into performance, rapport with the audience is readily established. It is the kind of material that encourages an audience to overt response. After the first few minutes the actors have the audience with them all the way, laughing at the humorous touches, gasping indignantly at the shocking behavior of the Commander, and freely applauding the set speeches, songs, and dances.

The cast must be warned not to expect much praise from the newspaper critics. The audience may be swept away but the critics are not so easily won and tend to be contemptuous toward a play that appeals so frankly to emotion. This is not an intellectual play. All the meaning in it is forthright and plainly evident, leaving a critic little opportunity to display his erudition or exercise his literary panache. The result is that he is likely to deprecate the whole thing as melodramatic and simplistic as if those were qualities not in its favor. I mention this here because performers are usually depressed by unfavorable reviews. Perhaps if they are warned in advance they will be able to discount the reviews and take satisfaction instead from the pleasure they can see that they are giving their audiences.

NOTES ON STAGING

The Commander with his soldiers enters twice during a celebration of the villagers, and the play gains from a strong contrast between the two entrances. The first time he is returning victorious from the taking of Ciudad Real with flags flying to a town waiting to greet him and celebrate his triumph. In the second entrance he appears unexpectedly with the remants of his defeated army, banners shredded and finery torn and smoke-stained. The villagers in their holiday best are celebrating the wedding of Laurencia and Frondoso, and when he departs, taking Laurencia with him by force, the stage is set for the revolt that follows.

The climax of the play comes in the next scene during the town meeting when the men argue whether to leave the place forever or appeal to Ferdinand and Isabella for succor. Into this meeting staggers Laurencia who has escaped from her tormentors, her hair down and her wedding gown disheveled, to burst forth with one of the most stirring speeches ever composed for the stage: "O, well named this town, 'the Sheep Well,' for none but sheep dwell here!" etc., creating a general uproar and cries of "Down with Calatrava!" and "Death to Fernando Gómez!"

Setting off such scenes and generally alternating with them are the light, jocular ones, like the betrothal (Scene Seven), tender, like the reunion of Frondoso and Laurencia after the rebellion (Scene Fifteen), or comical, like Mengo's recovery from the judge's questioning when the villagers ply him with food and drink until he can scarcely stagger off the stage.

PART FOUR

Later Comedy

CHAPTER 11

The Satires of Jonson and Molière

Satire, especially in premodern drama, is so often mishandled that a word of warning must be given to anyone considering producing a play by Ben Jonson or Molière which was either composed as satire or which contains any very pronounced elements of satire.

The common mistake in theatrical production is to treat satire too broadly, thus depriving it of its characteristic effect, which is the delight of discovering absurdities in the behavior of others. When too broadly done the discovery is forced upon one; one is denied the opportunity of making one's own discovery. The mistake is an easy one for the producer to make because satire always involves heightened situation and characterization and the producer, recognizing this, tends to proceed in the same direction, giving to the whole creation a very broad treatment. He is encouraged in this by the response of the audience which is always quicker and more vigorous for the broader effects.

Satire in drama is different from literary satire and even more different from satire as practiced in the graphic arts, for in both of these the satire is accomplished by means of exaggeration. The opposite is true of the best dramatic satire. It employs a light touch and goes only far enough to put its satiric point within reach of the audience, taking care not to make the point too obvious. Some of the best dramatic satire to be seen on the stage today occurs not in plays at all but in the mime of artists like Marcel Marceau. By comparison with the work of Marceau the best satire of most contemporary playwrights seems heavy handed. This is because Marceau has known for some time what most playwrights have either forgotten or not yet learned: that the art of theatrical satire is to manage the presentation in such a way that the observer discovers for himself those ironies and absurdities which the artist wants him to know.

Dramatic satire is usually defined as comic effect arising from the comparison and descrepancy between what we think ought to be and what we actually find in the behavior of people. Aristotle noted this when he described comedy as the representation of "men as they are."

Two things are thus placed in juxtaposition: ideality and actuality. Both must be valid. The idea as to how men should behave is one to which all members of the audience subscribe. The behavior represented as absurd is always some extreme, aberration, or inconsistency in relation to that idea. One essential of true satire is a fundamental plausibility of character and situation. The characters bear a readily recognizable resemblance to the same kinds of people in the world around us. The situations are the same kinds of situations as we might expect to find them in.

In drama pure satire is rare. *Volpone, Tartuffe, The Alchemist,* and *The School for Scandal* are all basically satiric, but all contain elements of farce, fantasy, and in the case of *The School for Scandal,* even romance. The blending of satire with farce is the commonest mixture. When artfully done, as in the table scene in *Tartuffe* or the second courtroom scene in *Volpone,* it gives to the work a seasoning which could not be equalled by any other means. However, the number of dramatists who have been able to make this blend work at its best have never been numerous and probably never will be, for it demands an extraordinary degree of artistry not only on the part of the author but also on the part of the performer who interprets the work.

Satire in drama reached the pinnacle of its development in the seventeenth and eighteenth centuries as the product of a mature and urbane culture in a time when society was well ordered and stable and values seemed as permanent as bed rock. In such a time the behavior of men could be measured against standards generally accepted by all men, or at least by all educated men. The appeal of satire was then and has been ever since to the more literate and thoughtful members of society, for its enjoyment requires some exertion of the intellect and is increased by the possession of a wide frame of reference.

When all is said and done there is perhaps no pleasure in theatre-going equal to the delight of experiencing one of the great satiric comedies performed with skill and good taste. When this is done we see through and around the characters, penetrating their affectations, rationalizations, and vacillations. We see what the characters themselves do not suspect, that their motives are mixed and their objectives impracticable or contradictory. We view their foibles with an Olympian perspective, exercising our intellects and our sense of proportion. The result is very gratifying, a sensation of superiority, of balance, and of smug satisfaction of a kind seldom experienced in real life.

CHAPTER 12

Volpone: A Problem of Contrasts

This play is studied by practically every undergraduate whose path is crossed by a course in Elizabethan Drama, but it has received far fewer productions than it deserves. The reason for this is not hard to determine. It is a difficult play to read—overlength, wordy, and loaded with topical allusions and classical references which repeatedly force the reader to interrupt himself in order to scrutinize the fine print of the footnotes. The songs are there with indications as to who sings what but the music is missing and only to be found in another book. Altogether it is as if the author had gone out of his way to confront the student with a test of his powers of endurance and concentration.

In performance the effect is entirely different. The language when spoken is brilliant—elegant, vivid, and fluent in utterance. The opulence of Renaissance Venice pervades the play with a great golden glow. The characters are imaginative, energetic, purposeful, and unhindered for the most part by moral scruples. The plot is never still but always on the move, evolving from one bold scheme to another even more daring.

HOW LONG IS TOO LONG?

This is not to say that the production of the play is not without its problems. The biggest problem, though not the most difficult, is the length. It is half again as long as it need be or should be. Ben Jonson edited his plays, not as performance pieces that had delighted audiences in the theatre, but as poetry to be appreciated by the reading gentry whose education was largely classical. He wanted renown as a poet, not as a playwright. As a result his plays, while they appear in exceptionally clean printings with few of the omissions, changes, and marginal notes which clutter the playhouse scripts, are also expanded and elaborated in language far beyond what could conceivably be performed under the playhouse conditions of his time.

Fortunately most of this expansion takes place in the expository first third of the work and can be trimmed down without impairing either intelligibility or plot. The rest of the amplified text is employed to make sure that Sir Politic Would-Be and his lady are really as tedious as the other characters say they are. Whether Jonson's audiences really enjoyed the garrulity which makes the Would-Be's boring to everyone else is questionable. Boring to the others they may be, and may even be amusing while doing so, but they cannot be permitted to bore the audience, so their lines must be reduced to a safe number.

More difficult is the problem which seems to be present in all of Ben Jonson's plays: the characters are hard for the actors to master. Rehearsing is hard work. Only by degrees do the characters come to life and only through the most determined effort. In the finished performance they are so vivid and have so much bounce that it is hard to believe that the actors ever had to labor over them. But labor they did. Mastering one of Jonson's characters is like chiseling a human likeness out of a block of granite. The less experienced actor, up against this for the first time, becomes discouraged and wonders if he will ever be able to bring the character to life. With the director's help and encouragement he will eventually succeed, but there will be many times during rehearsals when he will seem to be getting nowhere. There is a compensation however in another related quality of Jonson's creation: once the character does take shape it stays that way; it does not fade or slip away during successive performances. Like a portrait in marble it retains its finest lines regardless of differences in audience response and the varying moods of the performer.

The third problem is not unique with this play. It is common in comedy. But it might as well be mentioned here because we may not permit ourselves to forget that it is always lying in wait. This is the tendency of comedy, especially in those scenes which elicit the greatest audience response, to expand and lengthen, gaining a little each performance until it has to be put back into rehearsal and shrunk to its original dimensions. The tendency of some scenes to swell in performance must be checked because it not only throws the progression out of balance but also makes the play last too long so that the scenes coming close to the finale suffer.

CHARACTERS AND CASTING

Volpone

The actor who is cast for this part is going to play four distinct roles: Volpone himself; Volpone the invalid; Volpone the Mountebank, "Scoto of Mantua;" and Volpone the Commandadore, or bailiff. For the parts of the Mountebank and Commandadore he is going to have to be acrobatically agile. As Volpone himself he is going to have to be able to brag about his good looks and sing a lovely song. He boasts to Celia that he played Antinous in a masque at court, which if true would indicate that he possesses a better than average physique, so maybe he is handsome as well as versatile.

Although his suitors speak of him as "old Volpone," it seems clear that he cannot at the oldest be much beyond middle age. When he is pretending to be at death's door he acts old, but this is only his act; in reality there is no reason for him to be elderly. He delights in his quick wit and gets his greatest pleasure from deceiving his suitors. He loves his possessions and the fact that he is able to combine deception with acquisition is the source of intense satisfaction to him. But although greedy he is not miserly. His riches, however acquired, are valuable to him for the sensual pleasures they enable him to enjoy. To sum up, he is sensual, vain, avaricious, cowardly, and entirely without conscience. On paper this does not add up to a very admirable character, but on stage his imagination and vivacity make him continually fascinating to watch.

Mosca

Mosca's function is that of agent. He implements Volpone's decisions and wishes. In most of the scenes in which he appears he is manipulating someone and the person upon whom he is working is the center of interest. A common mistake is to allow Mosca to upstage the other characters and dominate the scene. The reason it is a mistake is that if the attention is allowed to linger too long on Mosca he becomes tiresome; at the same time the important decisions of the primary characters are obscured so that the transitions by means of which we follow and enjoy the intricate plot are blurred. In consequence clarity is lost and the play as a whole loses brilliance. The actor auditioning for the role of Mosca must understand that his is not the leading part in spite of the fact that he is on stage most of the time.

There is nothing in the play to tell us who Mosca is or where he came from. We do know from his actions that he is extremely glib and quick thinking. He turns to advantage every reversal except the very last one. Nothing indicates his age but it seems unlikely that such a wordly wise person would be a youth. The part requires a naturally deft actor and above all a very smart one. Cast the brightest one in the company for this role.

Voltore, the Lawyer

Voltore is as clever and unscrupulous as anyone of the suitors but he also projects an aura of danger. This heightens the excitement of Mosca's attempted deception of him. In the finale Voltore very nearly proves the undoing of Volpone and everyone else. The funny thing about him is that he desires above all to be honored and respected, to have dignity and be trusted and looked up to, and in order to achieve this he is willing to sacrifice everything, including that same integrity which is the basis of respect.

Corbaccio, The Old Miser

This one is old, close-fisted, and suspicious of everyone. The lines describe him as "four-eyed," deaf, toothless, with "three legs," and on the edge of his grave. His age and infirmities provide for innumerable gags. We have to be careful that the actor does not overdo the part. Because his traits are many, and from the point of view of the actor technically simple, the role does not demand as much of the actor as some of the other parts and can be given to one of the less experienced performers. Whoever plays the part is certain to be a favorite of audiences and remembered by all with pleasure for years afterward.

Corvino, the Merchant

This is an insecure man, brassy and aggressive when the wind is with him, but easily discouraged and deflated by the slightest obstacle to his ambitions. He alternates mercurially between hope and despair with no middle ground, and Mosca, sensing this, feeds him ideas which push him from one to the other. He thinks habitually in terms of trading and sharp dealing; his principles, such as they are, never stand in the way of what he regards as a good exchange.

Celia, Corvino's Chaste Wife

If Mosca's description of her is to be borne out by her appearance she is going to have to be a real beauty. But with the resources the costume designer and makeup artist can bring to bear this should present no problem if she has an agreeable voice and some grace of movement. There is a danger here in the fact that young attractive performers tend to attract sympathy from the audience and sympathy for Celia runs counter to the detachment essential to satire. Her predicament when threatened by Volpone with rape is not going to be as hilarious as Jonson intended if we sympathize with her. We dare not forget that the part was written to be played by a man.

Can it be made clear to an audience that Celia is virtuous in the narrowest possible sense, that she is good because she has no appetite for sensual pleasure, that it is the absence of feeling that makes her incorruptible fully as much as her moral or religious convictions? If this can be accomplished without making her seem stupid or merely a naive and tearful booby, we shall be able to keep the satire in balance.

Bonario

A similar problem exists with Corbaccio's son except that nothing in the text requires us to make him handsome. He might be a knock-kneed Aguecheek or a short tubby schoolboy of sixteen. In any case his Quixotic southern-gentleman style as he offers Celia his arm to escort her from Volpone's house is going to be very funny. The quality to work for in Bonario is that of naive highmindedness that is quite impracticable among sharpers like Voltore and Mosca.

Sir Politic Would-Be

Many a reader has wondered why Sir Pol and his fatuous lady are in this play. Except for Lady Would-Be's not very important testimony in the first trial scene neither of them has much to do with the main line of action. If they were omitted entirely the progression would be unaffected. In fact, the play is produced without them about as often as with them.

Comparing productions in which these creatures figured with those from which they were cut, it is clear that their presence enhances the play. Like Celia and Bonario, they provide a contrast which sets off to advantage the sharp practice of the principals. All of the major characters are unscrupulous, crafty, and cunning. In order for us to appreciate them their activities must be seen in contrast to those of people of ordinary morals. Celia and Bonario are high-principled but naive, while the Would-Be's are worldly and unprincipled but imperceptive. Together the two couples form a background against which the roguery of the others is set off to shine in its greatest brilliance. Consequently, the play as a whole is much better with them than without them, provided only that we do not have to see too much of them, for they are all fundamentally dull. Neither goodness nor stupidity is ever as interesting as wickedness and wit.

Sir Pol seems to combine a sort of affable congeniality with a conspiratorial need to confide. The important air which he gives to his confidences is belied by the triviality of the things he confides. No matter how he is played he is sure to remind us of someone who buttonholed us recently. There is no specific physical type for this kind of person so the task of the actor will be to achieve the essential quality of the species.

Lady Would-Be

The garrulous female is amusing on the stage but only for a short while, after which she begins to annoy the audience. So she must seem to be boring without actually being boring. Part of the problem is in the cutting and part is in the way the character is played.

It takes a really good actress and careful direction to bring this character to life. In addition to being tedious she is vain, affected, greedy, and if we are to judge from her hints to Mosca, eager to give away something that nobody wants. The part plays best if the actress is shapeless and homely.

Nano, Castrone, and Androgyno

Whether to make these the grotesques that Jonson describes will have to depend on the talent available. It is much more important that they be able to sing and dance well than that they be as grotesque as their names imply. Nano is the one who carries the greatest burden of mimicry and musical numbers and therefore needs to be the one most carefully cast.

COSTUMING

Because of the names Jonson has given his characters, costume designers have often been inspired to dress them in such a way as to make them resemble the subhuman creatures whose names they bear. Volpone, for example, is sometimes put into a reddish wig and beard and given pointed features to make him resemble a fox. Mosca is garbed in irridescent greenish black with wing-like sleeves to suggest a gadfly. Voltore is made up with a bald head with a ruff and cape shaped to recall the feathers and shape of a vulture. In some productions I have seen the characters even tried to simulate the movement characteristics of fox, gadfly, and vulture.

Such a treatment misses the satiric point of the play. Jonson has named his characters after animals in order to emphasize their predatory characteristics. This suggestion is enough. To go further and try to make them look like the creatures whose names they bear is belaboring the obvious. Not only is it superfluous for the audience but it makes the actors' task infinitely more difficult. Satiric effect depends upon close resemblance of characters to people around us. The characters should look like these people, not like animals. There have been satires from the time of Aesop to the present—witness *The Insect Comedy* and *The Animal Farm*—in which the characters were animals or insects behaving like human beings, but these are fantasies deriving their wit from the resemblance of their characters to humans. To reverse the picture and make humans look like animals is absurd. It serves no useful purpose and it obscures and coarsens many of the fine points of the satire.

Volpone's basic costume consists of a doublet or shirt worn with trunk-hose, stockings, and shoes. Over this he puts the robe he wears while reclining as an invalid, together with a nightcap and some sort of lap robe. The same outfit will serve for his appearance in the first court scene.

For the mountebank scene Volpone and his helpers will need outfits which conceal their identities yet permit them unlimited action. The Callot etchings of mountebanks, although a century later, are useful guides for these costumes. The grotesque masks which accompany the Callot costumes are helpful, provided they are constructed so as not to interfere with the actor's singing, speaking, or acrobatics.

As Commandadore, Volpone would be wearing the red cassock and cap of the typical Venetian bailiff. This makes an ideal outfit for the finale when Volpone suddenly rips off his disguise and reveals himself to the court. Velcro fastenings makes this easy to do.

At some point before the reading of the will we should see Volpone in his handsome *clarissimo* gown. This should be a different gown than the one he wears as an invalid. The gown of a *clarissimo* would be of rich crimson velvet trimmed with marten or mink. There is a distinctive head piece that accompanies the gown. It might be donned once by Volpone so that we would recognize it as his when Mosca comes into court wearing it. If there is any very great difference in sizes between Volpone and Mosca it would be better to have two outfits, one for each, so that Mosca can look really elegant when he comes into court and not look as if he is wearing garments too big or too small for him. There is a satiric point here that being a *clarissimo* is mainly a matter of being properly dressed.

Voltore, Corbaccio, and Corvino all wear gowns appropriate to their wealth and station. Corvino, the youngest of the trio, might also be the most lavishly costumed. All need purses in which they carry the various coins, papers, gifts, and so on which they use in the stage business.

Lady Would-Be might well be garbed in some fussy frilly outfit with lots of rings, bracelets, and artificial curls. She carries an enormous reticule into which she dives repeatedly for medicines, books, lorgnette, et cetera.

Sir Pol's tortoise costume consists of a carapace, or shell, with attached sleeves and trousers ending in flippers, with a cap which, when he lowers his head, looks like the head of a tortoise. This costume is so ridiculous that it always brings down the house. It is a sight gag, impossible to describe.

SETTING AND PROPERTIES

The physical requirements of the setting are simple: an entrance on either side of the acting area, a generous apron to facilitate the asides and the bi-polar scenes, and a reasonably high window or balcony for Celia's appearance in the mountebank scene. The courtroom scene requires an elevation of some sort to give height to the judges. The seduction scene needs a door or draperies through which Bonario can make a sudden entrance.

There is a good deal of moving of furniture on and off the stage: Volpone's couch, the chest containing his treasure, the mountebank's platform, the judges' chairs and platform in the courtroom scene, and the table, chair, and folding screen for the will-reading scene.

The appearance of the set should be elegant, with plenty of marble, gilt, carvings, and rich brocaded draperies. To what extent specific locales should be indicated is something to be decided by the designer. If desired, the play can be presented in a single formal setting with nothing but set properties such as the couch, screen, and judges' chairs to indicate locales. More detailed suggestion of locale would certainly add variety to the visual scheme provided the changes can be accomplished without interrupting the progression by curtain waits or dim-outs, for this is a play that must unfold continuously without pause or break of any kind between the successive actions.

The formal façade which Inigo Jones designed for the Cockpit-in-Court has been used for this play several times with considerable success. The design has been reproduced in many books on Elizabethan and Stuart staging. It has a large acting area and five entrances, including a central arch with a window or balcony over it and niches on either side of the second story which could be opened up into windows if needed. The architectural style is Palladian. With draw draperies or doors on the entrances the set accommodates all of the required action of *Volpone*. It could also be used for a number of other plays of this period and for practically everything Molière wrote.

NOTES ON STAGING

Only about two-thirds of the Prologue is needed. One could keep the first ten lines, the last seven lines, and only enough in between to provide the transitions.

(Act I–scene ii): A couch is much better here than a bed because it can be placed close enough to the audience for easy delivery of Volpone's asides and also because the characters approaching him can then play upstage of him and facing the audience. An alternative would be the chair that Elizabethans often favor for stage invalids.

(Act III–scene viii): This is a bi-polar scene with Corvino and Celia on one side, Mosca and Volpone on the other, and as much space in between as the width of the stage allows. The further apart they are, the easier Volpone's asides become and the more amusing the whole.

Volpone's wooing of Celia should not be allowed to turn into a farcical tussle. The satiric quality is better when the courtship is leisurely, the song fully developed, and Celia's incomprehension complete. Not until she offers to pray for his soul does he realize his mistake.

(Act V–scene ii): At what point does Mosca realize that Volpone's recklessness is presenting him with an opportunity to usurp his patron's position and wealth? This is the turning point of the Mosca-Volpone plot line.

(Act V–scene iii): It is easier for Volpone to spy on the reading of the will from behind a screen than from behind a traverse. This is another bi-polar scene, with Volpone and Mosca on one side and the readers of the will on the other.

(Act V–scene iv): The tortoise costume is hard to wear and requires an inordinate amount of rehearsal but is worth every minute of it.

(Act V–scene xi): The final courtroom scene is so complex, with so many asides and quick shifts of attention that one should consider rehearsing it until it runs smoothly before tackling any of the rest of the play. Once the actors have mastered this scene they will feel ready for anything.

CHAPTER 13

The Alchemist: A Problem of Tempo

The Alchemist is Jonson's most successful play. Its plot is a marvel of complexity made perfectly clear and continually intriguing, gaining momentum as it unfolds and coming around finally to a deft unequivocal conclusion. The scene is a dwelling in the Blackfriar's district of Jonson's London. The action, in unbroken progression, occupies only as much time as the performance itself. Greed, lust, superstition, false piety, and self-serving social ambition are satirized through the impostures of three clever rogues upon five sets of victims, while the rogues, after betraying each other, gain nothing and are obliged to consider themselves fortunate to escape punishment.

Upon reading this work one naturally compares it with Jonson's *Volpone*, written four years earlier. Both satirize common foibles through the impostures of the unscrupulous upon the gullible and greedy. In both the rogues fall out with each other and lose their ill-gotten gains. Both works observe the unities of time, place, and action and are constructed upon an accelerating sequence with the outcome unknown until the last few lines. And both allow the principals a variety of contrasting roles through the use of disguises and costume changes.

Like *Volpone*, the text of *The Alchemist* is exceptionally clean, exhibiting Jonson's usual care that his work should look good in print. It is also like *Volpone* in that it is from five hundred to a thousand lines longer than can be comfortably performed in two and a half to three hours. This means that as much as one-third of the text will have to be cut before casting begins. Fortunately this is not as difficult as it sounds. Most of the excessive length occurs in the expository scenes or in descriptive speeches that are much longer than necessary, mostly as a result of Jonson's attempt to make a more richly readable (and more readily salable) playbook.

Most of the other differences are what one might expect to find in the later of two similar works. For one thing, the plot is much more complex. There are three rogues instead of two and a much greater variety of fraudulent schemes afoot. Classical allusions are more numerous. There is a great deal more use of foreign terms, both Latin and Spanish. The effect of acceleration is heightened by a new device: the interruption of one plot line by another, usually by a second group of over-eager gulls appearing on the scene before the preceding ones are finished.

Surprisingly, there are no songs or dances such as enhance the earlier work. Nor are there many places where music or dance could be introduced to advantage. And the language, although fluent and varied, seems not to endow the play with that air of magnificence which the splendid lines of *Volpone* provided.

Altogether, the two plays are more nearly equal in performance effectiveness than a study of their texts might suggest, and the differences in performance quality are more dependent upon the skill of the performers. If one has at his disposal a large group of able actors *The Alchemist* is the better choice because there are more good roles more evenly distributed than in *Volpone*.

CHARACTERS AND CASTING

As with most plays of this period about twenty actors are needed, in this instance twelve principals and seven to nine minor characters, walk-ons, and supers. Unlike most of the other plays, opportunities for doubling of actors between roles are practically nonexistent.

Subtle

From what we learn about this creature during the opening quarrel, he is one of those "masterless" men who wandered from town to town, indentured to no guild master, servant to no householder, ineligible for military service by reason of age or simple cowardice, a vagabond living from day to day by his wits, unhoused, half clothed, and often hungry. When we meet him he is well fed, well dressed and prosperous, having settled down for an indefinite period to the lucrative occupation of stripping money and goods from gullible Londoners by appealing to their greed, superstition, or lust.

His name comes not from the modern meaning of the word but from the Elizabethan in which one who is cunning, wily, and deceitful is called "subtle." His particular forte is that he is able to assume the role of clergyman, necromancer, or physician with such conviction that none question his authority. Part of this conviction comes from his bearing. The other part is an encyclopedic knowledge of the arts he pretends to practice, or at least a mastery of the professional jargon. His description of the alchemical process by which the application of constantly increasing heat turns lead into tin, tin into copper, copper into silver, and silver into gold, is so logical that I have seen modern audiences follow it with rapt attention, all disbelief quite obviously suspended. Clearly it is his manner that makes people believe him: grave, self-assured, and sympathetic to the needs of his listeners. He is a "sincere" man.

Where could he have acquired his learning? He seems to know something of everything: Latin, Greek, alchemy, mythology, the scriptures, duelling lore, and a smattering of Spanish and Italian. His speech reveals no characteristics of class or region—no cockney, and no brogue. His vocabulary equals that of the best educated men of his time.

His age is not indicated. He seems to be older than Face, especially when he is impersonating the friar, but I think it less effective to play him as elderly than as middle aged, for if he is not elderly he can more easily offer his various impersonations as being of different ages and thereby gain a greater degree of variety and contrast between them.

In contrast to Subtle's "sincerity" and gravity in his various disguises is his swaggering insouciance when acting in his own character. Not only is he entirely unscrupulous but he takes the greatest delight in deception. Having existed most of his life as an underdog, he now occupies, however briefly, a position in which he can do as he likes with members of those classes who abused him most in the past, so now he is making the most of his opportunities and enjoying every minute of it.

In casting one should look for an actor who is a quick study with an inventive turn of mind, the sort who is always off his book and into stage business a week ahead of his fellow-workers. The part allows for almost unlimited invention and the more of it originates with the performer himself the better it usually turns out.

Subtle dominates every scene in which he appears. It is to him that Face brings the gullible ones gathered from tavern and street and it is he who impresses them with his mastery of science and art; in other words it is Subtle's acting in various roles that convinces the gulls of their imminent gains and separates them from their money. Subtle's part is thus the pole around which most of the action revolves. If the actor playing Subtle is strong in his part and ahead of the others in his development of it, the rest will have to work to catch up; they dare not lag very far behind in rehearsal. So Subtle becomes in a sense the bell-wether that sets the pace. If he is well cast the rest comes much easier; if he is less than outstanding the work of rehearsal is certain to be longer and harder and much less fun.

Face

Face's true character is that of the serving-man Jeremy who does not appear until the fifth act. But this is the person upon whom the actor must base his development of the role. The script calls him "housekeeper" because of his assignment of tending the house during his master's absence. His regular position is probably that of a footman. Like Subtle he derives immense satisfaction from the pretence which permits him to mingle as an equal with those from whom he is usually obliged to take orders and to defraud them while enjoying their trust and confidence.

Face does not have nearly as large a vocabulary as Subtle nor does he give evidence of much formal education. What he does know are the taverns and alleyways of London, meeting places like Paul's, and all the varied life that swarms there. Until recently he has known this life only from the underside as it were, from the viewpoint of the errand-boy, groom, or waiter. Now, with the help of Subtle, he assumes the dress and airs of a gentleman and hob-nobs with merchants and gentry as if he were one of them.

As a servant he developed an affable manner and eagerness to please which unfailingly endears the underling to his master. As Captain Face he now capitalizes on this manner, needing only to embellish it with the breezy air of the professional soldier and perennial gambler, strutting about in his finery, standing to treat to all and sundry and acting like every man's friend. Being naturally gregarious, this comes easily to him.

To make the actor's work more interesting, Jonson has given him the additional role of the drudge, Lungs, in every particular the diametric opposite of the carefree Captain: humble, earnest, and dull of wit. Since, in the space of a few lines, he must change from Face to Lungs and back again, the difference between the two is mainly a matter of contrast in behavior and speech, aided by some garment that can be donned in a trice, for there is not time for any change of makeup.

From the return of Lovewit onward the clamor of the neighbors and gulled clients presents Jeremy-Face with a series of challenges which he is barely able to meet, each more difficult than its predecessor. This requires an actor with an exquisite sense of timing, for the tempo of the denouement depends almost entirely on him. In casting therefore an instinct for timing and an ability to control and sustain the scene are of primary importance, taking precedence over appearance, experience, and everything else.

Doll Common

Doll is a prostitute, apparently one whom Subtle knew before he met Face. Together the two men have brought her into the house and set her up in business there. Subtle has taught her how to speak and act like a lady, just as he has taught Face how to behave like a captain. By putting her in fine clothes and passing her off as a great lady possessing the idiosyncrasy of liking to bed with strangers, they have been able to collect far more for her services than she could ever have commanded as a common streetwalker. Face acts as her pimp, passing the word to likely prospects and arranging her assignations.

At heart Doll is as coarse as they come, but she possesses a remarkable gift of mimicry, as we see when she impersonates first the great lady and immediately afterward the Queen of Faery. She has the ability to put aside her gutter speech and assume the accents of the high born or the brogue of faeryland as the occasion demands. She seems to revel in the excitement of the frauds they practice but she also seems easily bored by inactivity, repetition, or naivete in others. These are all traits consistent with the notions of Jonson's time regarding bawdry and fickleness which were thought to go hand in hand.

The fact that Sir Epicure Mammon is smitten with longing after his first glimpse of her would seem to indicate that she possesses a face and figure handsome enough to turn heads. Part of this effect might be achieved through costume and makeup—an elegant gown (Face says it is velvet), fine complexion, and attractive hairdo. Prostitutes on the stage are conventionally represented as overdressed or underdressed and wearing excessive makeup, but if the imposture Doll practices upon Mammon is to be plausible she should not look, act, or speak like the trull she really is. If before she dresses for her encounter with Mammon—during the inital quarrel perhaps—we were to see her in her shift or wrapper with her hair uncombed the contrast between her true nature and her assumed one might be more easily visualized.

Most actresses essaying prostitute roles overplay them rather badly, as if determined to make sure that no member of the audience should fail to get the idea. This is unnecessary in *The Alchemist*. From the first moment Doll appears the dullest spectator could scarcely fail to recognize her kind, either from her lines or her actions. There is nothing intrinsically funny in this. What is amusing is Doll's particular nature: the total absence of scruple, the delight in being able to impersonate gentry and the Faery Queen, and finally the innate fickleness which causes her to become bored with people and places as soon as the novelty begins to fade.

When we recall that the original Doll was played by a man, we may be able to picture her as Jonson saw the character, two hundred years before the romantic movement encouraged audiences to view prostitutes sympathetically. In the scenes where Doll appears as herself a man would probably have exaggerated both her femininity of manner in general and her coarseness of speech and gesture. With a woman in the role the first becomes unnecessary and the second leads so easily to overplaying that one is left with no option but a straightforward unforced impersonation.

In casting this part an actress with an ever-ready infectious laugh is worth looking for. The easier and more confident Doll seems the better she registers. It is also helpful to have an actress who can play some sort of stringed instrument which can serve for the specified "sittern."

Sir Epicure Mammon

This is one of the best acting parts in the comedy of the period and one which audiences remember most fondly. It is not a particularly difficult role; the lines "speak" themselves well and Mammon has no very difficult action to perform. So for the actor who plays it, this part is a genuine "plum." He would have to fumble badly in order to have it emerge as anything less than memorable.

Jonson uses the part to show off his own classical erudition, especially his vast acquaintance with the many forms of Roman vice. As a result Sir Epicure emerges as a sybarite whose imagined pleasures beggar description. When we first meet him he is on his way to Subtle's supposed alchemical lab, having been promised that this day will witness the turning into gold of all the household iron and brass which he has previously brought here. To his friend, Surly, an out-of-luck gambler, he boasts of what he will do with his wealth and the more he talks the more widely his imagination ranges.

From his many references to antiquity we conclude that he is well educated and that he has read extensively in the Greek and Latin authors. From the number of alchemical terms he uses we know that he is either well read in the subject or that he has picked up a remarkable amount of jargon during his brief association with Subtle. From the freedom with which he distributes largess we may also infer that he is quite well off. He gives Doll a diamond ring from his own finger and he repeatedly tips Lungs various small sums. His wooing of Doll, believing her to be a great lady, is courtly as befits a gentleman. All this would of course be very amusing to an Elizabethan audience to whom confusion of social status was always an unfailing source of hilarity.

What is it that makes Sir Epicure Mammon such a good part? I believe it is his unbridled imagination which repeatedly astounds us, leaping from one fantasy to another even more preposterous. I have seen him played as a gouty old codger and the resulting character was not very amusing. Nor is it effective to present him as a creature dominated entirely by lust. This man has an imagination of quicksilver. Notice the alacrity with which he takes the bait in the matter of Doll, and having taken it how he expands and elaborates the possibilities. In order to be so suggestible he must have a quick mind—shallow perhaps, but quick, very quick. It is this which makes him come so completely alive on the stage.

Pertinax Surly

The companion of Sir Epicure, as lean as the knight is fat, Surly is a sour sceptical man with no illusions or superstitions. He sees through Subtle's imposture from the first and does his best to caution Mammon against it but to no avail. Finally, determined to expose the fraud, he assumes the disguise of a Spanish don and allows himself to be solicited by Face who lures him to the house with promise of an assignation with the great lady (Doll).

One of the best scenes in the play occurs when Surly is brought in disguised as the Spaniard, unrecognized by either Subtle or Face who, thinking him unable to understand English, ridicule him, make fun of his clothing, complexion, language, and manner, while he is forced to endure the ridicule, unable to respond without giving away his game.

The actor who plays Surly thus has two roles quite distinct one from another. It is desirable therefore to have an actor who can speak Spanish fluently and who can differentiate sharply between the caustic Surly and the grandiloquent Don. It will help also if his appearance is in contrast with Mammon's when the two are first seen side by side.

Dapper

Dapper is a quite young man, a lawyer's clerk, and something of a man about town. Apparently he is also an incorrigible gambler and like many gamblers, superstitious. From the name Jonson has given him we may expect something of a dandy, hair and beard neatly trimmed and dress as rich as the sumptuary laws will allow—not as richly dressed as Mammon or Kastril, of course, but probably more fashionable than either and with more fanciful accessories. He should contrast strongly with Drugger in manner and dress, being as affected and elegant as the grocer is simple and shabby.

Abel Drugger

Drugger is in and out of the scene oftener than any of the other gulls. In spite of this I find I have more difficulty remembering his performance in detail than almost any other character in the play. Yet this is the role in which Garrick is reported to have scored one of his greatest triumphs. Perhaps some day I will see this character presented in just such a memorable way. Until then I can only wait and hope. My guess is that Garrick endowed him with some especially amusing idiosyncrasies of his own invention.

Drugger is a young, naive, inexperienced tradesman who is about to open a shop nearby. He comes to ask Subtle to cast a horoscope showing him how best to arrange his shop in order to capitalize on the destiny predicted for him by the stars. Promising to make him rich and marry him to a wealthy widow, Face turns him into an errand boy, using him to bring in more victims and ultimately to back him up in the accusations with which he discredits Surly.

From the way in which the rogues refer to Drugger it seems as if he has scraped and saved for years in order to be able finally to establish his own shop. From what they say of his diet he must by now be half-starved. We might expect therefore to see a shabby underfed creature whose obsequious behavior betrays a keen appreciation of the benefits to be gained from his association with those whom he considers to be gentry and therefore superior to him.

Kastril

A kastrel is a small bird of prey, a species of hawk. The name appears to be used here to indicate a quarrelsome choleric headstrong youth. He seems to have come of age quite recently. He is rough in manner and dress and reeks of the countryside from which he has come. He constantly bullies his eighteen-year-old sister, Dame Pliant. In most productions he is played with a rural accent.

The problem of the actor playing Kastril is to find ways of giving him some variety, for Jonson, who introduces him mainly to implement the marriage of

Dame Pliant to Lovewit, has given him very little and even though he has a few lines the fact that he continually repeats himself is likely to make him tiresome to an audience.

Dame Pliant

Subtle calls Dame Pliant "my plump and buxom widow" and Drugger tells us that she is "but nineteen at the most" and that she wears her clothes unfashionably. What we have then is an attractive young girl, perhaps a bit on the plain side as far as manner and dress are concerned, but otherwise definitely attractive. Some actresses have played her as if she were mentally retarded, but it is much better to portray her as innocently wide-eyed at the wonders of city life. Her part has few lines but it should not for that reason be given to an inexperienced actress. She may not have much to say but she is on stage a good deal and the fact that she is so much talked about makes her the object of much audience interest. Her reactions to Subtle's warm welcome, to Surly's revelation of the fraud, and to Lovewit's impulsive winning of her hand, are certain to make her delightful to watch.

Ananias and Tribulation Wholesome

In these two Puritans we have another pair of gulls seen often together and contrasting sharply in appearance and manner. Ananias is a lowly brother with pious manner and shabby clothes, intolerant and unforgiving, rejecting everything not in accord with his very literal interpretation of his Holy Book. Tribulation is a senior member of the church council, more worldy and considerably more prosperous. To heighten the contrast, Ananias might be lean and hungry looking while Tribulation is portly, pink-faced, and benignly confident.

Lovewit

As is usually the case with the *deus ex machina* role, a strong, self-assured performer is needed here. From the moment he appears, Lovewit dominates the scene and controls the pace of the progression as it comes round to its conclusion. It will help if he is a big man with a voice that can easily be heard above the clamor and confusion of the final scenes.

He seems mature and although Face promises that marriage with Dame Pliant will make him fifteen years younger, he should not be gray-haired or elderly, but vigorously in his prime. A touch of silver in his hair may perhaps add dignity but his appearance should be determined by the basic necessity for him to act and speak with authority. He seems to be a confident, good-humored sort. The fact that he has been recently widowed seems not to have depressed him much. The alacrity with which he takes up Face's advice about marrying Dame Pliant, and the ease with which he pardons his servant after he learns of that creatures misdeeds, suggest a genial nature.

The Neighbors

The neighbors who inform Lovewit of the strange goings-on in his house and who hang around him afterward to see what he does about it should be represented not as a ragged stage mob but as good solid householders of the toney Blackfriars' district. One must be careful not to cast too many inexperienced actors for this group, for the shifts of audience attention come very fast; one is going to need a group of supers who know how to "give" to the central character and direct the eye of the spectator.

COSTUMING

Although the action of the play is localized in the Blackfriars district and is intended by its author to be contemporaneous, it is not absolutely necessary that a modern producer costume it in the dress of 1610. The Old Vic once put it into eighteenth-century garb and had a very successful production. There are, however, some limits as to period and style, springing from the urbane and amoral nature of the satire, which seem to confine it to some period when society is relatively stable. This rules out modern dress, and most periods preceding the Elizabethan. To put it into the costume of non-European cultures would introduce an element of the bizarre which, while it might add visual variety, would certainly obscure many points depending on familiar behavior and customs, for the play is very English.

Disguise is one of the most consistent characteristics of dramatic satire which repeatedly features multiple-role characters who change costumes to assist their impostures. In The Alchemist five of the principals appear in more than one guise. Subtle appears first as himself, and afterward as a doctor of physic, a holy man, and a priest of faery. Face and Doll each have two disguises. Lovewit and Surly both disguise themselves as Spanish dons. The costume changes of Face and Subtle are so numerous and so fast—many of them having to be made in view of the audience—that no changes of makeup are possible. The entire imposture therefore has to be made convincing by means of the costume and the manner in which it is worn.

In his own form, before he assumes any disguise, Subtle seems to be dark complected and bearded. In the first scene Face refers to his sallow complexion, and further on he calls him "black boy," black is the common Elizabethan term for brunette. Before he assumes any of his disguises he is seen in trunk hose and shirt or something similar which will make it easy for him to slip into the robes that cover him from head to foot, first as the learned doctor and afterward as the holy man and finally as the priest of faery. For the conference with Dapper he puts on the doctor's robes and the "broad velvet head" or flat cap which goes with them. The gown can be any color; it is easier to manage with the lighting if it something other than black. As an added touch he might wear spectacles.

In order to receive Mammon he changes from the doctor's outfit into the costume of some sort of hermit or holy man. This is better as a friar's robe than as a Church of England cleric and it is also better white or gray than black or brown, since the dark shades make it more difficult for the actor to dominate the scene. Face speaks of Subtle in the hermit's guise as being threadbare, as if he cared for little but the results of his alchemy.

Jonson's stage direction calls for Subtle to enter for the gulling of Dapper disguised as a "Priest of Faery," this gives the actor an opportunity to display his virtuousity by impersonating one more character distinct from the three we have already seen. Dapper however hardly has time to appreciate the change because fifteen lines after Subtle appears the two rogues put the poor man into his blindfold.

Through the first four acts Face alternates between the guise of the swaggering Captain and that of the poor dull drudge, Lungs. Then he shaves off his beard and appears for the rest of the play as the housekeeper, Jeremy. In the last his garb is the discreet livery of the servant, which might be the familiar many-buttoned bluecoat, perhaps even with the badge of his master's house on it. Whatever he wears must include a pocket or two for keys and so on. As Captain Face he wears a beard of military cut and a sword with which he threatens Subtle. The remainder of this costume might include such details as would support the military rank which he claims: plumed hat, baldric or military sash, and perhaps a cassock or tabard with appropriate insignia. If the play is costumed in eighteenth- or late-seventeenth-century clothes, he could be given the red coat which came into existence as English uniform around the middle of the seventeenth century. Ordinarily one would expect to see him in boots and spurs, but these might interfere with the fast changes he has to make. As Lungs he could cover his captain's outfit, all but the feet, with a voluminous smock— probably smudged and blackened from his supposed furnace tending. Some sort of skullcap together with dark glasses would complete the picture.

Doll's most important costume is her first one for this is the only time we see her as the trull she really is. She might well be in some sort of frowsy undress—slovenly morning wrapper or petticoat and corset—with her hair unkempt as if not yet curled and combed for the day. She has plenty of time to change after this and when next we see her the change is impressive for now she appears as the great lady in a velvet gown with her hair handsomely done up and her hands covered with rings. Her third costume as the Queen of Faery appears to be something that goes on over her velvet gown for she gets in and out of it easily. When she appears the second time as Queen of Faery she makes a grand entrance, so probably a train should be part of this.

The fourth character to assume disguise is Surly, the gambler. Except for Doll's mention of the "lean gentleman" accompanying Sir Epicure Mammon there is nothing to tell us what Surly looks like in his own person. We tend to think of gamblers as somewhat debonair and flashy in dress with conspicuous display of jewelry carried over from their prosperous times. We also think of them as worldy wise, which Surly certainly is. There is much more to go on when he disguises himself as the Spaniard. He dyes his beard black (which would suggest that his natural coloring is lighter), trims it to the "Spanish cut" and darkens his complexion to a "scurvy yellow Madrid face," apparently the olive coloring of the Spaniard, so different from that of the pink-cheeked English-men. Subtle and Face are amused by his fluted cartwheel ruff which makes him look "like a head on a platter." His breeches are so voluminous that Face can feel his pockets for coins without his being aware of it. Since they accept him immediately as one of the gentry the fabrics in which he is clothed must be quite rich. At the time Jonson wrote the play it was customary for Spanish gentlemen to dress entirely in black.

The problem with Surly's disguise is that it must deceive Subtle and Face but be transparent to the spectators who have to recognize Surly in order to enjoy the joke. I have seen several productions in which Surly, when he came on as the Spaniard, was disguised so completely that no one in the audience knew who he was, and I have seen others in which his disguise was so thin that neither Subtle nor Face could possibly have failed to see through it, but I have never seen one which struck the right balance although I am sure it can be done.

When Surly uncovers himself, what does he do? He could rip off his big ruff, and if he has assumed a wig and false beard he could rip that off too. It all has to be done in an instant, the more sudden the more dramatic.

Lovewit's Spanish disguise is apparently much simpler since it need convince only the naive and untraveled Dame Pliant. He certainly does not have time to alter his complexion or the cut of his beard. Whatever disguise he assumes will probably have to go over his regular costume. And what would Lovewit's regular costume be? That of any well-to-do, middle-aged London gentleman, no doubt. Since he must dominate the stage in every scene in which he ap-pears it will help him if he can be put into some strong color that will stand out amid all the hurly-burly. Beyond this he must appear substantial and hand-some (since he marries the only eligible woman) but not fanciful in the sense that the younger men are. He wears a sword; we know this because he chal-lenges Kastril and puts him down.

In contrast to Lovewit stands "the fat knight" Mammon, obviously and os-tentatiously rich, with a great diamond on his finger and a plump purse from which he repeatedly tips the obsequious Lungs. He might carry a staff but he certainly wears no sword; it would be a nuisance in his wooing of Doll.

Ananias and Tribulation need to be recognized as Puritans by their familiar falling bands and plain cassocks. Beyond this, the contrast between the two of them should be striking: Ananias poor and threadbare against Tribulation in fine broadcloth with satin-lined cape, silver shoe-buckles, and silk stockings. For both of these characters dark gray would be better than black and would be better capable of showing up the difference in the quality of fabric, Ananias' coarse and faded, Tribulation's rich with a sheen of newness.

Abel Drugger seems to be outfitting his shop with money he has scrimped and saved over a long time. It seems likely therefore that he would be poorly dressed in simple, drab, and shabby clothing, perhaps with a shopkeeper's apron to mark him as a tradesman. He has pockets or wears a purse, for Face repeatedly wrings from him various small coins for one thing or another.

Kastril, being a gentleman, wears a sword proudly with his countrified clothing. What would this clothing be? Boots perhaps, with leather breeches, a sturdy serviceable cassock or doublet, and a hat lacking the smartness of the more elegant headgear of the other gentlemen.

Dame Pliant presents something of a problem since she must be at one and the same time both attractive to all the men who see her and also plain and out of fashion in her manner of dress. She is described as wearing a hood which is recognized as being unfashionable even by Drugger, but I see no way in which the effect of this can be brought home to a modern audience. A clever costumer may contrive, however, some acceptable equivalent. The women of Jonson's time had an almost unlimited variety of lace caps, many of which can be seen in the work of the Dutch painters. For the rest, her country look may be a matter of dull fabric and demure neckline, neither of which conceals the pronounced curves of the "soft and buxom widow."

The neighbors are a mixed lot, all ages and occupations (no children however), mostly prosperous bourgeois folk as might be expected in the Blackfriars which was one of the better neighborhoods of London. These will serve their function best if there are among them no very large areas of bright color. The scenes in which they appear are very busy and the focus of interest is difficult enough to maintain without having to compete with background supernumeraries.

The officers who come in response to the call of the townspeople would not be in uniform but they would need to be identified by some badge of office. Staves are useful for them in restraining and controlling the crowd. Some dun color will do nicely for these; we do not want to challenge the attention which should go to Lovewit and Jeremy-Face.

SETTING AND PROPERTIES

The requirements of the setting for this play are much simpler than those for *Volpone* and also simpler than those of most other plays of this period. The general visual character of the setting, whether the stage is an open one or framed by a proscenium, must be unmistakably rich. Whether this is achieved with expensive looking draperies, carving, or floor coverings, is immaterial. The important thing is to carry out the idea that the rogues' impostures are possible because they have Lovewit's fine house with which to impress their victims. I have seen this play produced on apron stages made to resemble an Elizabethan inn yard theatre, with wattle and daub walls and half-timbered upper storey, too crude by far. Lovewit's house impresses poor Drugger, convinces Dapper, and makes even the rich Sir Epicure Mammon feel right at home. Wattle and daub will not do this. Grinling Gibbon carvings might.

Of the physical requirements the most urgent is for at least four entrances: a front door, an entrance from the laboratory, one from the garden, and another which seems to come from upstairs. All these are necessary to keep apart the comings and goings of the various gulls. Having a newel post visible as part of a staircase will make it easier for Sir Epicure to seem to take Doll upstairs with obvious intentions.

The front door needs a peep-hole or window through which the inmates can look out and see other characters approaching. Some space for the approach, from vomitory or side entrances, should suggest the street outside. On their first entrance Mammon and Surly have over a hundred lines before they enter the house. A good deal of action in the fifth act takes place in the street as the neighbors and gulls converge on the house, Lovewit temporizes, and Face tries to quiet Subtle by whispering through the keyhole. There are several means by which this complicated action might be provided for. In an open theatre with an apron stage and vomitory entrances the characters supposedly coming along the street could come up from the vomitories. Action taking place in the "street" could be assigned to the ditch, the steps between ditch and apron, or even the outer edge of the apron. The door could be a skeleton frame slender enough not to obscure action or it even could be imaginary, like the door which Tyrone Guthrie contrived for *The Miser* in Minneapolis. That door consisted of a creaking sound borrowed from the conventional creaking door of Roman comedy and the actors' pantomimed actions of opening and closing, listening through the door held ajar, and so on. It was a very imaginative treatment of a difficult problem. One great virtue of it was that it never obstructed the sight line.

In a proscenium theatre a transparent curtain on a track is sometimes used to separate the forward part of the stage which serves as the street from the middle and upper parts suggesting the house interior. Other possibilities include the use of a stage divided horizontally, such as Mielziner designed for *The Death of a Salesman* and *The Glass Menagerie*, although this arrangement has the disadvantage of favoring one side of the audience with a better sight line.

Occasionally, in productions featuring an approximation of an Elizabethan stage, upper and lower levels have been used, with the outer rim of the main stage serving as the street and the upper level as part of the house interior. This is visually convincing but it has the disadvantage of putting the upstairs action so far from most of the spectators as to make the actors' task extremely difficult.

Ben Jonson's plays as a rule require few set props and those specified, such as Volpone's couch or Sir Politic Would-Be's tortoise shell, are easy to manage in scene changes. Beyond the specified props very little is needed either for atmosphere or set dressing. In *The Alchemist* the properties are almost all carried on and off by the performers. On stage a couple of benches that can be moved around are capable of fulfilling every requirement in the furniture department. I sometimes wonder, remembering Jonson's feud with the spectacle-obsessed

Inigo Jones, whether this feud might not have caused the poet to veer away from the marvels of stage machinery toward a style of production which, although complicated as to plot and filled with lively, almost frantic, stage business, depended less upon trick props and visual marvels than those of most other writers of his time.

This question is especially pertinent to our understanding of alchemy as practiced by Subtle. Like American auto mechanics, he does not encourage his customers to watch him working. Instead we are given an elaborate account of the process of transmutation and there is a good deal of discussion of the progress of the process by which Mammon's housewares are being turned into gold. But we see none of this, no furnace, no retorts, no glowing crucibles, only Subtle's flask of "good strong water" in the first scene, and the nearly endless procession of andirons, kettles, pots, warming pans, candlesticks, and so on which are carried across the stage, ostensibly to feed the process. I have seen several productions in which attempts were made to show something of the alchemy by means of some property man's juggernaut wheeled in to huff and puff, glow red, and finally explode, but none of these ever provided as good a scene as when the laboratory, with its final immolation, remained entirely off stage, with Mammon and Subtle on stage as the center of attention.

Those properties which are indispensable are all fairly simple. There is Doll's musical instrument, called a "sittern," for which a zither or mandolin will serve, both being among the easiest instruments to master. Kastril, Lovewit, and Captain Face carry weapons; if the play is costumed as of 1610 these would be rapier-and-dagger. Subtle has that flask with which he threatens Face, and later on he might be given an elaborate chart which he can unroll and display in order to illustrate for Mammon the process by means of which he turns base metals into gold. Dapper needs his "fly" in a bag suspended from a cord or chain around his neck, and later on, a blindfold and a gag of ginger bread. Drugger brings in a "paper of tobacco" and then a bolt of fine damask which comes unwound during the hurly-burly and engulfs the stage. Then there is the "third neighbor," apparently a locksmith, who helpfully brings his tools to open Lovewit's door. Finally there is the trunk that Subtle drags in, containing the loot, many items of which are described and displayed before Face takes the keys from Subtle and locks them up. Purses with coins in them are needed by Sir Epicure Mammon, Dapper, and Drugger. Sir Epicure's coins are mostly gold and silver; those of the others are all sizes and all metals.

NOTES ON STAGING

The Prologue is usually spoken by Lovewit, matching his speech to the audience at the end of the play, his manner in both instances being easy and informal.

(Act I–scene i): Here is one of the most difficult pieces of exposition one is likely ever to encounter. The intensity of the quarrel tends to hurry the actors and blur important points. The struggle in rehearsal is always to balance stage business with the necessity of putting the audience in possession of information they are going to need in order to understand the character and opening situation. The temptation to overbusiness should be resisted.

(Act II–scene iii): The pseudo Latin and Greek in Subtle's discourse looks like gibberish on the printed page but it is marvelously effective in performance. These lines should not be abridged until after they have been tested in rehearsal.

(Act IV–scene i): The joke of Mammon's wooing of Doll is better the more courtly his behavior. To make sure the audience gets the joke Doll sometimes offers visual asides to remind us that underneath her velvets she is still the common trull whom we met in the first scene.

(Act IV–scene iii): It is important that Surly's Spanish be spoken correctly. Some members of the audience are certain to understand the language.

(Act IV–scene v): The explosion off stage requires some ingenious sound effects: splintering timbers, breaking glass, falling metal, and plenty of smoke.

(Act V–scene v): The finale, with so many characters in action at one time, is, as usual, the most difficult scene to stage. As with the similar finale in *Volpone*, one might consider rehearsing it first until all are secure in order to gain the advantage of familiarity each time it comes up afterward during the rehearsal period.

CHAPTER 14

Molière's Art and Typical Problems in Staging his Plays

A really good performance of a Molière comedy is indescribably delightful. Nothing else is ever quite like it. Its characteristic quality is a kind of shimmering quicksilver brilliance that makes it seem always too brief and its high moments too fleeting to be fully grasped. The course of the action as it unrolls never stumbles or wanders, yet it is full of surprises. Characters are often marvelously transparent. All in all, there are few experiences in the theatre equal to the enjoyment of Molière at his best.

Theatre people who know this potential are irresistably drawn to Molière. Sooner or later everyone will attempt one or another of his comedies, and having achieved it will be led to essay another and still another, always hoping to improve on the lessons learned from the earlier effort. For there will always be, along with the gratification that comes from achievement, the feeling that it could have been better. The plays are so strongly put together that their performance seldom fails to engage the interest of the audience, seemingly no matter how they are done or by whom; they are seldom spoiled by ineptitude, and their success is not very chancy. But afterward one usually feels that one ought to have attained a greater finesse, and resolves to achieve it the next time.

CHARACTERISTICS OF MOLIÈRE'S COMEDY

The brilliance of Molière's comedy springs from a happy union of proved forms from classical comedy with the improvisational art of the Italian *commedia*. The opportunities it provides for molding the comic scene to the mood of a particular audience give to the whole work an air of spontaneity, while the firm substructure of classical character and plot makes sure that the effects will occur in the best possible sequence, will set off one another, and will also build to a satisfying conclusion.

In their original texts Molière's plays have no stage directions beyond "enter," and "exit," with no descriptions of person or place except those voiced in the lines. The stage business of such great passages as the table scene in *Tartuffe* or the sack scene in *Scapin* is barely hinted at in the play. One has to study the descriptions of performances, the reviews of the critics, and the memoirs of actors in order to find out what actions accompany the lines or amplify the big scenes. But since the text represents the work of the author himself and reveals his intent in regard to the whole, it is the text with which we have to begin. Later we can augment our understanding of the author's intent with a study of the various things that directors and actors have done to bring that text to life in performance.

Economy of Means

The first thing to note in Molière's comedies is the classical characteristic of composition which includes in the play nothing that can be dispensed with and omits nothing that is essential. Each play observes the so-called unities, occupying only that space of time actually required for the performance. From the opening scene to the finale the play proceeds without pause, imaginary time lapses, changes of scene, or flashback. The only intervals occur between acts when for a moment or two the stage is unoccupied, rather like the brief breathing space that separates the movements of a concerto; an aesthetic device that divides the whole into assimilable portions. No words are wasted telling us where we are, what time of day it is or whether the season is autumn or springtime. When it matters, the locale of the action becomes apparent from what the characters do. Weather and time of year, being irrelevant, are never mentioned.

Consistent with the economy of action is the fact that there are no extra characters. No deaf spinsters, drunken servants, or precocious youngsters are introduced to pass the time, provide a laugh or two, and then be forgotten. No friar comes on in the final scene to recapitulate the events which we have already witnessed. No chorus opens the play with an elaborate introduction, reappears briefly at the beginning of the second act and then disappears forever, leaving us wondering for the rest of the play when we will see him again.

At the same time nothing is missing that is needed to make the progression perfectly clear. What we have been led to expect never fails to happen and we see it before our eyes. No obligatory action is overlooked. Whatever is important is played out before our eyes, not hinted at, told by a messenger, or pantomimed without explanation. How different all this is from the practice of other playwrights! How often in the plays of others are we vaguely aware that something is missing. How often are we confronted by actions which we only partially comprehend. Not so with Molière. Whatever we need to know is made known to us; what we need to see is always shown; what we need to understand is always crystal clear. So consistent is Molière in making everything clear that we scarcely think of it as being art at all. It seems merely to be as it ought to be. Not until we compare his workmanship with that of others do we realize how much more skillful he is.

Plot Symmetry

One of the most striking characteristics of classical art is its fondness for symmetry: compositions consisting of similar halves balanced upon a central fulcrum. In Molière's work we see this kind of composition employed in two ways. In one way he balances characters against some central figure. Thus, in *Les Précieuses ridicules* he gives us two young ladies, their two suitors, and the two servants of the young men who, posing as dandies, impose upon the young women. Through most of the action the livelier of the imposters acts as the fulcrum of the action, motivating and dominating the behavior of the others until he is exposed and thrown out. In *Les Fourberies de Scapin* it is the clever servant who functions as the fulcrum between the opposing interests of a pair of young men and their miserly fathers.

The other kind of symmetry is temporal and comes into being as the play progresses, when one kind of scene is followed by another repeating the outlines of the first in somewhat the same way as a passage in music is repeated before the composition moves on to a new passage. For example, in *Scapin* a scene between one of the parents and Scapin is followed by a scene between Scapin and the other parent. A scene between one of the young men and Scapin is followed similarly by a scene with Scapin and the other young man, then by a scene with Scapin and both the young men. This kind of symmetry emerges gradually as the play unfolds. When we are reading the play it may strike us as an obvious formalizing device, so obvious that it seems artificial and often somewhat too patently contrived for our modern taste. In performance, however, it is far less obvious and it tends to seem logical and natural because it confers order upon the progression. This sense of order satisfies some need within us, in drama as in music. An orderly, sometimes even a predictable progression, seems to ring true aesthetically.

Accelerating Action

Molière's conscious artistry is nowhere more clearly revealed than in his mastery of the temporal progression. During performance of one of his plays we seldom have the feeling that a scene is dragging or that it is not going somewhere. All of his plays are constructed in such a way that the progression accelerates as it unrolls, with the longer and slower scenes near the beginning and the shorter and faster ones nearer the end. Interest is not allowed to diminish, for each new turn comes upon the heels of its predecessor a bit sooner than we expect it. The acceleration is not mechanically regular either for within the whole he alternates the longer more verbal scenes with the shorter more active ones.

Another factor in his management of the temporal character of the work comes in what musical-revue people call "spotting," the art of putting the right number in the best spot for it and for its effect on the whole. Producers of revues, for example, avoid putting their best numbers in the opening spot, preferring to have them later when the effect will be greater. If, during rehearsals, certain acts emerge as potential show-stoppers, they are shifted in the sequence until they reach the strongest position for their effect on the whole, usually by being placed closer to the finale. Molière does somewhat the same sort of thing. In farces like *Scapin* the funniest scenes are quite far along in the progression while the lesser ones are earlier. Upon studying the scene sequence one realizes that the principal reason for a scene being where it is lies in its effect, or rather the effect of its position, upon the sequence as a whole. Cause and effect relationships are relatively unimportant. A given scene could often have been positioned in any one of several places in the sequence without violating logic. But to put a hilarious scene like the sack scene in *Scapin* early in the play would be like having a winning touchdown in the first quarter of a football game instead of in the last two minutes. The final score might be the same but the game would be considerably less dramatic.

Molière articulates his scene sequences, not by the logic of cause and effect but by the simpler device of having one or more characters continue from one scene to another. One scene follows another quite naturally with the entrance of a new character or group of characters, one or more having remained on stage from the preceding scene. At the end of an act all characters exit, the stage is empty, there is a pause, then someone enters and the new act begins. Seldom do characters tell us why they exit, where they are going, or, when they enter, where they have come from or why they are coming here now. They simply appear when they are needed, very conveniently. For example, Scapin tells us of his plan to get even with Géronte and, as he finishes, he sees the old man approaching, just in time, as always. It seems natural enough because it is so *apt*. Its logic is aesthetic; it satisfies our craving for balance and is therefore acceptable and ultimately right.

Deus ex Machina *Endings*

Most of Molière's plays end rather abruptly with the introduction of some new character who supplies information that solves a dilemma or resolves a conflict. In *Scapin* the old nurse, Nerine, comes in looking for her master with news of his family. In *Tartuffe* the King's messenger, M. Exempt, accompanies Tartuffe, ostensibly to arrest Orgon for treason but actually to expose Tartuffe's impostures. This is the *deus ex machina* in it simplest and baldest form. It is not inevitable, necessary, or causally connected to previous action; it is simply a way of bringing the play to an end. Molière begins a play with a certain situation, rings all the changes he can, squeezes from it all the comic possibilities, and when he has wrung it dry he brings on his *deus ex machina* which he has kept waiting in the wings, to bring the play to a quick and complete end.

Classical Characterization

Molière's characters, whether old or young, never change, grow, reform, or see the error of their ways. All are firmly set in their ways. They never learn from their mistakes. Orgon at the end of *Tartuffe* is no wiser than he was at the beginning. He merely goes from the extreme of credulity to the extreme of scepticism. Like Orgon, Molière's characters are never neutral. He never creates any of those vague underdeveloped recessive characters that sometimes make other playwrights' work so difficult to bring to life. All of his characters are marvelously alive. Whether they are rogues, lovelorn youths, or miserly old men, all are intense in their desires, single-minded in their thinking, desperate in their actions, and furious at their frustrations. No one is ever seen in repose. No one ever gets tired or needs to relax. Hardly anyone ever even sits down except to jump up again.

As in the comedies of Plautus and Terence from whom he borrows so much, Molière's elderly people are cross, cowardly, greedy, and selfish. The older they are the more inflexible they are. Age never mellows; it only fixes more firmly whatever attitudes a character already possesses.

Nor is youth or young love romanticized. The young may be handsome, nice to look at, and pleasant to hear, especially when singing, but their infatuations are presented to us as obsessions, mild insanities intended to amuse us, but not by any means to be viewed sympathetically.

Young and old alike are portrayed as they are, not so much out of cynicism or because the author holds a jaundiced view of life but because a certain degree of detachment enables us to see the characters from an advantageous point of view which makes their behavior amusing to watch. Sympathy is foreign to Molière's comedy. Sympathy draws us closer to a character, causing us to feel as he feels, destroying the detachment which is indispensable if we are to appreciate his foibles to the fullest.

SOME TYPICAL PROBLEMS OF STAGING

The Tirade

One of the most difficult staging problems is the long and elaborate speech called in French the *tirade*. Plainly these are intended to amuse, but they seldom seem very amusing on the printed page. Rather, they seem rather to pose several difficult problems. How shall one vary and sustain passages of such ponderous length? One's first impulse is to contrive some ingenious stage business to accompany the tirade and take the audience's mind off its length, or else to vary it by heightening the responses of the listening characters. Such treatment seldom helps. Instead it seems only to distract the attention and diffuse the effect. I suspect that this is because the tirade is fundamentally verbal, with its comic effect in what is being said rather than the manner in which it is said.

For example, Béralde's lecture to Argan in *Le Malade imaginaire*, although it has the superficial sound of sense in English translation, is in actuality as ridiculous as the condition it seeks to remedy. I have seen productions in which this speech was punctuated with so much stage business that Béralde seemed to be the only sensible person in the play when he is in fact as peculiar as any.

The seasoned actor often finds that the tirades give him some of his best opportunities. The inexperienced actor, although he may enjoy having so many lines, often finds it difficult to hold his audience throughout. For the skillful actor the longer the speech the more effective it is likely to be. The difference between the two may be that the experienced actor is more likely to envisate the speech as a whole and use it to build, step-by-step, to a powerful climax; while the novice actor, taking the speech piece by piece, fragments it and is therefore unable to sustain interest, and then when he senses his grip on the audience slipping he tries even harder, and, as a result his delivery becomes labored, losing that quality of nimbleness which the comic tirade requires.

I hope no one, having read this, will ever make the mistake of abridging one of these tirades. They cannot be trimmed. There is nothing, not a phrase nor a repeated word, that can be cut out. Every word is part of the total effect and an integral part of the structure of the speech. Not one syllable is superfluous. Nothing can be deleted.

Repetition and Echo Phrasing

Another problem arises from Molière's frequent use of repetition and echo phrasing in his dialogue. He uses this device like a night-club comedian to make sure that the audience follows the drift of the joke while he is building it to its climax. The danger in this technique—with young actors—is that they might allow the repetition to become mechanical when in fact each element of the repetitive passage expresses some variant in the mental inflexibility of the character speaking. Since we in the audience grasp the point being made long before he does, his difficulty amuses us.

The Silent Central Character

Reading a play of Molière's one enjoys the lines and visualizes the speakers, but not until the characters take their places on the stage does one recognize the presence of one of the most powerful of dramatic devices, the silent character who is central to a crucial scene. This device, the "silent-center" scene, is common in the drama of antiquity, both tragedy and comedy, and Molière probably learned it from there, but it is rare in modern drama and for that reason easily overlooked or badly staged.

In the silent-center scene our attention is held by a central character who says nothing while those around him are revealing, intentionally or unintentionally, facts that will affect him. The important thing about this kind of scene is that the silent character is intended to be the center of interest while the other characters are subsidiary. Whatever they say or do, they are only the *agents* of the effect; their speeches and actions move the scene forward, we see them and hear them, but it is the silent-central character upon whom our attention is fixed because it is what *he* finally says or does that will cap the sequence. Circumstances are such that we know he is going to have to do *something* sooner or later. The longer he remains silent the funnier the scene becomes. There is one or more of these scenes in every play of Molière's. In *Tartuffe* there are three of them: one when Damis denounces Tartuffe to his father, one when M. Exempt denounces Tartuffe at the end of the play, and one when Orgon is hidden under the table while Tartuffe attempts to seduce his wife. In the last instance Orgon is often invisible, being completely concealed by the tablecloth, and this is always best for our eyes are fixed on it to catch some movement which will give us a hint as to how he is reacting. But the less we see and the less he does the better the scene always plays. I have witnessed productions of *Tartuffe* in which Orgon remained visible, mugging like mad or pretending nonchalant disbelief, but the scene was never as funny as when we were forced to imagine his responses because we could not see them.

Other silent-center scenes almost as good are those in *Le Malade imaginaire* and *Les Fourberies de Scapin*. In the former, Argan, in order to test the affection of his young wife, Béline, pretends to be dead. Instead of the grief he had expected from her however he hears her exult in her deliverance from the burden of a cranky, medicine-gulping tyrant. He then repeats the ruse with his daughter and is rewarded by discovering that her grief is genuine and her desolation sincere. In both scenes Argan himself, although motionless, is the center of interest as we wait to see how long he can continue his pretense.

Scapin has two good silent-center scenes. In one of them Zerbinette, who has just been told a funny story, finds it so hilarious that she cannot resist repeating it to the first person she meets, who is of course none other than old Géronte whose humiliation has been the subject of the story. While Zerbinette, laughing so hard she can barely get the words out, describes the event, Géronte, speechless with anger, is forced to listen. In this instance it is Géronte who is the center of interest. Zerbinette, being the agent, functions as a sort of "straight man," unwittingly fuelling his increasing fury.

The other scene in *Scapin* is more like the table scene in *Tartuffe* and the tortoise-shell scene in *Volpone* in that the central character is completely concealed. Scapin tells Géronte that some ruffians are after him and offers to hide him in a large laundry bag which he just "happens" to have with him. Géronte, terrified, slips quickly into the bag. Whereupon Scapin, pretending through changes of voice to be first one ruffian and then another, gives him a beating. The contortions of the sack, its changes of contour, its reactions to the blows, and its frantic efforts to crawl out of the way or to hide, becomes the center of interest while the actions and ventriloquism supplement it. The sack is such a strange looking thing, a huge worm one minute, a flat pancake the next, quaking in terror or freezing motionless in the hope of passing notice, that its possibilities are practically endless.

The Terminal Scene

In any play possessing a complicated plot the concluding scene is certain to present a difficult problem of staging. The problem is much more acute in Molière's plays as a rule because his final scenes are usually short, with a series of entrances building to the conclusion and attention focussed firmly on each new character in turn. The more characters there are on the stage the more difficult the problem becomes and it is especially taxing when, as in *Tartuffe*, the central character must be silent. Because the terminal scene is often technically the hardest scene in the play to stage some directors follow the practice here, as in Jonson's comedies, of beginning rehearsals with the final scene and working on it until the worst problems are smoothed out before going on to the easier scenes which form the rest of the play. Thereafter when, several weeks later, the scenes are rehearsed in sequence, the actors approach the final scene like colts coming into the home stretch and they sail down to the finish line in great style.

Problems of Setting

There is no reason why Molière's plays have to be performed in historically correct settings, nor is anything to be gained from attempting the kind of circumstantial production that occasionally proves so effective with Shakespeare's plays. In his own day, Molière put on his plays just about anywhere that the court entertainment of Louis XIV required, out-of-doors on the lawn or indoors on a platform in the banquet hall. In his own theatre he seems to have preferred some sort of formal setting with plenty of entrances and not much else. Very little furniture is required and not many hand properties.

Wherever his company performed it usually played among rather than in front of its audience, with spectators on three sides of the acting area. This situation allowed an easy rapport and made exaggeration unnecessary. The first necessity in the setting therefore is to make the actor's contact with his audience easy so that his anxieties and surprises can be readily shared. Beyond this the best setting physically is the one which provides for the greatest variety in action and groupings. For the farces moreover it is desirable to have solidly built set elements such as balustrades, doors, columns, and steps so that the action need not be restrained.

The symmetry of the plots seems at first glance to demand a comparable symmetry in the setting, but a set generally sustains interest longer when it goes counter to the form of the plot. A good rule of thumb for the designer is that when the plot is strongly symmetrical, as in *Scapin*, to make the set asymmetrical and irregular in order to avoid the curse of excessive formality. With an asymmetrical setting moreover the successive parallel scenes can be blocked in such a way as to emphasize the differences as well as the similarities. It is not necessary to point out the similarities because the playwright has already done this. It is far more artful to enliven the comparisons with a wealth of subtle contrasts.

When it comes to deciding the visual style of the setting, lightness is what counts above everything else: lightness of coloring, of architecture, of decoration, of illumination. The actual architecture of seventeenth-century France is characterized by weight, elaboration, and formal balance, all qualities inappropriate to comedy. It is necessary, therefore, to simplify and lighten the setting when elements of it have to be drawn from Molière's own time. When the action takes place indoors, as in *Le Bourgeois gentilhomme*, the interior needs to be lighter than that of the period in which the play was composed. The heavy fabrics, dark woodwork, and massive carved furniture must be lightened or avoided altogether. Sometimes an acceptable style can be achieved by adopting the features of interiors about a century later when delicate lines and lighter colors had become fashionable.

The lighting must take into account two needs: the need of the audience to see the actors' facial expression without effort and the need of the actor to see the facial expressions of his auditors. Molière wrote for a situation in which his players could see all the members of the audience as easily as the audience could see them. When performance was indoors the auditorium was lighted as brightly as the stage. It is worth while to consider performing his plays with the house lights on; it certainly makes the actors' task infinitely easier. It is hard to do Molière when the spectators are too dark to be seen.

Problems of Costuming

The costumes of seventeenth-century France are difficult to act in, even for the most accomplished of English-speaking performers. Probably only the *sociétaires* of the *Comédie-Française* are ever really at home in the dress of this period. Sometimes it seems to me that if the devil himself had set out to devise a mode of dress specifically aimed at making life miserable for the actor, he could scarcely have hit upon anything surer than the costumes of Molière's own day, with their profile-hiding wigs, hand-obscuring lace, and fussy ribbons. It is natural therefore to wonder whether all of Molière's plays have to be performed in the dress of his day. Once the question is asked, we see that only a few of the plays belong inseparably to their own time. Certain ones, which satirize follies peculiar to the era, such as *Les Précieuses ridicules* and *Le Bourgeois gentilhomme,* lose something when presented in the dress of any period in which society is not highly stratified. But most of the rest of the canon make fun of absurdities that are to be found in every age. Many of the plays therefore can be costumed in any period within two hundred years of Molière in either direction. However, contemporary modern dress may not be used successfully. There is an elegance about Molière which the more informal styles of our time cannot support. His works lend themselves poorly to modern-dress treatment, and when such treatment has been given them the plays have invariably fallen short of expectations.

Practical requirements of the action make the costumes complicated regardless of the period in which they are to be done. Pockets are many, and there are numerous accessories such as swords, purses, papers, cloaks, and walking sticks. Many of the garments have to be carefully designed to withstand vigorous activity and to accommodate lightning changes or superimposed disguises.

Special Problems Confronting the Actor

Actors of different cultures and training systems succeed to markedly different degrees in externalizing Molière's characters to the extent demanded by his very explicit texts. The French, as one might expect, succeed superlatively well. The Japanese, influenced perhaps by the elegant acting style of their own classical drama, are almost as good. The American, however, often experiences a great deal of difficulty. Insufficiently externalized, his presentation of a Molière character often seems fuzzy and imprecise. Or else, having acquired a knack for performing this kind of material, he gives us something so broad and so "busy" that the result lacks finesse. Basically, one problem of playing Molière, at least for Americans, is not only to externalize sufficiently but to externalize with the right degree of control.

But the right degree for one actor may not be right for another; it depends on appearance, physique, diction, manner of movement, and the force of his personality. Also, Molière's characters are not drawn with a uniformly bold hand. Tartuffe, for example, is infinitely more subtle than Sganarelle in *Le Medecin malgre lui*, so some of the actor's art lies in achieving the degree of externalization appropriate to the individual character.

Certain kinds of scenes require more externalization than others. Those scenes predominently of physical activity such as the sack scene, or Silvestre's impersonation of the ruffian, in *Scapin*, Argan's mock deaths in *Le Malade imaginaire*, the table scene in *Tartuffe*, and the fencing and dancing lessons in *Le Bourgeois gentilhomme*, appear to have been intended as opportunities for mimetic improvisation.

Then there are the scenes of another kind, verbal rather than physical, whose true wit emerges only through the most meticulous craftsmanship in phrasing, pointing, and building to perfectly proportioned subordinate and ultimate climaxes. The "galley" scene in *Scapin* is one of these, as is the scene in which Scapin describes to Argante all the hazards of recourse to legal action. The prelude to the table scene, in which Tartuffe rationalizes his courtship of Elmire, is certainly another. And in *Le Malade imaginaire* we have two beauties, one in Doctor Diafoirus' description of the education of his son, the other in M. Purgon's towering malediction. All of these and many others like them are scenes in which delivery is paramount and which are easily diffused and deprived of impact by too much stage business.

CHAPTER 15

Les Fourberies de Scapin: Problems of Sequential Progression

Here is certainly one of the cleverest farces ever composed, although at first reading one might not be inclined to think so. The title is hard to translate into English. It has been known variously as *The Trickery of Scapin*, *The Cheats of Scapin*, *The Mischief-Maker*, *Scapino*, and just plain *Scapin*. Many brilliant and memorable productions have been given this work (and also, alas, a few rather dull ones). It has been brilliant when imaginative directors and versatile actors have done it and dull when produced too broadly with lumpish horse-play. There are some who believe that farce consists entirely of continuous supercharged bustle and ingenious stage business; these people miss the fact that the sequence demands above all great variety in tone and tempo; thus they ruin the scenes of wit with over-activity.

As always, it is difficult to say what makes a play good when it is at its best. One thing, certainly, is that it contains several of the funniest scenes ever witnessed on any stage. None is entirely original and each had probably been done many times in earlier plays and in the *Commedia dell' Arte*. But Molière's versions are far the best, the result of years of refinement and gradual perfection, until each stands as the pinnacle of its particular kind. No one since has been able to improve any of them and even today if a performer skips a line, or introduces an uncalled-for pause or irrelevant business the loss is noticeable.

As is often the case with Molière, the prize scenes are very different from one and another as to the way in which laughter is provoked. One is built on a sight gag of the broadest physical buffoonery. Another, a diatribe on the courts, lawyers, and legal system, is mainly satirical. Another describes the agony of a penny-pinching miser trapped in a dilemma that is certain to cost him a good deal of money no matter what he decides. Of the other scenes, which may or may not be hilarious depending on the skill of the actors, one involves the spectacle of a dull-witted fellow who, upon being disguised as a bravado, becomes so carried away with his role that he puts the lives of his friends in jeopardy. Another, which requires an actress with a hearty and infectious laugh, consists of the reactions of a vain man upon being forced to listen to a mocking description of his humiliation from one who has just heard about it but does not know who he is.

These scenes are tied together with a plot which introduces and identifies the principals, moves briskly from one scene to another still funnier until the best of the comic possibilities have been exhausted, then brings it all around to a quick surprise conclusion.

CHARACTERS AND CASTING

As we often find in classical comedy, the principal characters are neatly paired: two young men, two young girls whom the men adore, two miserly fathers, and two servants. The only unmatched characters are the old woman who acts as *deus ex machina* and a servant who functions as messenger when someone is needed to come running in with startling news. The two families involved are thus perfectly symmetrical, each having one parent, one servant, one young man, and one (long-lost) daughter.

With this small number of characters there is little danger of confusing one with another, but there is the question as to whether the paired characters should be differentiated or made to resemble one another.

The Lovers

For the sake of variety it is probably best not to deal similarly with all pairs. With the young people it is certainly best if both the young men can be tall and handsome and the girls equally graceful and pretty. Side by side the girls should not in any way put each other at a disadvantage. It is common in such cases to make one a luscious blonde and the other a luscious brunette. Red hair should be avoided as it tends to be more interesting on stage than either light or dark hair. The same applies to the young men. If the blonde-brunette contrast is used for them it might be possible to have it as a family trait, so that the girl who turns out to be the daughter of Argante, for example, might have the same hair color as her brother, Octave.

The Servants

With the servants, Scapin and Silvestre, as with the parents, Argante and Géronte, the more strikingly they are differentiated the more amusing they usually are. The text makes it clear that Scapin is intended to be smarter than anyone else in the play, while his friend Silvestre combines extraordinary stupidity with an imaginative and extremely suggestible nature. This makes Silvestre the natural instrument by means of which Scapin carries out his stratagems. I started to say "perfect instrument" but Silvestre's enthusiasum almost wrecks the proceedings. In any case, the greater the contrast between them the funnier they are. Contrasting appearance enhances the effect. If Scapin is short, a tall actor should be cast as Silvestre. If Scapin is played as something of a dandy, vain of his appearance as of his wit, Silvestre might be naive and uncouth in appearance.

The role of Nerine is functional; mainly that of bringing the news that makes possible the conclusion of the play, but there is no reason why she should not be played as an eccentric. Different actresses have done different things to individualize her, from giving her a funny walk to making her preposterously nearsighted. But she must not be played as so old or infirm as to arouse sympathy. Nor can she be played with a stutter, an accent, or any other peculiarity of speech since this would interfere with the exposition which is her main reason for being.

The Old Men

The old men, Argante and Géronte, are not sharply differentiated in the text, but their parts always go better when there are strong contrasts in their appearance and behavior. They are alike in their miserliness and in their determination to have their own way with their sons. Both are cowardly. But superficially at least Argante appears to be more logical minded and Géronte more emotional. If Géronte also appears to have more concern for dignity and the way he stands in the eyes of others, this will heighten his part in both the laughing and sack scenes.

Supers and Walk-ons

In addition to Scapin, Silvestre, and Carle, there must be at least two other servants to carry on Scapin at the end when all the principals are already on stage. Once these have been cast many other uses will be found for them in the course of rehearsals, especially if they are good dancers who can add a balletic flourish to their various duties.

SETTING: POSSIBILITIES

This play needs about five different entrances to accommodate the many actions in which characters meet by chance or exit hurriedly to avoid being seen by someone else. A house with a door is useful for Zerbinette's entrance in the laughing scene. Sometimes this turns out to be a two-shutter Dutch door because of the comic possibilities of a door in two halves. Some arches, porches, or columns will help to make the many overhearings and chases more interesting. I have seen the setting equipped in various productions with quite a wide variety of hazards for Géronte in the sack scene. One production had a fountain into which he tumbled while trying to grope his way out of the reach of his tormentor. Another had an ornmental balustrade with a conventional loop for him to get stuck in. The most useful element of the setting, aside from the numerous entrances, is an apron projecting well out into the audience in order to make the asides and soliloquies easier as well as heightening by proximity the effect of the several beatings. A few steps, not too steep, in an irregular arrangement, will provide the comedians with opportunities to develop during rehearsals.

As this is a rather informal sort of play, the setting should not be symmetrical nor provided with any very rigid architectural elements. Sometimes it is detailed as a town square, or as a waterfront esplanade with alleys and houses on either side and ships in the background. Such extensive detailing is not at all necessary, however, for the comedy plays just as well on a bare platform without localization. But whatever is provided should also be provided with some means of changing its appearance in order to forestall the visual tedium which is the frequent curse of the one-set production, especially the one-set comedy.

As to color and lighting, about all that is required is that the tone of the set provide a comfortable background against which the faces can always be be seen without effort and which will also set off the costumes to advantage. As for the lighting, its principal function is to make sure that the spectators can see the slightest change of facial expression at all times and of every character.

COSTUMES AND PROPERTIES

The dress of Molière's time is not required in this play and would in any case probably be more of a hindrance than a help to the actors. The comedy has been done quite successfully in *Commedia* costumes, with the girls in eighteenth-century Watteau-style gowns and the young men in the very becoming knee breeches and skirted coats of the same period. The young men should of course be very handsomely done up and the girls should be neat and trim in gauzy stuffs of pink, pale yellow, or peach (never in blue or gray, for these hues tend to make young women look older; for the same reason powdered wigs should be avoided on both sexes). Scapin has often been costumed in a Harlequin-like outfit. Silvestre has often been dressed to resemble the character called Zanni, and for his swashbuckling act he has often assumed the guise of the Capitano. The costumes of both old men have often been rendered as versions of the familiar Pantalone.

Pockets are needed in the costumes of both old men, both young men, and Scapin, in order to accommodate the required purses and papers. The old men often carry walking sticks and these are useful for all sorts of stage business. The young men carry swords—the slender lightweight court swords of the eighteenth century are best—with which they threaten Scapin and possibly quarrel with one another. No furniture of any kind is needed, but there might be a bench or shelf somewhere for Silvestre and Carle to sit on during those scenes when they have to be present but are not involved in the action.

Silvestre, when disguised as the ruffian, needs a large hat, a false mustache, a gigantic saber or scimiter, and a voluminous cloak. Sometimes the hat has a floppy brim which keeps falling down in front of his eyes. The cloak is often as big as a tent and keeps tripping him as he tries to strut, falling down over his sword hand, muffling his more extravagant gestures, and catching on the point of his weapon.

The sack into which Scapin puts Géronte needs to be big enough so that the old man can step easily into it and also get out of it quickly at the end of the scene. I have seen productions in which Géronte went into the sack with his hat on and his walking stick in his hand——and in one case even an umbrella— and came out after all the tumbling and beating without being disheveled. This was the result of extraordinary skill on the part of the costumer who built a costume so sturdy that it fell right back into place in spite of the violence of the action. The sack must be made of some porous loose-woven fabric so that the actor will not suffocate while inside it. It should also be made light enough so that Scapin can fold it and carry it unobtrusively until the time comes to use it. It needs to be bright—white, yellow, or pink—so as to be easily seen at all times in spite of its many changes in shape and location. Whether to have a draw string closure depends on the actor who has to work inside, but it is easy to make the sack with provision for draw string and add it later if rehearsals justify.

For the scene in which Scapin tries to frighten Argante out of going to court, some directors have introduced papers or a scroll for him to use in illustrating his points. I have seen this scroll stretched out to fifteen or twenty feet to be used for ingenious stage business, Argante having to put on glasses to read it, and so on. Others have had the servants bring in enormous law books, one after another, blow the dust off them, and in one production a mouse ran out.

It has become almost traditional for the purse that Géronte extracts so painfully from his breast pocket to be made of red velvet in the shape of a heart. During his charge to Scapin he inadvertently puts the purse back into his pocket so that when Scapin reminds him that he has not been paid the whole painful process has to be repeated.

In some productions both Scapin and Silvestre, like their *Commedia* counterparts, carry slap-sticks in their belts. These can be used for the beatings they receive from their masters and also for the beating Scapin gives to Géronte in the sack scene. The slap-stick is a wonderful prop for this kind of comedy. It looks dangerous but it does not hurt and it makes a terrific clatter so that the cringing and wincing of the victim is amply motivated. In addition to being useful for the sack scene the slap-stick can be used instead of a sword in the scene where Léandre beats Scapin. During the course of rehearsals other places will be found where the slap-sticks can be used effectively.

NOTES ON STAGING

(Scene i): This scene with its curious "reverse dialogue" is quite different from most opening scenes and difficult to make natural. A great many devices have been tried, such as having the dull Silvestre take so long in trying to get the lines out that Octave repeatedly takes the words out of his mouth, or by having him keep looking around for help until it arrives in the form of Scapin.

(Scene ii): Octave's lengthy narrative provides him with an excellent opportunity to impersonate all the people and emotions as he describes them.

(Scene x): Carried away by his own brilliance, Scapin turns into the various court functionaries one by one as he describes them to Argante: the stern judge, the cunning lawyer, the crabby clerk, the bluff bailiff, and so on—quite a gallery of characters.

(Scene xi): The frightening ruffian so recklessly flourishing that glittering sword is of course none other than Silvestre, so in love with his role that he nearly kills both his master and friend before Scapin reminds him who he is. Whereupon, completely deflated, he shambles out in an ignominious exit, tripping over his cape, bumping into the scenery, or falling off the stage into the bass drum.

(Scene xii): The famous "galley scene." The more deliberately Scapin manipulates the old man the funnier the scene becomes. The focus of attention is mainly on Géronte and his suffering. Scapin is only the agent in this scene; Géronte is the object of our attention.

(Scene xv): The "sack scene." Two comic devices make this one of the best farce scenes of all time. One is Scapin's impersonation of the successive ruffians supposedly seeking Géronte. The other is the visual effect of the sack with the old man inside trying to escape the blows of the unseen assailant. The "discovery" at the end of the scene is quite difficult as to timing. In general, the slower it is played and the longer before Scapin realizes that Géronte is on to his trickery the better it usually goes.

(Scene xvi): The "laughing scene." Once Zerbinette has achieved an acceptable laugh the main comic effect comes from focussing attention on Géronte throughout.

(Scene xx): The scene is best when Scapin really looks and acts as if he were mortally wounded. His babbling recitation of his impostures needs to be very carefully pointed if Géronte's embarassment is to be fully motivated.

The play sometimes ends with music and dance, pairing off the young couples, the parents, and the servants, leaving Scapin as soloist and to take the final bow.

CHAPTER 16

Tartuffe: A Problem of Clarity

The study of *Tartuffe*, whether as an exercise in criticism or a preliminary to production, always raises more questions than it answers. Upon first reading, and sometimes upon first seeing also, the play is deceptively simple. The head of a family plans to marry his daughter to a recent acquaintance whose piety has made a profound impression on him. The pleas of family fail to dissuade him. Not until he is forced to witness the friend's attempt to seduce his wife does he realize that he has been imposed on. But by then it is too late, for he has entrusted to the imposter all his possessions. He is saved from destitution only by the timely intervention of a wise and all-seeing monarch.

The comic quality of the play springs first from the father's obsession, from the manner in which he dotes on his saintly friend, disregarding the warnings of his relatives and the desires of his daughter, and, later, from the train of unpleasant surprises which follows the discovery that he has been duped. One of the greatest comic scenes in all drama occurs when the wife in her attempt to unmask the imposter hides her husband under a table while she encourages the advances of his friend. Basically this scene is farcical, but as Molière manages it, it combines farce, satire, suspense, and surprise, providing an unlimited range of possibilities for interpretation and staging. Throughout the play from beginning to end there are many amusing or outright comical touches that reveal the hand of a master and the viewpoint of one acutely aware of the absurdities of human behavior.

The other quality of the play, one which intrigues the critic, the actor, and everyone else who comes to know the work intimately, is not comical but psychological, for the comic action that Molière has given us is only the visible tip of the iceberg, protruding a surface beneath which lies an infinity of motives, morals, emotions, and reasons for the action which we see. The behavior of the father is so preposterous that we feel the actor must show us reasons for it, for we feel that what is puzzling in life ought to be explained to us by the artist who represents it on the stage. The ability to do this is what makes him an artist and earns our respect for him.

HYPOCRISY: THE DOUBLE MIRROR

Tartuffe himself is endlessly fascinating because although we know him to be a hypocrite we seem never to be sure whether we are seeing one of his various masks or looking at the man behind them. Thus the role of Tartuffe provides splendid opportunities for an actor. It is, furthermore, one of those creations whose dominent traits can be made to conform to the nature and style of every actor who essays the role. No matter who plays it or how, the character always rings true. This is doubly interesting when we recall that he is presented to us as a master of falsification. Tartuffe has become one, therefore, of the best comic acting parts of all time, esteemed equally with Falstaff, Volpone, and Sir Giles Overreach; it has attracted one after another of the greatest actors of each generation.

The play as we have it now represents Molière's second attempt to dramatize the subject. From what has come down to us through the accounts of contemporaries and the author's own preface to the present text, the original appears to have been a shorter work consisting of three acts instead of five. Molière is believed to have expanded the action and added acts one and two plus the *deus ex machina* ending. Knowing of the Jesuits' objection to the first version and its suppression as a result of their influence, one may guess that the earlier work made more of Tartuffe's religiosity; that his hypocrisy may have been somewhat less a reflection of Orgon's attitudes and more a matter of employing the formalities of religion to mask his lust and greed. Molière in his preface insists that it is Tartuffe's hypocrisy and not his religiosity which is central. It seems likely therefore that Molière made the play acceptable by reducing the emphasis on religion as the base for Tartuffe's hypocrisy and ended by adding the flattering representation of the all-powerful monarch who sees through all pretense and intervenes to punish the imposter.

At first glance it looks as if the direction of the rewriting was toward making Tartuffe's hypocrisy more obvious but this is improbable. The reworking of a complex piece generally tends toward the refining rather than the simplification of the work. Both playwright and actor are inclined to broaden and strengthen the motivation in order to give greater dimension and subtlety to a character, not less.

But if this is the case, how are we to manage those scenes which are plainly farcical, such as the famous table scene? Are the farcical elements to be played down and the satirical ones played up? Apparently so. But the manner and degree must be determined by the personality and skill of the actor who plays the part.

It has often been pointed out that Orgon, and not Tartuffe, is the central character. But this is not the way it appears to the audience in the theatre. Tartuffe is such a vivid character that he holds attention in every scene in which he appears. Orgon, no matter how skillful the actor who plays him, seems more an accessory to the action than the center of it. After a performance it is often difficult to recall exactly what Orgon did at certain critical points or how he reacted to each of the successive reversals, but it is easy to remember everything that Tartuffe did: how he looked, and how he spoke his lines in every crisis. In fact, it is difficult to forget Tartuffe's behavior and when one has seen a dozen Tartuffes one can still remember distinctly each one for years afterward. With Orgon it is the other way around; with the passage of time it becomes increasingly difficult to differentiate one Orgon from the others and after a while they all begin to look and sound alike.

Anyone trying to rationalize the plot is certain to be confused. The play is not constructed as a progression of events related by cause and effect. There are many memorable scenes which could be cut without having any effect on the outcome. The quarrel between Marianne and Valère contributes nothing to the progression although it does provide a delightful interlude. The cheerful intrusion of M. Loyal affects neither the course of action nor the attitudes of the family but it does give us an amusing glimpse of the bureacracy in motion. Madame Pernelle's refusal to believe Orgon's discovery of Tartuffe's imposture is not in any way essential to the denouement but it adds a clever grace note.

All in all, the structure of the play is probably best understood if we view it as a series of scenes related to Tartuffe's presence in the house of Orgon, exemplifying various absurdities of human behavior. Richard Wilbur, whose translation of the play is generally regarded as the best since the eighteenth century, calls it "a comic study of the misuse of the highest values—religion, the natural bonds of family life, patriotism—for self-serving motives," and we might well think of it as such rather than as a conventionally plotted comedy.

Of all premodern dramas *Tartuffe* is the least typical. It contains no music or dance and no opportunities for their interpolation. As far as we know it was never intended for outdoor performance. Three of the four female parts were written to be played by women. The language is poetic only in the sense that it is composed according to the classical principles of form, not in the sense of being imaginatively colored. And although Molière in his preface to the play is explicit as to his intentions, the play itself encourages an unusually wide range of interpretations at the same time allowing for nuances of a kind not seen in most early dramas.

Yet *Tartuffe* is in no sense modern, nor has it ever been viewed as a forerunner of anything modern. For while its problems may not be typical of those of premodern drama its form and point of view are quite typical of its own time, a time when art owed much to antiquity. *Tartuffe* is typically neoclassical: in its economy of form and its observance of the unities, in its representation of human foibles, in its attitude toward the young lovers, and in its assumption of a society harmonious and stable under the rule of a benign and all-seeing monarch. The principal problem then in producing *Tartuffe* today is the problem of bringing to life a neoclassical satirical comedy on a modern stage for an English-speaking audience without falsifying its viewpoint or lessening its sophistication.

Productions of this play by American companies tend to overplay the farce and overbusiness everything else, as if there were no comedy without an abundance of bustle. Productions by French companies are generally more subtle and less busy. Their total effect is that of a tighter, neater, and smoother progression and one which grips the attention more continually. English-speaking companies tend to play the table scene as farce; the same scene by a French company comes across more like high comedy.

From this I think we can see the direction which the production ought to take. The problem is a difficult one and its solution demands an extraordinary degree of artistry. The result moreover is going to have to stand comparison with some of the best work of the greatest theatre talent of ten generations. But when has this ever prevented anyone from undertaking the production of a really great play?

CHARACTERIZATION AND ACTING

The worst problem in *Tartuffe* is that the vivid characters like Dorine, M. Loyal, and Tartuffe himself tend to overshadow the others and make them seem two-dimensional. The result is that it becomes extremely difficult to make the recessive characters lifelike enough for the satire to bite. One cannot satirize cardboard characters. For satiric comedy to take hold the people in it must in every instance be acceptably human. They may be recognizable as types but they must still be believable as people.

This problem is especially acute in the relationship between Orgon and Tartuffe. In regard to the plot Orgon's character is central. His taking Tartuffe into his home precipitates the conflict, his decision to marry his daughter to him sets off the rebellion of daughter, son, and wife, and his gift of his property and secret papers nearly ruins them all. Orgon dominates every scene in which he appears when Tartuffe is elsewhere, yet he becomes a secondary character the minute Tartuffe enters the scene and he does not regain his dominence until Tartuffe is finally silenced by the King's officer.

With Dorine the problem is slightly different. Early in the play she emerges as the liveliest and most perceptive character. Because of this she tends to monopolize the interest of the audience and make the characters with whom she appears, such as Mariane, seem less vigorous. After Tartuffe makes his appearance the importance of her part diminishes. The problem here is to manage things so that the audience does not continue to expect her to participate prominently in every scene in which she appears. Unless this is done a feeling of disappointment develops when in later scenes she is not as amusing as before.

The vigor with which Tartuffe and Dorine have been endowed by the playwright and the ease with which they dominate the scenes in which they appear has had the unfortunate effect of encouraging performers to overact these parts, spelling out for us many points which we can easily see for ourselves.

Tartuffe

One of the things that makes Tartuffe fascinating as a character is that he has in performance much more substance and subtlety than one could imagine from reading the play. Another thing is that he takes on the nature and style of each actor who undertakes the part, so that no matter how many Tartuffes you see you will never see two alike. The Tartuffe of John Wood is an entirely different character from that of William Hutt and neither of them bears any resemblance to the famous Tartuffe created by Louis Jouvet.

Jouvet attempted to create a more real Tartuffe by presenting him as a genuinely devout man betrayed into his attempt upon Elmire by the irresponsible urging of his all-too-human flesh and sincerely repentant when he realized what he had done. His behavior following the confrontation with Orgon was played as if he believed he was really doing Orgon a favor by removing from his control those worldly possessions which stood between him and eternal salvation. Audiences were startled by the lifelikeness of Jouvet's Tartuffe at the same time that they were horrified and repelled by it.

Great as was Jouvet's creation, it could have been accomplished only by ignoring Molière's description of Tartuffe as a hypocrite. Hypocrisy is pretense, the assumption of a mask of sincerity for the promotion of some ulterior purpose. There is no such thing as sincere hypocrisy, inadvertent hypocrisy, or unconscious hypocrisy, since it is the deliberateness of the pretense which makes it hypocritical. "Sincere hypocrisy" is a contradiction in terms. A sincere man whose public behavior is at odds with his private beliefs can only be called inconsistent if he is unaware of the descrepancy. In order to be a hypocrite he must be aware of the descrepancy.

The art in playing Tartuffe is to show unequivocally the contrast between the real person and the various masks he assumes without making the difference too obvious. The spectator must believe that it is himself who is seeing through the sham and not that it is being shown to him by the art of the actor. The more subtly the actor is able to slip from one to the other, from the apparent to the real Tartuffe while keeping each distinct and clear, the greater is his achievement.

Which aspect of the Tartuffe we see can be counted as real? Certainly his lust for Elmire is real, and his greed is real, judging from the alacrity with which he accepts the deed to Orgon's property. His capacity for treachery is shown to be real when he betrays his patron to the authorities. The speed with which he moves to profit from the advantage he has gained seems also to reveal a genuine (and somewhat pathetic) longing for rank and social position. Yet, in spite of his lowly origins he seems to lack nothing in self-assurance or confidence in his ability to manipulate events to his own advantage. But above all these is one even greater reality: his opportunism. Every turn of events he manages to shape to his own advantage; every action of Orgon's except one he adapts to his own ends. There seems to be no evidence that he plans ahead or attempts to anticipate the course of events; he merely takes events as they come, seeing the possibilities before others do and making the most of the opportunities which open up for him. Tartuffe's is a hand-to-mouth existence such as a gambler, beggar, or mountebank might have. He lives wholly in the present and takes whatever comes his way. He meets the needs of the moment by assuming whatever guise will best serve the occasion. If piety is in favor he can kneel and pray with the best of them. If humble subservience to the wishes of his patron will pay off he can be the humblest person alive. If aggressive and elegantly phrased courtship will win the heart of his mistress he can be the most articulate lover imaginable. If conspicuous loyalty to his sovereign will help to confirm him in his newly acquired social station his loyalty will outshine others.

The real Tartuffe then is unscrupulous, treacherous, lecherous, and greedy. His hypocrisy lies in the extraordinary facility with which he dons the mask which will yield the most immediate gain at any given moment.

Some actors have presented Tartuffe as a wily schemer but this interpretation is not borne out by the text. Besides, it is much more interesting to watch the activity of a deft opportunist than that of a schemer.

Orgon

What of Orgon? What is it about him that makes him such an easy mark for Tartuffe? He gives no sign of being a particularly religious man, so why is he so deeply impressed by Tartuffe's piety? Richard Wilbur sees him as a *pater familias* whose problems in controlling his family have led him to use religiosity as a weapon and Tartuffe as his agent and supporter. Organ may not be religious at heart but he is obsessed with religion because it serves his purpose. Wilbur believes, with some insight, that if Orgon had been obsessed with politics Tartuffe would have been an idealogue, and if he had been obsessed with erudition Tartuffe would have posed as a scholar. Orgon has become a tyrant because only through tyranny can he continue to rule his small domain; Tartuffe is for the moment the instrument of his tyranny.

Interesting as this analysis is, it does not give the actor the kind of material he needs to make Orgon believably human. If he represents Orgon merely as an irascible tyrant of fixed purpose, deaf to the needs of his family, we have only a *commedia* parent no different from that of the crudest Italianate farce. If Orgon is to come anywhere near to holding his own against the fascination that Tartuffe has for the spectators he will have to be more than a mere tyrant.

When a character as written seems two-dimensional the most profitable course is often to turn the character around and look for his other, complementary, side. What is the complementary side of the tyrannical parent? Usually the belief that he knows better than son, daughter, or wife what is best for them all; in other words, misconceived concern for their welfare. He thinks of himself as a man of experience and principle acting out of conviction in the best interests of those whom he loves. In the case of Orgon this means marrying his daughter to Tartuffe because he really believes that in the long run she will be happier thus. In his insistence upon this he need not always be dictatorial. He can be loving and gentle because he knows that what he is doing is best for her and that if she fails to show enthusiasum it is only because she is too young to see the future as clearly as he does. Such an approach would give us a different and more human Orgon than we usually see and one which could be made readily acceptable.

It would be difficult for Orgon to adopt the same attitude toward Damis' denunciation of Tartuffe, but a hint of fatherly concern for a son whose eyes and ears have misled him would give a better tone to the scene than to have him explode in anger against his son immediately upon hearing Tartuffe's penitential confession.

It is interesting to note that the thought never seems to cross Orgon's mind that Elmire could be unfaithful to him, with Tartuffe or anyone else. This is to his credit for it shows a commendable confidence in his own appeal for her. He offers no objection when she makes him get under the table, and none when she explains how she intends to go about rekindling Tartuffe's passion for her. Orgon's behavior is quite different from what we have been accustomed to expect from husbands in such situations, so jealousy is obviously not one of his faults as a husband. Some actors play Orgon as if he were indifferent to Elmire, as if he did not care whether she was unfaithful or not, but such an interpretation does not yield a very interesting character.

Some critics, seeing Orgon as a curmudgeon, wonder why Elmire would ever have married him and remain faithful. Others wonder how such a woodenheaded person could have accumulated or held on to the substantial fortune which seems to be his. Strictly speaking, such questions are not part of the play. Orgon's wealth and the relationship between him and Elmire are simply part of the *donnée* or given situation with which the play begins. It is useful for the actor however to search for some means of filling out these aspects of Orgon's existence. An interpretation that indicates any kind of rapport or feeling of tenderness between Orgon and Elmire will greatly strengthen the production.

At the end of the play we are given nothing to suggest that Orgon's experience with Tartuffe has mellowed his nature or changed his outlook in any significant way. At the end he is just as much an extremist as ever and just as quick to anger or irrational action as he ever was. But it is gratifying to discover that his piety has not been a fleeting obsession when he invites his family to kneel in prayer of thanksgiving for their deliverance. And his reaffirmation of the marriage contract between Mariane and Valére at least puts to rights the worst wrong that he perpetrated when he tried to separate them.

Elmire

The character of Elmire is fairly straightforward. Her principal concern is for the happiness of her step-children, especially Mariane. Next to that is her concern for Orgon and her determination to find some means for protecting him from exploitation by Tartuffe. I think we may discount Madame Pernelle's criticism—that Elmire is vain, overdressed, and careless with money—for nothing we see in the course of the play bears this out. Most likely this is merely the way Elmire seems to the older woman. On both occasions when Tartuffe makes advances to her she expresses feelings of guilt for having encouraged him. On the second occasion in particular when she has coyly led him to reveal himself to Orgon she seems to feel that there was something shameful in her deception for which she must apologize. This is not the action of a true coquette.

The lines of the play make it clear that Elmire is Orgon's second wife and suggest that she is somewhat younger than he. Her youthfulness in relation to him is dictated by the nature of the plot: the younger, prettier, and seemingly unappreciated she is the more plausible Tartuffe's attempt becomes.

In casting this role it is important that Elmire be played by an actress of exceptional beauty and charm. A plain woman, no matter how good an actress, is simply swallowed up by the part, attention going instead to the more vivid Tartuffe, the more individual Dorine and the more attractive Mariane. Nor should Dorine's description of her illness the night before be taken literally enough to affect her appearance; if she looks pale or ill she cannot hold her own.

Elmire should convey the appeal of a mature woman accustomed to the ways of the world. Tartuffe's proposition is not a novel experience for her nor one she is not perfectly capable of handling without outside help. It helps enormously if she also possesses the coloring, figure, and graceful bearing of a woman of unmistakable sex appeal, for it is this quality which makes Tartuffe's attraction toward her seemingly inevitable, and believable.

Cléante

Orgon's sensible brother-in-law is probably the most difficult part in this play. He has the longest speeches and their substance seems to make sense but they make no impression on the people to whom they are directed, Orgon and Tartuffe. What worse task could an actor be given than to deliver a number of lengthy, well-composed speeches to listeners who are hostile, obviously bored, and impatient to be about something else? In spite of this, audiences generally favor Cléante and some very good performances have been given in this part.

Molière does not tell us whether Cléante is older or younger than Orgon, but because of his sententiousness he seems older, and in performance he can be made up to seem somewhat older.

Dorine

The character of Dorine stands for a kind of servant rather than an individual: the family retainer who has grown up in service—nurse, maid, companion, and confidante—and who has, over the years, acquired a special place in the household that allows her to speak her mind as she pleases, offering criticism and advice regardless of whether she has been asked for it. The actress who plays Dorine must above all be one with exceptional timing who can manage the many asides and interjections to perfection, giving them that air of spontaneity and aptitude that makes them come alive. These asides and offhand interjections have always been the most difficult kind of lines to deliver effectively. Not many performers ever develop the knack. Some never do. Others seem almost as if they had been born with the gift. It is one of the latter that we will need for this part regardless of size, shape, age, or general appearance.

The part is often mistakenly cast as a soubrette, with a young, pretty, and saucy impersonation. Such casting ruins the part, which properly belongs to an older and wiser woman, who, being in the same age bracket as Orgon and Cléante, can speak her mind fearlessly in their presence. Furthermore, we must have only one mature beauty in this play and that must be Elmire; there must be no other woman of comparable age or appeal to qualify our interest in her. Dorine can be downright homely. It is not her appearance that counts.

M. Exempt

In plays with *deus ex machina* endings the actor who performs this function must always be one of the strongest in the company, impressive in appearance, with strong stage presence and flawless diction. It is important to keep this in mind during auditions so that no outstanding possibilities are overlooked. The role of the King's Officer, or M. Exempt as he is sometimes called, is not a demanding one. He has only one entrance and one long speech. He seldom needs to report for rehearsal at any other time than when the finale is being worked on unless there are calls for fittings or photographs. These requirements sometimes help to make it easier to secure an actor of the first rank for this brief but very important part.

COSTUMING

Since this is not a play about historical events or a satire of the mores of any specific period, historically accurate costumes are not needed. The bourgeois dress of Parisians during the reign of Louis XIV is interesting and colorful, but only French actors are usually at home in the costumes of the time. With a gifted costumer, unlimited budget, and ample rehearsal time, one might attempt to emulate the French. Otherwise it would be better to dress the play in the costumes of some other period.

What else could it be? Certainly not modern, for our marriage customs are quite different and the satire of fake religiosity in this day of many strange sects might strike some too close to home. But the style of dress could be Georgian, Empire, Regency, Victorian, or even Edwardian, all of which are periods easier to simulate than the late seventeenth century in France. Empire and Regency clothes are especially handsome and have the further virtue of improving the appearance of all who wear them.

Madame Pernelle, being an elderly lady and widowed, might be expected to appear in black, but since this is a comedy some shade of gray would be better. Rich materials, good style, and fine workmanship in her garments mark her as a woman of substance and affluence.

At the opposite extreme of age we have Mariane, still in her teens, just old enough to put her hair up and begin to dress like a woman instead of a schoolgirl. The more prettily she is dressed the more appalled we will be at the prospect of seeing her married to Tartuffe.

Elmire and Dorine are both mature women, with an important difference. Elmire is handsomely gowned and coiffured as befits her station, while Dorine's clothing is noticeably plainer. As Dorine's position in the family is not quite the same as a servant's, a bunch of keys at her waist might help to make this clear. Actresses always like to appear a bit younger than they actually are and so tend to play both Elmire and Dorine too young. They should look and act their age, that is, old enough to be sensible, which in the play they both are.

Tartuffe mentions the fine lace on Elmire's collar and the rich material of her gown, so both should support the reference. Some costumer's provide her with laced bodice and shoes which Tartuffe can try to unlace while he is wooing her.

As to Dorine's decolletege which so offends Tartuffe that he offers her his handkerchief and insists that she cover her bosom with it, this probably exists more in Tartuffe's mind than anywhere else. I have seen Dorines with necklines so low that they hardly dared to bend over. This interferes with the play by distracting the audience. Nor is it probable that a domestic would be dressed so.

All that we are told about Orgon indicates that he is quite well to do. We do not know his rank if any, his occupation, nor the source of his income. We are told that the King knows him and remembers him favorably from his part in the civil wars. From this we would expect to see him well dressed in handsome but not frivolous clothes, a good substantial citizen who knows his worth and makes no attempt to conceal it.

As Cléante seems older and more sober it would seem appropriate for him to be dressed in the same general manner as Orgon but perhaps a trifle more soberly.

Damis and Valére, being very young men, would be more elaborately dressed than the others, with more extremely cut coats, waistcoats, and breeches and more touches of youthful fancy. It is important that they be clearly distinguished one from another since neither is on stage much. One of the best ways to do this is to make one fair and the other dark.

The little bailiff, M. Loyal, apparently has nothing about him to suggest his profession because when he reveals his mission it comes as a surprise to everyone present. Otherwise, the only requirement of his costume is that it be less elegant than those of the principals.

The Officer of the King, M. Exempt, should be handsomely and impressively costumed, with some conspicuous badge of office, and if appropriate, plumed hat and sword. If the period is eighteenth century he could wear a powdered wig, a gorget, and a military sash with a sword. If the period chosen were Empire or later he would show up very well in one of the many handsome military uniforms of that time. The officers or soldiers accompanying him could be similarly costumed, only a little less brilliantly. In the Stratford production these were outfitted as privates of the Brigade of Guards, in red coats with white cross belts and Tower muskets; picturesque, but not very French.

The costume of Tartuffe allows for wide differences in style. Lately he has taken to appearing in rather austere clerical black with a white neckcloth vaguely suggesting some sort of ministry. Along with this he usually has pale makeup and lanky hair. This get-up seems to have originated with Louis Jouvet. Previously the traditional Tartuffe was plump and pink-cheeked in accordance with Dorine's description of him and he seldom wore black although he was occasionally put into rusty and run-down clothing in spite of the lines telling us that Orgon has clothed him like a gentleman. In the Stratford production he was dressed like an impoverished English country squire and for some unexplained reason wore leggins of the same cut and color as those worn by the Americans in World War II. Since, according to Orgon, he claims to be a dispossessed nobleman, it is plausible for him to look somewhat down at heels in spite of Orgon's help. But he certainly should not be garbed as either cleric or pauper. I think it poor practice to put him in black, for not only is the use of black questionable in comedy but to have him the one black-garbed character in the play encourages comparison with a certain great tragedy and this is misleading, for it can do no good whatsoever to the utterly different Tartuffe.

When Tartuffe makes his entrance with the King's Officer in the last act he often appears in a handsome new outfit suitable to his improved social position, so that the contrast between this arrogant person and the humble creature of earlier scenes is revealing and highly dramatic. The one thing we have to make sure of is that if he is given an elegant new costume it should not in any way interfere with his immediate recognition. Audiences recognize characters by their whole appearance, including the cut and color of their costumes. Any very striking change of costume late in the play always raises the danger that the character may not be recognized at once. In a short climactic scene this could be disastrous. No one in the audience should have the slightest doubt as to who Tartuffe is when he suddenly enters blocking the path of Orgon's escape.

The resurgence of the fashion for beards has given us a few bearded Tartuffes. Unfortunately, the beard seriously interferes with facial expression, especially when combined with any sort of wig. If an actor under consideration for the role has a beard and is unwilling to part with it, it would be better to look for another actor not so adorned.

SETTING

The setting for a comedy ought to look like a place where amusing, delightful, and often absurd things can happen. Too often the setting for *Tartuffe* has been one in which anything at all could happen, where on first glance there was nothing to tell whether the imminent action was to be serious or comical. In part this has been due to the designer's attempt to convey an impression of period style by using features of seventeenth-century architecture and decoration, features which in their weight, coloring and general elaborateness are grossly unsuited to comedy.

Period style is not important in *Tartuffe* as it is in some of Molière's other plays. The foibles that *Tartuffe* exposes are not peculiar to seventeenth-century France. Any period of conspicuous religious fervor in which the authority of the parent is absolute will serve as well as that in which the play was composed. But whatever the period style, lightness and brightness are indispensable to the setting, for this is comedy, satiric comedy to be sure, but still comedy. Light and lively is the password. Let the somber and weighty settings be saved for somber and weighty subjects.

As to the physique of the setting, the requirements are few. Unfortunately they are not also simple. One problem is that the demands of the first and last acts are opposed to those of the rest of the play. These two acts need a feeling of openness and space, the others a definite sense of intimacy. In the first act all but three of the principals are assembled while Madame Pernelle scolds each in turn and then makes a grand exit. In the last act all the principals are present when Tartuffe and the Officer make their grand entrance. Both acts need space for many characters and provision for impressive entrances and exits. If we were to think of the setting as any sort of specific locale it would be the spacious foyer of a large house. But such a locale will not do for the scenes in which Tartuffe attempts to seduce Elmire, especially the second attempt when he is so concerned about being overheard or interrupted. Seduction implies privacy. Is it likely that Tartuffe would attempt it in the most heavily trafficked room in the house? Most of the other scenes in the three middle acts are small scenes involving two or three characters only. Act two is entirely concerned with Mariane, first in her relationship with her father and then with her lover, Valère. Act three embodies Tartuffe's first overture to Elmire, his discovery by Damis, and his forgiveness by Orgon. Act four consists of the table scene and the preparations for it.

On an open stage the feeling of locale is conveyed by the manner of the performers with the help of a few pieces of appropriate furniture, provided of course that the background is not embellished with more specific details. On a proscenium stage the sense of place is created by the scenic elements surrounding the players and tends to be more specific because of the fact that it exists within an enclosure. Were one producing *Tartuffe* on a proscenium stage one might do well to consider changing the setting, using one set for acts one and five and another smaller one for acts two, three, and four. Such a change would have the further advantage of introducing visual variety into a play that needs it.

The other physical requirements are less problematical. One must provide an exit for Madame Pernelle in act one which will not cause the audience to wonder why she does not on her way out meet Orgon coming in, and an exit in act five which will work the opposite way, causing Orgon to collide with Tartuffe and the Officer as they make their entrance. At least one place must be provided from which a character can overhear and perhaps also see action on the central stage area. Some designers have contrived a room with a balcony for this purpose. Many of them unfortunately have tried to use the same set for the table scene, which is illogical and also makes the scene harder to play.

NOTES ON STAGING

(Act I–scene i): One is tempted to provide some stage business to make Madame Pernelle's indifference to the arguments of her family more plausible, such as giving her an ear trumpet. But a little goes a long way here. The exposition is what matters; it tells us a lot and it requires close listening. Save the ingenious business for later when it may be needed to sharpen interest; nobody ever gets bored during the first ten minutes of a play.

(Act I–scene v): How can we convey Orgon's inattention and still keep the attention of the audience on Cléante's argument?

(Act II–scene ii): I have never seen a production in which the exchange between Orgon and Dorine here was as amusing as it is in the script. Fortunately, coming early in the play it is readily forgotten.

(Act III–scene i): The locale now shifts to some more intimate interior room. Problem: where to hide the eavesdropping Damis? We do not want to anticipate the table scene.

(Act III–scene iii): Tartuffe's intentions should be made clear but there is no reason for him to abandon his charm; rather the reverse.

(Act IV–scene iv): Our eyes will keep going back to the table to see if Orgon is responding. The effect of the scene is best when there is absolutely nothing, no action of any kind, to indicate what is going on in Orgon's mind. Some directors seem to think that the more business they can cram into this scene the better it is going to be; a serious mistake.

One of the best uncoverings I have ever seen was accomplished by putting the table on casters so that it could be rolled away, leaving Orgon sitting there, stunned by what he has heard, until Elmire rouses him to action.

How does Tartuffe react to Orgon's confrontation? With humble prayer, repeating III–iii? And when prayer fails, how does he accomplish the transition into the relentless tyrant?

(Act V–scene iv): The pleasanter and more courteous M. Loyal, the funnier this scene.

(Act V–scene vii): When unmasked, what does Tartuffe do? Does he try to pray again? What is he now: the martyr, the defiant rogue, or the unappreciated benefactor?

CHAPTER 17

She Stoops to Conquer: A Problem of Coherence

She Stoops to Conquer was one of the first plays I came to know intimately. From watching it through weeks of rehearsal and studying it nightly in performance I formed some definite opinions as to its strengths and weaknesses and where the problems were. Several years went by before I happened to see another first-class production. Then, to my surprise, many of what I had marked down as weak spots turned out to be among the best parts and some of what I had thought to be strong points proved almost the opposite. As time passed and I saw more different productions I realized that what had originally appeared to be strengths and weaknesses were in actuality only variations in effectiveness of individual scenes and characters attributable to casting or to the temper of a particular audience. Now, each new production has its surprises. The quality of the production may be consistent but characters and scenes that are brilliant in one production are seldom the same as those most successful in another by a different company.

A STURDY CHAMELEON

One enjoys the play more each time one sees a new production in spite of the fact that one becomes increasingly demanding and less easily satisfied, one of the proofs, I suppose, of its position as a classic. In almost any hands the play turns out well and seems to leave the audience satisfied.

Many of what I once thought to be problems evaporate in the hands of a skillful director. Others however have persisted and continue to lie in wait to puzzle and trip the unwary. I have yet to see a production in which all characters are equally interesting or all scenes equally effective. Now that I know how good each can be when circumstances are favorable I am still looking forward to a production in which every element achieves its potential.

Some of the more persistent difficulties arise from certain mistakes repeatedly made in defining the author's intention. The worst of these have come from misperceiving the nature of the play and consequently attempting to make it into something it is not. For example, everyone knows that Goldsmith, bored by the artificiality of the popular "sentimental" comedy of his time and out of patience with its insistence on "genteel" elegance, parodied it in a number of places in this play. Yet, to attempt to treat any part of *She Stoops* as satire is invariably disastrous, for one cannot parody a parody, especially when the object of ridicule is as remote from the experience of modern audiences as the sentimental comedy of the eighteenth century.

Another common mistake is to attempt to mock the manner and style of eighteenth-century acting: the soliloquies, asides, overhearings, and so on. This only succeeds in emphasizing conventions that seemed natural enough to the audiences for whom the play was written but which seem artificial to us. The result is to remove the play further from our taste, making it seem more remote when one ought to be working to make it more immediate. Quaint acting conventions of another age are interesting but not very funny and cannot be made to sustain humor long enough to keep the quaintness from cloying long before the play reaches its final scene.

Some productions have taken an opposite tack which is almost as bad. Noticing that the play has an exceptionally large number of references to manners, dress, and decor of its time, director and designer join forces to give us a genre picture of eighteenth-century country life. But *She Stoops* is not a documentary, nor did its author intend it as such. It is merely a mistaken-identity comedy that happens to take place in a country house. Circumstantial details of architecture and furniture may be interesting at first glance but after that they only clutter the scene; the visual detail steals attention from the performer and wears out the eye long before the play is over. In the theatre for which Goldsmith wrote the scenery was beautifully painted, but being lit only by candlelight it was also much less obtrusive than modern scene painting. Furthermore, the performers did the best part of their acting on the forefront of the apron where they were close to the audience and set off by the light from the footlights. The softness of the candlelight, the emphasis of the footlights and the proximity of the actor to his auditors all combined to give the intimate scenes considerable power. Surrounding the actors with realistic settings introduces a competing visual factor which the originals never had to contend with.

As far as I know, no one has ever attempted to produce this play in modern dress or any of the other bizarre costumings sometimes inflicted on English classics. I think this may be because the play is so completely of its own time and place. All of its best situations have been used again and again, but none of the copies or borrowings have ever carried the individual atmosphere and lifelike quality which made the original a classic.

GOLDSMITH'S SPECIAL ATMOSPHERE

She Stoops to Conquer is different from most comedies in the extent to which the author incorporates the locale, season, weather, and time of day into the total effect of the work. In most comedies locale is only sketchily indicated and then only when relevant to the action; otherwise it goes unmentioned. Weather is usually fair and time of day only figures when mistakes are about to occur because of darkness; and as for season, who can tell in what time of the year *Tartuffe* takes place, or *The Country Wife*, or *The Comedy of Errors*?

But in *She Stoops* the country setting is established with considerable care. Hardcastle's house is supposed to be some forty miles from London (although Marlow believes he has travelled nearer to sixty by the time he reaches the ale-house). The roads are rough and muddy. Tony boasts of going twenty-five miles in two and a half hours so this should provide a pretty good idea of the kind of roads Goldsmith had in mind.

The season is not mentioned by name but it is plainly not summer, and since there is no mention of frost, ice, or snow, it is certainly not in the depth of winter. Mrs. Hardcastle deplores "this raw evening," and tries to prevent Tony from going out in it. Later on, when old Hardcastle orders Marlow out of the house, the young man refuses to go, exclaiming, "What, at this time of the night, and such a night!" Hastings earlier speaks of the comforts of "a clean room and a good fire." When Constance Neville is making ready to depart her servant brings her cloak, fan, muff, and gloves, and reminds her that her hat is in the next room. Mrs. Hardcastle, who gets soaked in the horse pond, "up to the waist, like a mermaid," seems also to have caught cold, for she says, "I have caught my death in it," and some actresses amplify this by making her sneeze and cough through the rest of the play.

Less definite than the season is the time of day. The early scenes take place during daylight hours and the later ones at night, although it is impossible to determine at what point in the play we pass from the one to the other. Kate, in her first scene with her father, describes their agreement according to which she wears her best clothes during the day (in the "morning" she says) when most of her social activity is going on, and her plainer "house-wife's dress" in the evening at home. It is daylight when Marlow and Hastings stop at the ale-house to ask directions, for all the directions given them are visual. It is still daylight when they arrive at Hardcastle's, for Kate is still wearing her fine clothes when she first meets Marlow. Since it is still daylight one might wonder why the young men are concerned about sleeping accommodations, but then one remembers that horse-drawn vehicles can go only so far without either changing horses or stopping to rest them. After a forty mile trip over rough and muddy roads their horses would by now be nearly exhausted. They are able to continue to the "Old Buck's Head" inn only because it is but a mile further.

At the end of the play they all go in to supper, presumably to dine on the "made dishes" to which Marlow and Hastings objected at the beginning of the play, so the hour must still be this side of midnight.

If we keep in mind that dramatic time is always elastic, going fast or slow according to the liveliness of the action it encompasses, the whole play would appear to occupy less than eight hours. The action occurs on a gray day when the difference between daylight and dark is not very distinct.

More interesting to me than the question of season, weather, and time of day, is the dating of the action. By this I mean not the date of its composition but the date on which the events are supposed to occur, for Goldsmith seems to have placed his action a generation or so earlier than the one in which it took the stage. The play was produced in 1773 but its action does not take place then, nor is it in the ubiquitous "present."

The perspective of time is such that we habitually think of events of an earlier generation as occurring in a simpler and more spacious age. Thornton Wilder took advantage of this very effectively in *Our Town* when he placed it in the first decade of the twentieth century, thirty-five years earlier than the date of its production. These were the childhood years of most of the members of his audience. By placing his action in those years he gained a great advantage in atmosphere, especially in the feeling of warmth and simplicity generally associated with the years of our childhood. Goldsmith has done the same thing with *She Stoops*. The play takes place, not in 1773 but some twenty or thirty years earlier. The work is deliberately "old-fashioned" and designed to take advantage of happy associations of earlier times. Evidence of this is Hardcastle's reference to having served with the Duke of Marlborough, whose career ended sixty years before *She Stoops* was composed. Hardcastle is proud of having been present at the siege of Denain, which took place in 1712, and the battle of Belgrade, which was fought in 1717. His memory for details is not very good, for the English were beaten at Denain and Belgrade took place after Marlborough was relieved. But even so if he had been old enough to serve with Marlborough he would, by 1773, be too old to be a likely parent to a girl of eighteen. Another indication of earlier time is Mrs. Hardcastle's deprecation of her husband's fondness for his "great flaxen wig." The blonde, full-bottom wig reached the peak of its popularity around 1700. By 1745 a blond wig would have been a curiosity even in the country.

Goldsmith's references to historical events are not to be taken too literally, however. Hardcastle mentions as one of his reasons for withdrawing from politics the mistakes of the government in regard to India, naming two Indian princes, "Heyder Ally" and "Ally Cawn," (Haidar Ali, Sultan of Mysore, and Ali Khan, Nawab of Bengal) who were prominent in the 1760s. The song, "Water Parted," is from the opera *Artaxerxes*, which was produced in 1762, although the melody may have existed earlier. The intent of the author is nevertheless clear enough: to place the action in an earlier age than the one in which the play was composed.

THE PLOT

At first glance this looks like a fairly typical mistaken-identity plot, but on closer examination one sees the mistakes spring one from another in such a way that there are no options as to spotting of the good scenes. This sequential development is more typical of narrative than of drama, and it is also more typical of a novel than of a play. In most mistaken-identity plays the successive mistakes are arranged in sequence according to their effectiveness with the funniest ones coming last and the less amusing ones earlier. In this play the first error, mistaking Hardcastle's house for an inn, provides the foundation for Kate's impersonation of the barmaid two acts further on, after her first tete-a-tete with Marlow in her own character has failed to penetrate his shyness. Her impersonation of the barmaid is sustained only long enough to catch his interest. When she sees him again she has changed her impersonation to that of a poor relation of the family. Finally, she appears as herself, at which point their parents observe them together and insist on their betrothal. While Marlow is becoming more strongly attracted to her he falls further and further afoul of her father but Kate checks the progression by making her father promise to delay final judgment until he has observed her alone with the young man.

The secondary plot, the plan for the elopement of Hastings with Constance Neville, operates almost entirely without reference to the Marlow-Kate plot, serving mainly to introduce variety and put some space between Marlow's first notice of Kate and his subsequent encounters with her up to the final capitulation. Love affairs in drama cannot develop as they usually do in life or in novels, by degrees, but must be shown instead as a series of high points: wooings, quarrels, misunderstandings, and making up. Since the Kate-Marlow affair is one of continual change it must be alternated with some other action. Hence the business with the jewel-case and the attempt of Mrs. Hardcastle to separate Constance from Hastings by taking her away to old Aunt Pedigree's.

Tony is the prime agent who keeps the play in motion, first by misdirecting the young men, second by stealing the jewels, and finally by frustrating his mother's attempt to separate the lovers by taking her and her ward on a make-believe journey. The fact that Tony functions always as agent in a situation in which some other character must suffer, make decisions, or take action, gives us a clue to his proper place in the play. The character is so vividly drawn that there is always the danger that he will usurp the center of interest, for the play as a whole goes much better when the interest falls less on him and more on the character upon whom he is practicing.

Goldsmith makes his play move rather briskly by two means in particular, the first of which is an exceptionally free use of soliloquies to separate scenes and keep us informed of characters' feelings and developments of the plot. The soliloquies are generally brief and to the point. They carry the burden of exposition, which in a mistaken-identity plot is always considerable, and they save a great deal of time. Every major character except Constance and Mrs. Hardcastle has at least one soliloquy. The second means is his complete disregard for motivation in connection with exits and entrances. Unmotivated entrances and exits allow characters to appear and disappear as needed. In this play they are managed so well that we are scarcely aware of the mechanism. On a few rare occasions the characters tell us where they are going when they leave the stage or why they are coming here when they enter, but for the most part they come on when the situation requires their presence and when they are no longer needed they simply walk off.

TEXT AND LANGUAGE

The text of the play is in pretty good shape, and the dialogue is well knit and easy to speak. There are, however, several problems that must be solved before the play can be put into rehearsal. One of these comes from changes which have taken place in our language. Another comes from a peculiarity of the author's style.

One of Goldsmith's peculiarities is his fondness for quoting Shakespeare, usually inaccurately, and often inappropriately. For example, at the end of Kate's first scene she says, "would it were bed-time and all well." This is from *King Henry IV, Part One* (V-i–126) where Falstaff, just before the battle of Shrewsbury, says to Prince Hal, "I would 'twere bedtime, Hal, and all well." This hardly seems appropriate for Kate; she has no reason to look forward to bedtime, especially on this day of all days. The scene-ending is greatly improved if the line is simply cut. Another is uttered by Mrs, Hardcastle, when she calls Hastings "the pink of courtesy." This is from *Romeo and Juliet* (II-iv–63), where it is used by Mercutio to describe himself. Mrs. Hardcastle uses the term sarcastically after she has discovered Hastings' plan to elope with Miss Neville. In the earlier part of the play, when Tony tells Marlow and Hastings that they have lost their way, Marlow exclaims, "We wanted no ghost to tell us that." The line is from *Hamlet* (I-v–125). Tony could motivate Marlow's exclamation by delivering his cue, ". . . you have lost your way," in mock-heroic manner.

Some problems arise because of words whose meanings have changed since the lines were written. Mrs. Hardcastle says, "I vow, Mr. Hardcastle, you're very particular." What she means is that he is peculiar, and it would improve the sense of her line to change "particular" to "peculiar." Later on, speaking of Tony, she says, "I don't think a boy wants much learning to spend fifteen hundred a year." The line makes better sense if "wants" is replaced by "needs." In act three, Kate, speaking of Tony, says, "I don't wonder at his impudence," when what she means is that she is appalled by his impudence. It would be better if she simply said so. Later on, after having put on her "house-wife's dress" Kate asks her maid how she looks, and the woman replies, "It's the dress, madam, that every lady wears in the country but when she visits and receives company." What she means is that the garb is what country ladies wear except when they are receiving company or visiting. Substitute "except" for "but" and the line sounds right. In act four, Hastings says, "I quite forgot to tell her [Constance] that I intended to prepare at the bottom of the garden." What he means is that he intended to go to the bottom of the garden, or to wait for her there. If the word "prepare" is changed to "repair" it will make sense. In the same act Mrs. Hardcastle says to Constance, "The jewels, my dear Con, shall be yours incontinently." In this case we need only substitute "immediately" for "incontinently" and the line works out. Later in the same act Constance says to Marlow, "Mr. Marlow, we never kept on your mistake till it was too late to undeceive you." This is not a line that can be repaired by word substitution. Since Constance is in any case interrupted by the servant come to hurry her departure, it seems that the line could easily be cut and the servant allowed to interrupt Marlow instead.

Other problems arise because of the eighteenth-century habit of circumlocution. This makes for elegant speech but to our ears it sounds affected. The lines are well composed and easy to speak but they often seem to say more than the dialogue requires. Careful trimming can often sharpen the point of a scene and, without losing the flavor of the period, bring it closer to the manner of speech more likely to appeal to a modern audience. Here is an example from the fifth act, with the suggested excision indicated by parentheses:

Hastings: (My dear Constance, why will you deliberate thus?) If we delay a moment, all is lost forever. Pluck up a little resolution, and we shall soon be out of reach of her malignity.

Miss Neville: (I find it impossible.) My spirits are so sunk with the agitations I have suffered, that I am unable to face any new danger. (Two or three years' patience will at last crown us with happiness.)

Hastings: (Such a tedious delay is worse than inconstancy.) Let us fly, my charmer. Let us date our happiness from this very moment. (Perish fortune!) Love and content will increase what we possess beyond a monarch's revenue. (Let me prevail!)

Miss Neville: No, Mr. Hastings; no. (Prudence once more comes to my relief, and I will obey its dictates. In the moment of passion fortune may be despised, but it ever produces a lasting repentance.) I'm resolved to apply to Mr. Hardcastle's compassion and justice for redress.

Hastings: (But) though he had the will, he has not the power to relieve you.

Miss Neville: He has the influence, and upon that I am resolved to rely.

Hastings: (I have no hopes. But) since you persist, I must reluctantly obey you.

SETTING

The most important thing about the setting is that it changes instantly from one locale to another without a wait, interruption, or even dimming of lights. In the first act it changes from Mr. Hardcastle's house to the Alehouse and back again without a pause. In the fifth act it changes from Hardcastle's house to an exterior, "The Bottom of the Garden," and right back again. In the other acts there are several places where a change of scenery from one room in the house to a different one would help vary the visual progression and make the action also more plausible.

Such instantaneous changes were easily made in the theatre for which *She Stoops* was written because of the form which scenery had taken: wings and back-flats sliding in waxed grooves underfoot and overhead so that the locale could be changed by merely pushing the painted flats together or by pulling them apart to uncover another picture-locale immediately behind.

Some productions of this play feature scene changes effected by costumed servants. For the first few changes this is rather intriguing, but after a while it begins to grow tiresome, and because each such change holds up the progression, by the fifth act the whole business is unbearably tedious. This is what always happens when a continuity originally intended to proceed without interruption is held up, whether by interpolated business, drawing of curtains, or even by the briefest dimming of lights. No interruption of the forward movement has been allowed for in the original script and none can be added without impairing the effectiveness of the whole.

Neither the form of the scenery nor the manner of changing it had much effect on the acting style of the original since most of the performance took place on the forefront of the stage which projected some distance forward from the proscenium, placing the actor more nearly among his auditors than in front of them.

In the eighteenth-century scenery was only a background for the action, not an environment. It could be an attractive background, but it was always subordinated to the acting, being mellow of line and soft of color and less brightly lighted than the performers. Originally this subordination prevailed when both actors and settings were viewed under the soft light of candles and oil lamps. It remains basic to the setting and lighting of these plays today. For this reason it is possible to put on a very creditable production of *She Stoops* in an arena theatre without any scenery at all, using only furniture to suggest changes of locale.

Whatever furniture is used should be handsome. "Antique but creditable," is Hastings' appraisal. It might not be as elegant as that of Adam or Sheraton but it could be good Queen Anne walnut, nicely polished. In Mr. Hardcastle's house one might also expect gleaming brass and cut glass. Rusticity should be relegated to the Alehouse, with its oaken benches, deal tables, and pewter tankards.

The original production was untroubled by one problem which has come into being with modern lighting: the problem of playing a farcical scene in which the mistakes are caused by darkness. This is the problem we have in the scene "At the Bottom of the Garden," when Mrs. Hardcastle, after a long drive, arrives at the foot of her own back yard (thinking herself miles from home) and mistakes Mr. Hardcastle for a highwayman. In the original production the indication of night was merely a matter of painting on the back flats, the illumination of the acting area remaining unchanged, a convention similar to that which we now see in the cinema where night is indicated, not by a decrease in visibility, but by some alteration in the quality of the lighting. In modern productions when the text describes the scene as dark too often the lighting designer seems to feel that the audience need not see any better than the characters; when this happens the whole point of the scene is lost. I once sat behind a man at *She Stoops* who, toward the end of the garden scene, leaned over to his companion and whispered, "If the next scene is as dark as this I'll go blind."

COSTUMING

A number of specific items of dress are called for in the course of the play. The most important of these is Kate's change from the "superfluous silks" of her daytime attire to the plain house-wife's dress which she wears in the evening. The change is more difficult than it looks. Of the two outfits the house-wife costume is the more important because it is in this costume that she wins Marlow. Also, she has to wear it through most of the play, so we must not tire of it. In her "plain" dress, Kate must nevertheless be quite appealing, for once she has caught Marlow's eye he is irretrievably lost to her. Plain fabric would seem to be called for, with a minimum of frills and probably no jewelry, but the cut and fit of the garment must be artfully contrived for the actress who plays Kate so as to show off her figure to greatest advantage. Hemline, skirt fullness, waistline placement, and sleeve length are all critical since the optimum treatment of each will vary according to the physique of the individual actress. Many designers put Kate in a mob cap to carry out the idea of the housewife-barmaid, but it is difficult to design a mob cap which will enhance the features of the wearer; if the cap cannot improve her appearance it should not be used.

Kate's other costume, her morning outfit for visiting and receiving callers, can be made of rich fabric with abundant ornamentation. When she first meets Marlow the stage direction describes her "as returned from walking," which means that she still has her hat on, for later she says, "My bonnet would have kept him from seeing me." What kind of bonnet this would be, that could keep him from seeing her face and yet allow the audience to see her? Whether she would be wearing any sort of gloves, shawl, or muff can be determined by the designer. I have seen productions in which she also carried a furled parasol and used it very effectively.

Constance Neville's costume must be designed so as to make her appearance similar to that of Kate in her dress-up outfit, but different enough in color and general treatment so that the two girls set off each other to advantage. One way of doing this is to make sure that they do not have the same color of hair. I was surprised in a recent production otherwise very well done to see that the designer chose to put them both into blonde wigs. Each was attractive enough but both lost by it when they were on stage at the same time.

In the last act Constance is obliged to don hat, cloak, gloves, and muff for her journey and apparently she wears all this for the rest of the play since she has no opportunity to change. In which case the cloak, et cetera, should be designed with the requirements of her final appearance in mind.

Mrs. Hardcastle appears to have several outfits. First of all there is the one in which we first see her, which might be somewhat like Kate's house-wife dress, with a mob cap to cover her elaborate hairdo. Then there is the costume in which she welcomes Hastings and Marlow, her "full-dress" outfit. Next there is her traveling costume worn in the last act which seems to consist of a cloak, probably with a hood, plus muff, gloves and hat. Finally, in most productions she has a second traveling costume exactly like the first but stained, muddied, and disheveled, in which she appears after Tony has landed the coach in the horse pond. Her entrance thus in the garden scene always gets a laugh.

Mrs. Hardcastle is usually represented with an excess of frills, ruffles, and ribbons. One should think twice, however, before putting her into ugly lines or clashing colors as this may prove less comic than tiresome before the play is over.

Of Old Hardcastle's costume all we know is that his wife regards him as hopelessly out of fashion: too many buttons and a "great flaxen wig." Except for the wig, her description need not be taken too literally. He is quite well off and no doubt dresses the part. As to the wig which Mrs. Hardcastle so dislikes, I have seen him in one resembling the full-bottom wig worn by Dr. Johnson in the Joshua Reynolds portrait and he looked very good indeed at the same time that he exemplified the fashion to which his wife objected.

When we first meet Marlow and Hastings at the Alehouse they are in traveling clothes: boots, gloves, hats, and surcoats or cloaks. The next time we see them they have just arrived at the Hardcastles' so they would still be in their boots although they have already removed their cloaks and hats. Marlow says that he is thinking of changing his traveling dress, but the girls enter before the men have any opportunity to change so that Hastings' first meeting with Constance Neville and Marlow's initial encounter with Kate Hardcastle both take place while the men are still in the clothes they have been traveling in. Whether they change costumes afterward is uncertain. A little variety of dress would be welcome, but it is neither necessary nor likely. Hastings intends to elope with Constance as soon as their horses are sufficiently rested. He would hardly dress up for what is certain to be a hard and fast drive to the channel coast. Marlow on the other hand continues to think of himself as being at an inn until Kate undeceives him in act four. From then on he speaks only of getting away from the place as soon as possible. One would not expect him to change costume in order to resume his travel. The only change indicated occurs when he takes off his boots in the parlor while ordering Mr. Hardcastle to see them attended to. After removing the boots he probably puts on pumps.

Tony's appearance is nowhere indicated in the text except when he calls for his boots before starting out on the journey with his mother and Constance, and a little later when the stage direction calls for him to enter "booted and spattered," as he would be from riding postillion to the coach. In most productions he is costumed in rough country clothes of homespun and leather; occasionally in a red coat and jockey cap. The red coat is too bright for a character whose natural exuberance repeatedly aggravates the problem of keeping him in balance with the other characters.

The four servants whom Hardcastle is drilling at the beginning of Act two usually look best in livery, although not necessarily of the best fit. The scene is funnier if at first they appear to be almost acceptable as house servants and then by their behaviour make it gradually more and more improbable that Mr. Hardcastle's plan of increasing his household staff by bringing in men from the plough and the barn is going to have any chance of success.

CHARACTERS AND CASTING

The play can be produced with a full cast of twenty, or, if the minor characters are doubled, with as few as fourteen. Characters who appear only once, like Tony's alehouse companions, are logical candidates for doubling. In this instance the alehouse folk and Old Hardcastle's awkward squad can be played by the same four actors. The fact that the two scenes come so close together may be attributed to Goldsmith's inexperience as a playwright, but even so there is a space of three pages in which they can make the change, so the doubling is far from impossible.

Those who have not seen the same productions of this play will never be able to agree as to which character is the most delightful. In the original production one of the lesser actors of the company enjoyed a great success as Tony Lumpkin, much to the chagrin of Woodward, who had turned down the part. Since then different characters in the cast have carried the day in different stagings. In the first production I saw, Old Hardcastle appeared to be the star. More recently I have seen Mrs. Hardcastle emerge as the audience favorite, then Tony, and finally, in two successive productions on opposite sides of the Atlantic, Kate. The interesting thing about all this is that no matter who shines at the moment none of the others seems to suffer. At one time I believed it impossible to overact the part of Mrs. Hardcastle, the broadly played ones had been so successful. But since then I have seen her played in a rather subdued manner without any loss of interest and a definite gain in the balance of the whole.

Kate Hardcastle

When the play is announced for production the part of Kate attracts all the best actresses in the vicinity. So let us start with Kate. What do we have to begin with? We know that she is eighteen because she tells us so. We know she is Hardcastle's daughter by his first marriage, that her father would like nothing better than to see her married to the son of his lifelong friend, Sir Charles Marlow, but that her dowry is small. The only physical description of her comes, not very reliably, from Tony: "A tall, trapesing, trolloping, talkative maypole." This can hardly be regarded as accurate, seeing that he describes himself as "a pretty well-bred agreeable youth that everybody is fond of."

The quality that makes Kate charming as a character and gratifying to the actress who plays her is her emotional transparency. Her hopes, fears, frustrations, are all highly visible. When her father describes young Marlow she is delighted and makes no attempt to conceal her interest, but when he utters the words, "bashful and reserved," her interest evaporates and she is suddenly wary. A moment later, having reflected upon the situation, she changes her mind and decides to accept him after all. Then, to tease her, her father suggests that Young Marlow might not take to her. For a moment she is downcast at the thought. But only for a moment. Soon she is eager again, come what will. And so it goes with her: eager one moment, wary the next, confident one minute and unsure the next, first reckless, then calculating, and so on, so that during the course of the play she runs through a kaleidoscope of emotions.

The most delightful impersonations of this character have displayed a combination of unsureness (if only momentary) with a gambler's addiction to the excitement of chance. She is not at all sure, she says, that she will be able to "manage" Marlow, but she is nevertheless eager to try. There are many points at which it is evident that she is not at all certain that her scheme will succeed but she hazards everything on the next gambit regardless. She does not plan much beyond the next move, but is inclined rather to "trust to occurrences for success."

Some actresses play Kate too strongly, as if she were confident from the first that she could manipulate events to her liking. This makes a much less appealing character than the one who improvises from moment to moment, not always sure of the outcome but always thrilling to the excitement of the adventure.

Kate herself plays several parts. In the first act we see the affectionate obedient daughter. In the second act we see the well-brought-up young lady seeking some sort of common ground with the bashful Marlow. In the third act we see her assume the saucy manner of the barmaid. In the fourth she is no longer the barmaid but the honest industrious "poor relation appointed to keep the keys and see that the guests want nothing." In the last act she returns to the girl we saw at first but with an added mischievous touch once young Marlow is firmly secured.

Constance Neville

The problem of the actress playing Constance is to keep her from seeming too mature for her years. She seems to be about the same age as Kate, but the impression we get from her behavior, in spite of her determination to elope with Hastings, is that of a soberer and more sensible girl. Part of this is because she has few lines that could be considered humorous or whimsical. Perhaps if the actress were to look for lines and business such as that in her two scenes with Tony, in which she could express the delight she takes in deceiving Mrs. Hardcastle, this might lighten her role and help to give it a greater variety.

Mrs. Hardcastle

The part of Mrs. Hardcastle provides for plenty of laughs but no sympathy. If no attempt is made to develop sympathy the only alternative is to play her with such vigor that no one will be allowed to reflect on the fact that she is the butt of everyone's deception and that no one seems to care a fig for her feelings. This is the way most performers play her. It might however be worth the effort to experiment a little to see what might be done to make her more human; it would certainly do the play no harm.

Young Marlow

This is the most difficult part in the play. All his best lines and stage business come in the first half of the play. As he grows more serious in his pursuit of Kate the center of interest shifts to her, the scenes between them become her scenes, and he ends up playing straight man to her.

Marlow's phenomenal shyness in the presence of ladies and his boldness with servant girls must be made plausible. The most successful Marlows in this respect have been those who looked and acted more like boys than men: youthful, boisterous, boastful, easily deceived, and easily frustrated. Immaturity makes both bashfulness and boastfulness excusable. It seems likely that Marlow's account of his merry evenings at the Ladies' Club are intended to be taken by us with a grain of salt. His habit of addressing Kate in her barmaid role as "child" is all the more amusing if he is obviously not much older or more experienced than she.

Hastings

Hastings is often played as the more sophisticated of the two young men. This may be because of the more mature attitude he assumes in regard to Marlow's pursuit of the "barmaid." He generally plays better, however, if he is represented as somewhat juvenile in his outlook and especially in his romantic intention toward Constance Neville, traveling all the way into the countryside to steal her away from her guardian and carry her off to France. If the actor playing Hastings keeps his Romeo-like behavior uppermost and lets it show through his relations with the other characters whose actions are material to his success the role shapes up very nicely.

Tony Lumpkin

Tony Lumpkin needs to be able to sing. There is no point in attempting the song of "The Three Jolly Pigeons" unless it pleases the ear. There are directors now and then who seem to think that a song badly sung is funny, but few of the audience are likely to appreciate such a rendition.

As a comedian Tony's success seems to lie in his ability to convey the sheer joy he takes in mischief, his exaggerated self-esteem and his complete indifference to the anguish which he inflicts, first on Constance Neville and her lover and afterward on his mother. There is nothing subtle or complicated about Tony. He is not an imaginative creature like Bob Acres, sensitive to every nuance, and susceptible to every suggestion. Tony is a simple physical type, of inexhaustible energy, not very perceptive about anything but cock-fighting and horse-racing, but not stupid either. Cunning he is, in a rather primitive way, and that is about all.

Old Hardcastle

In spite of the fact that he is on stage more than anyone else and functions as pivot to most of the plot, the part of Hardcastle seems not to require an actor of very highly developed skill or great experience. I have seen him played by some of the least accomplished members of certain repertory companies without in any way impairing the production. On the other hand, some of the best actors, while very good in the part, were not much more effective than the least experienced ones. The quality of Hardcastle's character is such that he is more likely to be played by one of the older members who specializes in eccentrics and elderly men.

Sir Charles Marlow

Sir Charles does not appear until the fourth act and does not make his presence felt until the finale. His function is that of the *deus ex machina* whose appearance brings everything into balance and marks the end of the progression, and as is usually the case with this role, an actor of commanding presence and consummate skill is called for. So before all the roles have been assigned one of the strongest actors must be cast for this part.

In some productions Sir Charles is made to seem rather elegant and urbane in contrast to the Hardcastles. This is a mistake. The scenes in which the old men appear together always go better when they are represented as two of a kind, equally warm-hearted, equally old-fashioned, and equally forgiving.

Minor Characters

Of the servants and alehouse denizens, two points are worth mentioning. First, as to Kate's maid, who appears only twice, once to advise her on the barmaid impersonation and later to help Constance into her traveling garb. This maid plays best as a woman more mature than Kate, experienced enough to give advice on the manner of a barmaid, and sympathetic enough to show some reluctance at having to dress and hurry Constance for her unwanted separation from Hastings. Two pretty young ladies are enough; we want no young maid competing with them for audience interest.

The other point has to do with the balance between the comical servants' scenes early in the play and their later function as servants. The awkward-squad scene is delightful but coming so early in the play it creates difficulties further on because once we have seen these servants as clowns we expect them to do something funny whenever we see them again, but in all their later scenes they function not as clowns but as ordinary fetch-and-carry footmen. One can invent business for their later appearances but such business is out of place and distracts from the significant action at hand. Still, it seems unlikely that Hardcastle would have to recruit stable hands to wait table if he already had footmen. Careful directing can bring these requirements into harmony, but the treatment of the servants is a problem which has tripped more than one unwary director.

NOTES ON STAGING

(Act I-scene ii): A really well-sung song here will do wonders toward getting the play off to a good start.

(Act II): The scene with the servants is often grossly over-businessed. Overdoing it encourages the audience to expect comparable behavior whenever any of these servants appears again, only to be disappointed.

The meeting between Marlow and Kate is one of the most difficult; the performers will have to do a lot of extra work on this and they must support and aid one another.

(Act III): In contrast to the above, the scene between Marlow and Kate when he first sees her as barmaid is delightful and always goes well. Sometimes he picks her up and starts out only to come face to face with Old Hardcastle.

(Act V): With the improbability of Mrs. Hardcastle's mistaking her husband for a highwayman, I am always surprised when the scene "at the bottom of the garden" goes off well. It must be kept quite brightly lighted if the audience is to enjoy the mistake. Perhaps by using a dark background and rather contrasty lighting an adequate effect of night can be achieved.

The final scene between Kate and Marlow is most delightful when Kate makes sure that we know that she enjoys having the upper hand with no uncertainties as to the outcome of her ruse.

Both epilogues are too long, but by cutting each down to about ten lines they make a neat pair and provide an unusual conclusion to the performance.

CHAPTER 18

The Rivals: A Problem of Style

Actors love this play. It has enjoyed more all-star revivals than any other work in English. Reasons for this are not hard to find. It contains more good acting parts than almost any comedy one can name, and while all, from principals to walk-ons, are brilliantly realized, three of them, Bob Acres, Mrs. Malaprop, and Sir Lucius O'Trigger, have seldom been equalled. The others, while recognizable as stock figures, surpass their prototypes at every point.

Supporting these characters is the author's extraordinary facility with language. His people, regardless of station in life, are endowed with remarkably expressive vocabularies and remarkably graceful syntax. The most eloquent of course is Mrs. Malaprop, whose pride in her "parts of speech" carries her quite overboard. Not far behind comes Bob Acres with his unique oaths and Captain Jack Absolute with his courtly address, "the very pineapple of politeness," according to Mrs. Malaprop. On the printed page the language seems rather prolix, but it "speaks well" and lends itself well to the acting style which the play requires, a style characterized by elegance and decorum in speech, manners, and dress; a genuine elegance in most of the characters, an affectation only with Mrs. Malaprop and the valet, Fag.

Students take readily to *The Rivals* because Sheridan's point of view is definitely that of a very young man (he was only twenty-three when he wrote the play). He views the parental generation and the conventions of adult society with the sceptical eye of youth. Older people strike him as somewhat absurd, as do their customs. But no less absurd are the affectations of those five or six years younger than he: Lydia, Julia, and Faulkland. Beyond that the whole of the small world in which he lives is full of amusing incongruities, not quite serious enough for satire but just right for facetious representation.

The general characteristics of eighteenth-century English comedy are superlatively well served in this play. When fully understood and properly employed in performance they go far toward giving the play its true sparkle. Chief among these is the presentational mode that permits a character to share his thoughts and feelings with the audience. For modern actors the direct-address convention is difficult to manage with the smoothness and lightness of touch which the form demands. Those who emphasize the artifice only succeed in making the asides and soliloquies seem rather quaint, and after the fourth or fifth aside, rather tiresome. Others, who deliver the aside as a "throw-away," while they may make it appear more natural, often lose that clarity which gives to direct address its particular power. Theatres in the eighteenth century had stages with huge aprons which made it possible for an actor to play quite close to his audience so that he could deliver an aside as a thought shared with his hearers. It was not difficult for him to achieve confidentiality but it did require considerable skill and practice on his part to achieve the effect of intimacy *with the whole audience*. To seem confidential and yet reach everyone in the auditorium, this was the mark of his artistry.

OVERBURDENED DONNÉE, THIN SPOTS, LOOSE THREADS, AND WHO CARES?

The mistaken-identity plot here is ingenious but it seems subservient to the characterization, as if it were built around the situations and the characters' eccentricities rather than being developed as a continuum. In this play we do not have a steadily evolving cause-and-effect progression as we have in *She Stoops*, nor a mounting sequence of misunderstandings and deceptions as in *Scapin*. What we have instead are characters of extreme individuality involved in a series of contretemps that exploit their peculiarities. Not all the scenes give us the feeling that the play is moving forward; some in fact—the Faulkland-Julia scenes, for example—go nowhere.

With four plot lines the canvas is so crowded that the author omits several of what would ordinarily be regarded as obligatory scenes. We see nothing of Mrs. Malaprop's flirtation with Sir Lucius but only hear of it. Acres is a suitor of Lydia's but although he comes a long way to see her they never appear together until the finale and then only because they both happen to be on stage at the same time. We are never shown how Acres learned of his rival or are told whether the discovery prompted his journey to Bath. Jack Absolute proposes elopement to Lydia, Lydia agrees and Mrs. Malaprop encourages them but the plan once broached is never heard of again.

In composing the play Sheridan borrowed freely from his predecessors, using tried and true stage types, situations, and structural devices, and he used them brilliantly, weaving them together into a creation which excelled all its models. The problems that plague producers today arise from the imperfections of the fabric: overburdened donnée, neglected plot links, unresolved conflicts, and omitted obligatory scenes. These faults often combine to make the play in performance seldom as good as we feel it ought to be in spite of the fact that it always attracts good audiences and strongly appeals to actors. The actors, having played in it once, will want to do it again in order to do it better, and the audience, having seen how good some parts can be, will turn out for subsequent productions in the hope of seeing one in which all of the parts are as good as those they liked at first. The thin spots and loose threads in the fabric are only partially masked by the play's distinctive virtues. They can however be mitigated by skillful cutting, reinforcement through stage business, and artful pointing. If the remedial work is well done the performance can be greatly s!rengthened, creating a more satisfying total effect than could ever have been achieved with the unretouched original.

The Rivals is fun to rehearse. Its problems of style and delivery challenge the best efforts of actors who tackle them with considerable zest. Rehearsals are seldom fatiguing and tend to get livelier as they go on so that the players are often reluctant to stop when they should. Scheduling of rehearsals is easy because three-fourths of the scenes involve only two characters. This means that much time can be devoted to developing interplay, always enjoyable for the performers. Of the thirty-six French scenes that make up the play, twenty-seven are two-character scenes, four are three-character, four are for four-characters, and only one, the finale, requires the entire cast all at one time.

In performance the play holds its shape very well, with noticeable gains in finesse as the number of performances increases. Curiously, there is little inclination on the actors' part toward that progressive broadening which generally plagues comedies with very long runs. On the other hand, while style, pointing, and tempo hold up quite well, there is often a distinct slippage in stage business, which tends to become imprecise and to vary from night to night so that extra rehearsals are necessary at regular intervals to keep the business neat and on track.

CHARACTERS AND CASTING

The Rivals had its first production in the same theatre as She Stoops to Conquer (the Covent Garden) by a company which included many of the same actors. Edward Shuter, who had played Mr. Hardcastle, took the part of Sir Anthony Absolute. John Quick, who had been Tony Lumpkin, became Bob Acres. Mrs. Green had done Mrs. Hardcastle; now she appeared as Mrs. Malaprop. All of them had better parts in The Rivals except poor Mrs. Bulkley who, having scored as Kate Hardcastle, had to be content with the far less rewarding role of Julia and a part of the epilogue.

It would be a mistake to assume that because certain parts in different plays were taken by the same actors that the resulting characters would have resembled each other. An actor taking a part similar to one in an earlier work is less likely to repeat himself than to seek ways to differentiate the two characters. Individual members of an acting company may suffer limitations in the range of parts they can play because of such factors as stature, age, or vocal traits, but the better the actor is the more versatile he is and the greater the number of different characters he can make convincing without repeating himself. There is no reason to believe that this was any less true of actors in the eighteenth century than it is of actors today.

The characters of Acres, Malaprop, and Sir Lucius spring from established stage types, but they go far beyond the type in each instance so that in even a moderately well done production they impress us, not as stage types, but as highly original creations. Sheridan's use of type characters may make the casting easier for a modern producer but it is most likely to be successful in production if the type functions as the jumping-off place for the creation of a unique character. The young lovers—Jack, Lydia, Julia, and Faulkland—can be cast for their looks and general skill, but Mrs. Malaprop, Sir Lucius, and Bob Acres are going to have to be cast for their talent in comedy regardless of any other consideration.

Jack Absolute

Jack has the longest part in the play and the most complex. The quality that especially endears him to us is the mischievous delight he takes in aggravating the fears, disappointments, and chagrin of his father, Mrs. Malaprop, and Lydia. He is often puzzled by the turn of events and frequently forced to pretend to beliefs and feelings which he could not possibly possess. He is extremely articulate whether he is courting Lydia or flattering Mrs. Malaprop and he finds himself at a loss for words only in the presence of his father, and then only momentarily. He is always well mannered and never ill humored. So what does all this add up to? A character, apparently, so varied that little effort will be needed to keep him interesting from first to last, but one which, because of the many transitions he has to negotiate, is going to demand an actor of exceptionally good diction and sense of timing. His transitions are often so abrupt that unless the bridging and linkage is expertly managed his behavior may confuse an audience. In addition to this we are going to have to have an actor who is genuinely handsome, graceful in movement, and confident in bearing.

Sir Anthony Absolute

Sir Anthony is the choleric tyrannical parent, quick to anger and equally quick to laughter, accustomed to having his own way in everything. We tend to think of him as a man in his middle fifties with a portly figure and lordly bearing. Although he changes his moods he seems not to change much from the habitual wooden-headedness with which he confronts every situation, which indicates a problem in preserving him from monotony. He is certain to be interesting in his first few scenes, but how can we make him equally interesting in the last few? Perhaps some of the cues which Sheridan has provided, that Sir Anthony has an affable side, that he is not stingy, and that he feels genuine affection for Jack, can be exemplified to give him greater variety and warmth than one's initial reading of the part might at first suggest. He repeatedly warns Jack not to put him into a temper, creating an anticipation which is never fulfilled.

Mrs. Malaprop

Mrs. Malaprop's part is made difficult for her by the fact that most of her best lines and good scenes come early in the play, and while she has many good lines further on, an expectation is created at the outset which most actresses find hard to sustain. No actress ever fails in this part if she is able to make herself heard and her lines understood—the lines themselves provide most of the comic effect—but every once in a while an actress comes along who is able to give to the role an unforgettable vitality. Part of this seems to be in the aplomb with which she expresses herself and the unshakeable self-confidence with which she performs every action. This was true of the great Malaprops of the past. For the modern actress the heart of the role may be found in the finale when she coyly reveals her identity as "Delia" only to be brushed off by Sir Lucius and afterward consoled by Sir Anthony. Once she has solved the problem of how to play Mrs. Malaprop's disappointment without introducing an inappropriate pathos the other scenes in the play should be easier to manage; then the first impression can be brought into harmony with the rest of the role.

As to appearance, an actress of mature figure (as shapeless as possible) has a great advantage. A homely actress shows up better in the part than one who has to be made up to look homely. A small or dainty actress is at a great disadvantage here.

Bob Acres

The quality that distinguishes Acres, makes him delightful every minute he is before the audience, and sets him off as superior to all similar characters before or since, is his extremely kinetic imagination. Hand in hand with this goes his extraordinarily swift response to suggestion. Unlike most of his prototypes he has nothing mischievous about him, nothing small, and nothing petty. He is all cherubic good will with eager, puppy-like good humor, and he is as gullible as they come anywhere, city or country.

His determination to shine in society is of course quite plainly at odds with his country-bred nature, but he gives us no reason to fear that he will succeed in the attempt or become the man-about-town he admires. His eagerness to oblige Sir Lucius, whom he regards as his model of gentlemanly behavior, betrays him into affecting a bravado which he does not feel. The humor subsequently develops from the contrast between his increasing misgivings and the front with which he tries to conceal them.

Many an actor has given the finest performance of his career as Bob Acres and few if any have failed. The role is so rich in color and variety that it is almost impossible to mar it. And yet, though the part always comes alive in performance it is seldom as hilariously funny as one feels it ought to be. There is so much going on that Acres' predicament seems to unfold too fast to be fully appreciated. Only a very great actor can make the role register in detail as completely as one hopes for.

Sir Lucius O'Trigger

"Poor little dear Sir Lucius," as Mrs. Malaprop calls him, is a spirited fortune hunter whose immediate purpose in life is to marry an heiress, preferably a young and pretty one. His assets are his looks, his gift of blarney, his breezy manner, and his modest title. In the version of the play that has come down to us his being Irish is incidental so he needs no more than a hint of brogue in his speech, just enough to flavor his diction. Actors sometimes make the mistake of making him so Irish that we have difficulty understanding his lines.

The part was rewritten by Sheridan after first-night audiences objected to the crudity of the character, and John Lee, the original Sir Lucius, was replaced by Laurence Clinch, a more seasoned performer. We can only guess as to what made him seem crude but it was probably a thick brogue plus a conventionally broad representation of the "comic Irishman" stereotype. The revised character seems to have emerged as debonair instead of pugnacious, always in control of the situation and never the least discommoded or raffled or rude no matter what surprises confront him.

Lydia Languish

Lydia's surname is misleading. There is nothing languid about her. At first reading she seems like a peevish spoiled teenager, determined only to frustrate the expectations of her elders. But on seeing a really good actress in the part one discovers that there is much more to the character. For there are two Lydias, one who lives in the world of ten-penny romances, trying to recreate the tribulations of their heroines in her own well-ordered existence, and the other a seventeen-year-old who encounters real disappointments and surprises. The contrast between Lydia's real self and her romanticized mirror image is the source of the humor. This contrast is exceedingly difficult to maintain. If the audience responds well the actress may be inclined to overplay the artificial aspect of the character. If on the other hand the audience response is slow the actress is tempted to broaden her portrayal in order to reach her listeners. Either course tends to make her representation of the real Lydia disappear into something like parody with the result that the delightful contrast is lost. Any tyro can portray the artificial aspect; it takes a real artist to show the genuine Lydia underneath and then keep the two Lydias distinct and in balance.

Julia Melville

What is true of Lydia is equally true of Julia, for both girls' actions are influenced by the same notions of adult behavior gleaned from their lending-library reading. In performance Julia is often presented quite differently from Lydia so that she tends to lose affectation and to seem more genuine, more sincere, and, unfortunately, more mature. If this is allowed to happen poor Julia becomes a mere foil for the carryings-on of both Lydia and Faulkland; it makes her seem more sensible than they. Now, sensibility is an admirable trait for a character in a novel but it is not very interesting on the stage, especially in comedy. The problem with Julia therefore is exactly the opposite of that with Lydia: it is to make her seem on occasion more affected and more superficial than she might otherwise appear.

Faulkland

Faulkland's mercurial nature is the principal source of our amusement with him. The intensity of his feelings betrays him repeatedly, carrying him far beyond his objectives. The secret of making his role work as it should is to cast an actor of seemingly open, sincere, uncomplicated nature. Mere hair-tearing theatrics will not do it. He must be the kind of person we can believe in, sympathize with, and agree with up to the moment that the absurdity of his behavior becomes evident. He is always plausible in the beginning. His absurdity lies in the extremes to which he carries himself.

Lucy

Lucy is conspicuous in only two scenes. Thereafter when she appears it is only as a walk-on. Here is the role of the familiar intriguing servant who acts as go-between for lovers, all the while benefitting herself and her purse with the gratuities gained from her mistress' suitors. It is a typical soubrette part that gains most when cast with a pert, saucy, and preferably smaller than average actress. She does not have to be pretty; in fact it is better if she is not as attractive as either her mistress or Julia.

David and Fag

It is common in old comedy to have a pair of servants, one of whom is clever and the other dull-witted, and to develop various comic effects from the contrast between them. In this case the clever one is Jack's valet or batman, Fag, and the dull one is Bob Acres' manservant, David. Fag is usually presented as an overdressed, overmannered, imitation gentleman, and David as an amiable countrified lout. David has the more difficult of the two parts because he is the one who must bring to Sir Anthony the horrible news of the intended duel and thus initiate the chicken-little chase which carries the entire cast to the duelling ground for the finale.

SETTINGS AND SCENE CHANGES

In visualizing The Rivals one will come closest to the spirit of the original if one thinks of it as an exercise in high fashion. The late eighteenth century was a time when living accommodations of the upper classes were handsomer than they have ever been since. The clean lines of the classical revival in architecture plus the delicate colors and exquisite proportions of the interiors created by the brothers Adam set off their occupants to the best possible advantage. No doubt this is why whenever *The Rivals* is produced it is usually shown in the settings of its own time, or else in those of only a few years later, but seldom in the trappings of any other time or place.

The play requires thirteen or fourteen changes of scene employing nine different sets. Four of these are exteriors, the remainder are interiors. It is possible that the exterior scenes of the original production showed places in Bath readily recognized by most of the audience, as are certain locales in the same city today known to every tourist. The interiors need very little in the way of functional furniture and can therefore be designed with an eye primarily to pictorial effect and setting off the performers to advantage.

The one indispensable requirement of the setting is that it provide for continuous progression without dimouts, curtain waits, or pauses to shift furniture. As in Elizabethan drama, the exit of one group of characters coincident with the entrance of another group tells us that we have moved to a different locale. But in the eighteenth century the change, while taking no more time than before, is much more complete visually because it involves a complete change of scenery. The successive display of a large number of attractive picture-settings is an important part of the show. As far as action is concerned, *The Rivals* could just as easily be presented on a bare platform, or in a unit set, or in drapes, but such a presentation, unless carefully planned with an eye to style, yields only an impoverished version of a work intended to be handsomely visualized.

By 1775 scene painting, which had come into being during the Renaissance, had reached the pinnacle of its development in a form which encouraged almost unlimited pictorial effects. The mechanical device that made this possible was an ingenious system of flat, painted, canvas-covered frames which could be slid in from opposite sides of the stage to meet in the center and form a complete picture behind the performers. A dozen or more paired sets of frames could be used in a single performance, yielding as many different locales. The changes could be effected by as few as two stage hands, one on each side, and took no more than a moment while the action on the stage continued without interruption. Today only a few of these eighteenth-century theatres remain with their scenery and scene-shifting devices, but these few are enough to show how easily and smoothly the system operated.

Pictorially, many of the painted scenes from this period are undeniably handsome. The art of perspective was highly developed, and on the flat surface all sorts of vistas, ornamentation, and even sculpture, were painted with such cunning as to completely deceive the observer. Among the remaining examples are many instances where one cannot tell, from fifteen or twenty feet away, whether the elements of the setting are three-demensional or simulated in paint. And this is true even when the settings are studied under modern illumination. In 1775 stages were lighted by candles and oil lamps whose soft shadowless illumination must have greatly enhanced the illusions which the painter contrived.

COSTUMING

Because the play itself is light, it always looks best in light colored costumes, with no black anywhere and deeper shades replaced by tints of the same hues. As to periods, sometimes the characters are dressed in the costumes of 1775, when the play was written, and sometimes in the fashions of later years up to about 1815. Within the forty-year space between these two dates are some of the most attractive styles of dress ever developed. The lines of the garments are simple and direct without features which distort the human figure or falsify the silhouette. The waistlines of both men and women are rather high, making both sexes appear taller and slenderer. Toward the end of the period the women's styles are particularly attractive, with high waists, soft materials, and flowing, floor-length skirts.

Jack Absolute

Jack needs two costumes. When we first see him in his lodgings he might be expected to be dressed informally, more so than when he goes calling in the next act. At home in the morning he could be wearing a dressing gown over his shirt or he might be in one of those sleeved waistcoats favored by gentlemen for at-home attire. In some productions a good deal of stage business is introduced, while Jack converses with Faulkland, by having his servant bring in his street clothes garment by garment and prepare him for going out. This business has the drawback of taking the attention away from the exposition at the same time it calls attention to the mechanics of eighteenth-century clothing. If this were a realistic play the details of gentleman's dress might have some value; but it is not, and such extraneous business only distracts attention from more important considerations.

It is an open question whether Jack's second costume, which he wears throughout the rest of the play, should be his uniform as a captain of infantry or the civilian dress of a fashionable gentleman. Officers of the British army in that time seldom wore uniforms except on parade, so it is possible that he might be in mufti. Even in mufti, however, an officer would be recognizable as such by the cut and color of his attire and the accessories he favored, just as British officers are today, identifiable by the kinds of hats, ties and shoes they wear and the kind of umbrellas they carry. In act III–scene iii, when Lydia sees Jack when his back is toward her she exclaims, "There stands the hated rival—an officer, too;—but oh, how unlike my Beverley!" If he were in uniform it would be difficult to mistake him for an ensign, but in mufti the difference in rank would not be apparent.

In act IV-scene ii Lydia wonders why Mrs. Malaprop does not recognize

"Beverley" when Jack is brought in by his father. "Perhaps the regimentals are alike," she says. This it seems would indicate that the original Jack was in uniform. From the early eighteenth century onward uniforms had facings on collars, cuffs, and lapels, which were distinctively colored according to regiment.

The principal reason for considering putting Jack into civilian clothes rather than his uniform is that the scarlet coat of the British officer has such high attention-attracting powers that it makes consistent control of audience attention quite difficult. In order to keep the play moving one must be able, by various devices of grouping and movement, to fix the spectators' attention on significant action and speech. This is hard to do when one character, who may not always be the center of interest, is wearing bright red. Some designers have used the uniform but lightened the color of the coat to a sort of dusty pink. Others have put him in the green of the Rifle Regiment. None of these expedients allows as much control as is possible when he wears mufti.

In act V-scene ii, on his way to the duelling ground, Jack dons a greatcoat to hide the sword he is carrying. By 1775 the fashion of wearing swords, except at court ceremonies, had long since passed, and as he says, "A sword seen in the streets of Bath would raise as great an alarm as a mad dog," so Jack has to carry his weapon under his coat. The coat is discarded as soon as he reaches the King's Mead Fields where his opponent is waiting.

Lydia and Julia

Each of the young ladies needs two costumes, one for the morning, and one for the rest of the day. The morning gown in both instances is the simpler. When they leave their rooms to go to the King's Mead Fields they might be expected to throw something over their shoulders. Hats are never needed and should be avoided in any case because they obscure the features and interfere with the lighting.

By 1775 young women in England no longer wore wigs or powdered their hair except for state occasions, so the coiffures of both girls should appear simple and natural. White wigs are flattering in movies and televison because in the closeups they set off a fresh complexion rather nicely, but on stage the same white wigs make young women look like grandmothers and so should be avoided where possible.

If the play is costumed in a period later than that in which it was written, the high waisted Empire gowns are very attractive. The originals were often of very thin fabrics and it is possible to attain a similar effect by putting the girls into body stockings under the gauzy costumes. Then when one of them passes in front of a bright background the fleeting silhouette is guaranteed to make the dullest audience sit up and take notice. For the effect to work as it should it is essential that both Lydia and Julia be equally shapely, for if one has a better figure the contrast is not only unaesthetic but certain to cause unhappiness in the company.

Sir Anthony

The parental generation in a comedy always seems older because of the way it is contrasted with youth. In costuming Sir Anthony the question of the costumer is not so much what age as how old-fashioned he should appear to be. Neither his language nor his general behavior seems especially countrified. Nothing about him suggest a country squire of the Hardcastle type. The treatment given his costume therefore would seem most appropriate if there was nothing about it to indicate his age or background. He is certainly not a dandy in the way that Sir Lucius is, but he is a man of property to whom London and Bath are places in which he can feel right at home.

Mrs. Malaprop

This aunt-guardian of Lydia seems to belong to the same generation as Sir Anthony. Being widowed and apparently quite well off she is actively seeking another husband. At the moment it is Sir Lucius who has caught her fancy and she has been exchanging notes with him under an assumed name. Because of this we get the impression that she is trying to appear younger than she is and we might expect her to favor inappropriately youthful attire. Jack, in one of his letters to Lydia, describes her as an "old weather-beaten she-dragon," and refers to the "ridiculous vanity which makes her dress up her coarse features." This need not be taken literally, as Jack is making fun of her, but it does suggest the direction her costume should take.

It is really difficult to make an actress appear overly made up without approaching the grotesque, and grotesquery is out of place here. Beyond fifty feet we can scarcely make out facial expression; any makeup that would be bold enough to be visible at such a distance would have to be as broad as that of a clown. It might be better therefore to concentrate on Mrs. Malaprop's figure and hairdo, giving her girlish curls and a color of hair that could suggest it to be dyed, along with a figure padded out to be rather plump and shapeless. As to color of costume, there are few today which are regarded as inappropriate for mature women, but one might be able to find some patterned stuffs in which a full-figured woman would be poorly served. Excessive ornament in the form of bracelets and bangles which glitter and ring at every gesture might help. Accessories such as lorgnette, fan, and parasol, might also be tried.

Sir Lucius O'Trigger

The character of Sir Lucius is so vividly drawn that one might expect his costume to be equally vivid, but this is seldom the case. Costumers never seem to know quite what to do with him. Most of the time he turns up in a green coat (because he is Irish, no doubt) and sometimes he also has red hair, for since Sir Lucius has a volatile nature the red hair seems natural.

The rest of his costume should describe the debonair gentleman who is very much the adventurer, with fanciful touches to reveal the devil-may-care disposition of the man. Such men often put their last pennies on their backs. They may be stony broke or deeply in debt but their dress never shows it. Sir Lucius should appear to be dressed in the height of fashion, with clothes of the smartest cut and finest materials. If it is possible to identify him by means of his costume as the swaggering good-humored, fine-mannered gentleman adventurer, his role is certain to gain by it.

Faulkland

Faulkland is often done up as a dandy, but this has never made his difficult role any easier to play. That he is self-centered and inordinately conscious of his own emotional temperature is certainly evident, but nothing about him hints at any affectation in dress. Some costumers, noting this, have gone overboard in another direction and dressed him in black, like a preacher. But this has the disadvantage of introducing black into an ensemble where it is likely to play hob with the color scheme. The logical treatment for Faulkland, it would seem, lies somewhere between these two extremes. That his dress should be elegant and fashionable seems evident, but there is no reason for it to be striking in any way, and since his scenes are long and fairly difficult to play it would seem sensible not to burden him with any eccentricities of dress or manner which would distract from the subtleties of his presentation.

Lucy

A serving-maid's livery with smartly cut bodice, lace apron, and ankle-length skirt, topped off with a saucy mob cap, will do very nicely for Lucy and also for the other maid. Lucy's apron must have two pockets, one for her account book and one for the tips she collects in the course of her function as go-between for the various lovers.

Fag and David

Jack's manservant, Fag, imitates the dress and manner of the dandies he has seen in Bath. This creates a problem for the costumer who must accommodate this affectation without obscuring his servant's livery. Since Jack is an infantry captain, Fag must be his batman. To put him in uniform however would be undesirable for it would confront us with the same problem as that of Jack's. What Fag needs apparently is some rather elegant outfit which one can recognize both as livery and also as an imitation of the clothing worn by his peers. Who does Fag imitate? Sir Lucius? Faulkland? Jack? There would be no point in his imitating someone we never see. I vote for Sir Lucius.

David, Bob Acres' manservant, is usually contrasted with Fag, carrying out the classical pairing of servants, one clever and one stupid, and his costume should reflect this. David is costumed to appear countrified, in dull fabrics and loosely fitted coat and breeches with rather substantial clodhoppers instead of the neat buckled pumps worn by the city folk.

NOTES ON STAGING

(Prologue): The first prologue, by Jack Absolute, goes best if the dialogue is omitted, so that it begins with, "I know 'tis hard to deal," omits reference to the Drury Lane Theatre, then continues to the end. The second, by Julia, is intended to follow. About the first six lines of this are all that can be made intelligible to a modern audience.

(Act I–scene i): As a means of setting the tone of the play some productions begin with a street scene in which all of the principals are seen briefly, each in some characteristic activity.

(Act II–scene ii): If there are two intermissions the first usually follows this scene with the set remaining in place. The second intermission then comes after act III–scene iv.

(Act III–scene ii): The effectiveness of this scene is determined by the interplay between Julia and Faulkland and the degree to which they can contrast their suddenly changing moods.

(Act III–scene iii): Careful cutting might eliminate the elopement plan which always confuses an audience since no one ever mentions it again. The last part of the scene, the three-sided exchange between Jack, Lydia, and Mrs. Malaprop, is extremely difficult and needs extra rehearsal.

(Act III–scene iv–a): Make sure that Acres knows the actual steps of the dances he mentions; the real ones are genuinely funny and it is more amusing if he does them well rather than stumbling through them.

(Act IV–scene iii): The more elegantly polite the exchange the funnier the scene becomes. Most productions skip from the line just before Faulkland's servant's entrance to the closing lines of Faulkland's soliloquy.

(Act V–scene i): From Mrs. Malaprop's entrance onward this scene is difficult because of the excitement and fragmented dialogue, both of which make control of attention hard to achieve. Most directors use a good deal of flighty movement and this works well as long as each character in turn is enabled to speak from the downstage side of the furor and close to the audience.

(Act V–scene iii): Certainly one of the funniest scenes ever written. It works best when Acres takes his time and develops his reactions fully. The finale, like that of all plot comedies, poses many problems, not the least of which is the achieving of a free continuous flow from one couple to the next without any obvious gimmicks such as manipulated lighting or the "freezing" of characters momentarily uninvolved.

(Epilogue): Not all the lines Sheridan wrote need to be spoken. If the first six lines are joined to the last twelve the result makes sense and provides a neat closing of moderate length.

APPENDIX A

Notable Productions of the Premodern Plays Discussed Here

The finest productions of premodern plays are generally those of the state theatres in the country of origin: the National Theatre of Great Britain, the Comédie Française, the Greek National Theatre, and the Teatro Español. It is to these we must go to see the plays at their best: in their original language, relatively uncut, presented by artists thoroughly familiar with the material and possessing the technical maturity requisite to interpretation of classics.

Below are notes on the plays that have been given detailed treatment in the preceding text. The number of American productions here is greater because information on these is more readily available to readers and also because data in English on foreign-language productions is inevitably spotty.

Many of these plays, like classics everywhere, have also appeared in numerous adaptations, such as *The Old Fox* (*Volpone*) and *Scapino* (*Les Fourberies de Scapin*). There are so many of these that space limitations prevent us from listing them here.

The plays are listed alphabetically with the most recent productions first.

THE ALCHEMIST (1610)

Young Vic Company, London; season of 1971–1972. Twenty-eight performances in repertory.

Stratford (Ontario) Festival Company; season of 1969. In repertory, on tour. Director: Jean Gascon.

Repertory Company of Lincoln Center, New York; season of 1965–1966. Fifty-three performances beginning October 13. Director: Jules Irving.

Gate Theatre, New York; 1964. Forty-six performances beginning September 14. Director: Stephen Porter.

ANTIGONE (c. 441 B.C.)

Classic Stage Company at the Abbey Theatre, New York; 1981. Fifty-seven performances beginning October 30. Director: Christopher Martin.

Repertory Theatre of Lincoln Center, New York; 1971. Forty-six performances beginning May 13. Director: John Hirsch.

Sheridan Square Playhouse, New York; 1967. Five performances beginning January 13. Director: Therese Haydon.

ELECTRA (Sophocles) (c. 418 B.C.)

Greek Tragedy Theatre (Piraikon), at City Center, New York; 1964. Sixteen performances beginning August 31, followed by a national tour. Director: Dimitri Rondiris. In Greek.

New York Shakespeare Festival, at the Delacorte Theatre, Central Park, New York; August, 1964. Twenty-two performances in repertory. Director: Gerald Freedman.

DOCTOR FAUSTUS (c. 1588–1592)

Lyric Studio, Hammersmith, at the Fortune Theatre, London; March through May, 1980. A studio production with minimal spectacle; eight men playing all parts. Beautifully spoken.

Oregon Shakespeare Festival, Ashland, Oregon; 1979. Thirty-two performances beginning June 6. Director: Jerry Turner.

Guthrie Theatre Company at the Tyrone Guthrie Theatre, Minneapolis; 1976. Twenty-four performances beginning June 16. Director: Ken Ruta.

Royal Shakespeare Company at the Aldwych Theatre, London, following performances at the Edinburgh Festival and Stratford-upon-Avon; 1974. Thirty-seven performances in repertory beginning September 5. Directed by John Barton.

LES FOURBERIES DE SCAPIN (1671)

Comédie-Française at the City Center, New York; 1961. Eight performances beginning February 21, with Robert Hirsch as Scapin and Michel Aumont as Géronte. In French.

Comédie-Française in London during the season of 1958–1959, with Robert Hirsch as Scapin and M. Sereys as Géronte. In French.

Lyric Studio, Hammersmith, London, during the season of 1958–1959. Directed by Casper Wrede.

FUENTE OVEJUNA (1611–1618)

Except for productions at Northwestern University in 1965 and the University of Texas in 1963, I can find no record of this play having been produced in English. It appears from time to time in the repertory of the Teatro Español in Madrid, most recently in 1962–1963, directed by Victor Maria Cortezo. Since then it has received one production in Madrid, in 1978, at the Martín, directed by Vicente Sáinz de la Peña.

THE RIVALS (1775)

American Conservatory Theatre at the Geary Theatre, San Francisco; 1981. Twenty-six performances beginning May 10. Directed by David Hammond and John C. Fletcher.

Stratford (Ontario) Festival Company, Stratford, Canada; the 1981 season. In repertory at the Avon Theatre. Directed by Brian Bedford.

Guthrie Theatre Company at the Tyrone Guthrie Theatre, Minneapolis; 1979. Forty performances in repertory beginning May 31. Directed by Alvin Epstein.

A company headed by Ralph Richardson and Margaret Rutherford, in London during the season of 1966–1967. Two hundred sixty-one performances.

National Repertory Theatre, on tour of the United States during the season of 1965–1966. In repertory. Directed by Eva LeGallienne.

SHE STOOPS TO CONQUER (1777)

Guthrie Theatre Company at the Tyrone Guthrie Theatre, Minneapolis; 1978. Fifty-three performances in repertory beginning June 6. Directed by Michael Langham.

Stratford (Ontario) Festival Company, Stratford, Canada; seasons of 1972 and 1973. In repertory at the Festival Theatre. Directed by Michael Bawtree.

National Repertory Theatre; 1964–1965. Forty-six performances in repertory on tour. Directed by Jack Sydow.

Association of Producing Artists at the Phoenix Theatre, New York; 1960–1961. Forty-seven performances beginning in November, 1960, and ending in June, 1961. Directed by Stuart Vaughan.

TARTUFFE (1664)

Stratford (Ontario) Festival Company at the Festival Theatre. Thirty-five performances in repertory beginning August 2, 1983. Directed by John Hirsch, with Brian Bedford as Tartuffe.

The Circle in the Square, New York; 1977. Eighty-eight performances beginning September 7. Directed by Stephen Porter, with John Wood as Tartuffe.

Stratford (Ontario) Festival Company at the Festival Theatre. In repertory during the season of 1968 and again in 1969. Directed by Jean Gascon, with William Hutt as Tartuffe.

The American Conservatory Theatre, San Francisco, has produced *Tartuffe* repeatedly since its first offering of the play in New York in 1965. Directed by William Ball.

THE TROJAN WOMEN (415 b.c.)

The Royal Shakespeare Company at the Aldwych, London; season of 1979–1980. In repertory. Directed by John Barton, with Eliza Ward as Hecuba.

National Repertory Theatre, on tour of the United States during the season of 1965–1966. Directed by Jack Sydow, with Eva Le Gallienne as Hecuba.

The Circle in the Square, New York; 1963. Six hundred performances beginning in December. Directed by Michael Cacoyannis with Mildred Dunnock, and afterward, Carolyn Coates, as Hecuba.

VOLPONE (1605–1606)

National Theatre of Great Britain, London; 1977. In repertory beginning in April. Directed by Peter Hall, with Paul Scofield as Volpone and John Gielgud as Sir Politic Would-be.

Guthrie Theatre Company at the Tyrone Guthrie Theatre, Minneapolis; 1964. In repertory during the season. Directed by Douglas Campbell, with Douglas Campbell as Volpone and George Grizzard as Mosca.

APPENDIX B

Additional Premodern Plays Suitable for Modern Production

All but five of these are plays I have seen produced successfully at least once. Two of the five, *The Duchess of Malfi* and *The White Devil*, while providing challenging opportunities for theatre workers have yet to be received favorably by any audience of which I was a member. The other four are plays I believe worthy of production and capable of success but which I have not as yet seen performed; each of these is identified in the commentary.

Abraham and Isaac Anonymous. (fourteenth- or fifteenth-century English). A short play, very moving when performed in a church with appropriate organ accompaniment.

El Alcalde de Zalamea (The Mayor of Zalamea). Pedro Calderón de la Barca (1642). A tightly plotted conflict with a cliff-hanging finale and an abundance of music and dance.

Alcestis. Euripides (438 B.C.). This has long been a favorite in schools because the plot is interesting and the acting parts are well distributed.

Amphitryon. Plautus (c. 186 B.C.). An amusing "twin" play often recomposed by later playwrights. In its original form delightful and not very difficult to do.

L'Avare (The Miser). Molière (1669). Often produced and always successful.

Bacchae. Euripides (405 B.C.). An absorbing plot with a number of brilliant choruses lending themselves well to music and choreography.

The Beaux' Stratagem. George Farquhar (1706). Disguise, mistaken identity, countryhouse wooings, and invading highwaymen. Always a delight.

The Beggar's Opera. John Gay (1728). Clever satire of public morals. Filled with good musical numbers from popular ballads of the time. Best when cast with really good singers.

Birds. Aristophanes (414 B.C.). Like most of Aristophanes' comedies, this is really a musical show. Zany principals, imaginative plot, and fantastic costumes.

Le Bourgeois gentilhomme (The Would-be Gentleman; The Burger as Gentry, etc.). Molière (1670). In spite of its very seventeenth-century subject, this always goes well, whether because of the musical finale or the gallery of characters.

The Changeling. Thomas Middleton and William Rowley (c. 1632). Contrasting double plots of tragedy and comedy. A difficult play but one that has attracted actors for generations.

The Clandestine Marriage. George Colman and David Garrick (1766). A delightful, lively comedy with a wealth of good acting parts.

The Contrast. Royall Tyler (1787). An early American work contrasting honest citizens with affected fops and dull country louts. Many good roles.

The Country Wife. William Wycherley (c. 1674). Some of the best comic scenes ever composed.

The Duchess of Malfi. John Webster (c. 1612–1614). In spite of its poor track record the fascination that this play exerts for actors and directors brings it often to the stage.

L'Ecole des Femmes (The School for Wives). Molière (1662). Indestructible comedy about the old man with a young wife.

L'Ecole des Maris (The School for Husbands). Molière (1661). Somewhat more difficult than its counterpart, but with more music and dance and capable of delightful entertainment.

Epicoene, or the Silent Woman. Ben Jonson (1609). Part satire, part farce, and always successful, according to reports, for this is one comedy I have yet to see.

Erasmus Montanus. Ludvig Holberg (c. 1722). Affectations of the intelligentsia exposed in an earthy comedy-satire.

Everyman. Anonymous (fifteenth century). More dramatic in performance than a reading of the text could begin to suggest. Man's inevitable meeting with Death holds all audiences. Plays best in a church.

Frogs. Aristophanes (405 B.C.). An old favorite from the days when Greek and Latin were taught in schools. One of the easiest of Aristophanes' plays to produce.

Ion. Euripides (fifth century B.C., date uncertain). More of a melodramatic romance than a tragedy, its deft plot and vivid characters seldom fail to move audiences.

Iphigenia at Aulis. Euripides (c. 405 B.C.). Audiences are always moved by the plight of the young girl who goes to her death a victim of her father's weakness.

Jeppa paa bjerget (Jeppe of the Hill; Hillbilly Jeppe). Ludvig Holberg (1722). A drunken peasant is made to believe that he is really a lord. Full of good roles and hilarious action.

The Knight of the Burning Pestle. Frances Beaumont and John Fletcher (c. 1607–1610). Triple-plotted romp loaded with music, dance, and good parts for all.

La Locandiera (The Mistress of the Inn; The Landlady). Carlo Goldoni (1753). Light comedy with a stellar role for a versatile actress.

Lysistrata. Aristophanes (411 B.C.). Ribald musical show. Best with men taking the women's parts, as originally intended.

Mandragola. Niccolò Machiavelli (c. 1513–1520). Clever plot and sharply drawn comic characters.

Mary Stuart. Friedrich Schiller (1800). High romantic tragedy with splendid roles for two women.

Le Médecin malgré lui (The Doctor in Spite of Himself). Molière (1666). Farce with a touch of satire. Invariably delightful. Also good as a children's play.

Menaechmi (The Twins). Plautus (Date uncertain; late third century). Not as funny as its English mate, *The Comedy of Errors,* but infinitely easier to produce, and, with the original lyrics and good musical accompaniment, an entertaining piece.

A New Way to Pay Old Debts. Philip Massinger (1621–1625). For generations this has provided brilliant opportunities for actors. It requires mature skillful performers.

Oedipus Coloneus. Sophocles (401 B.C.). Many consider this Sophocles' finest work. Especially appealing to elderly audiences, probably because the author composed it in his ninetieth year, when he was beginning to feel the effects of age.

Oedipus Tyrannus. Sophocles (c. 403 B.C.). Being well known, this work always attracts good audiences, but it seldom receives favorable reviews. The qualities which give the play its peculiar power in Greek are seldom attained in English translation.

Old Fortunatus. Thomas Dekker (1599). Fantasy, romance, and adventure make this enjoyable in the theatre. Young audiences ought to like it, although I have never seen it done for them.

Oresteia. Aeschylus (458 B.C.). This trilogy, embracing *Agamemnon, Choephori, and Eumenides,* plays no longer in Greek than some plays by Shakespeare. In English the three, although somewhat lengthy together, make a very satisfying evening.

El perro del hortelano (The Gardener's Dog). Lope de Vega Carpio (c. 1615). One of Lope's lightest and most actable romances.

Les Précieuses ridicules (The Affected Young Ladies). Molière (1659). An amusing short play with five good roles.

Prometheus Bound. Aeschylus (c. 478 B.C.). This is less static in performance than it seems to the reader. Vivid characters and beautiful lines make it thoroughly enjoyable.

Revizor (The Inspector General). Nikolai Gogal (1836). One of the most original and hilarious of the mistaken-identity comedies.

The School for Scandal. Richard Brinsley Sheridan (1777). Somewhat less exuberant than *The Rivals* and considerably more difficult, but favored by companies wanting a vehicle to show off their talent and skill.

Il servatore de due Padroni (The Servant of Two Masters). Carlo Goldoni (c. 1750). In the manner of the *commedia dell' arte*: star-crossed lovers, stupid servants, crotchety parents, and many good scenes.

The Shoemakers' Holiday. Thomas Dekker (1559). Historical romance. Two pairs of lovers, King Henry VIII in his youth, and plenty of music and dance.

The Spanish Tragedy. Thomas Kyd (1592), with later additions by Ben Jonson. Rich in language and dramatic situation. The final scene, in the grand manner of the time, is difficult but powerful when properly done.

The Way of the World. William Congreve (1700). An exercise in style; capable, when in the hands of accomplished actors, of providing a delightful evening.

The White Devil. John Webster (1611). The vividness of its characters and its occasionally brilliant lines have intrigued actors for generations, but it has enjoyed few successful productions and remains a major challenge to the most adventurous performers.

A Woman Killed with Kindness. Thomas Heywood (1603). A well written double-plot domestic tragedy which I have yet to see on the stage. Why it has not been produced more often is a mystery to me for it has nothing about it that would make it particularly risky or difficult to do.

Bibliography of Production Aids and References

Outside the realm of Shakespearean scholarship there is surprisingly little material dealing specifically with the problems of producing premodern drama for modern audiences. Nor is much material available in English to help the producer of the plays of ancient Greece, the Spanish Golden Age, or even Molière. Most reference works are peripheral to the subject, treating some single aspect only, such as choreography, diction, stage convention, or theatre architecture. These works I have grouped in four categories: Acting and Stage Convention; Language, Diction, and Delivery; Music and Dance; and Stages, Stage Setting, and Stage Mechanics. Placed side by side they form a rather eclectic collection but anyone interested in producing old plays will find them worth his attention. I have listed no books on scene design, stage lighting, or costuming because, although many excellent works on these subjects have become available in recent years, none relate directly to the problem of producing premodern drama.

ACTING AND STAGE CONVENTION

Bradbrook, Muriel C. *The Growth and Structure of Elizabethan Comedy.* Berkeley: University of California Press, 1956. Emphasizes the oral nature of the drama and the free fluid nature of comic performance, its flexibility, its tendency toward improvisation, and the players' manipulation of the audience. Treatment of comic scenes and various comic styles is excellent but loses validity as it becomes apparent that the author is describing performances she has never seen on the stage.

Granville-Barker, Harley. *Prefaces to Shakespeare,* 2 vol. Vol. I, Introduction. Princeton: Princeton University Press, 1947. The introductory notes embodied in the first twenty-three pages have yet to be equalled for down-to-earth analysis of the practicalities of producing Elizabethan drama for modern audiences.

Harbage, Alfred. "Elizabethan Acting." *PMLA,* 54 (1939), 685 ff. Excellent description of presentative (rather than subjective-interpretive) acting as dictated by the rhetorical nature of Elizabethan acting as a logical product of the kind of material the actor had to present and the theatre in which he had to present it.

Herzel, Roger W. " 'Much Depends on the Acting': The Original Cast of *Le Misanthrope.*" *PMLA*, 95 (1980), 348–66. Description of the casting of Molière's original production in terms of the personalities and abilities of various members of the company.

———. *The Original Casting of Molière's Plays.* Ann Arbor: University of Michigan Research Press, 1982. Reviews all the existing original documents and cast lists of the *Comédie* from 1685 backward, reconstructing the casts for most of Molière's plays.

Hobbs, William. *Stage Combat.* New York: St. Martin's Press, 1981. Of the many books now available on stage fights, this is one of the best, covering a wide variety of ancient weapons and their use on the stage.

Joseph, B.L. *Elizabethan Acting.* London: Oxford University Press, 1951. The best detailed description to date of the rhetorical style of acting which prevailed in the sixteenth and seventeenth centuries.

Rennart, Hugo Albert. *The Spanish Stage in the Time of Lope de Vega.* New York: Hispanic Society of America, 1909. Covers the same material for the Spanish Theatre as E.K. Chambers does for the Elizabethan, but more condensed with a greater emphasis on the actor's craft. Invaluable to understanding of the plays of the Golden Age and the manner of their presentation.

Reynolds, George Fullmer. *The Staging of Elizabethan Plays at the Red Bull Theatre, 1605–1625.* New York: Modern Language Association and Oxford University Press, 1940. Although small, with a narrow field, this book goes much deeper into the aesthetics and techniques of open-stage acting and production than any comparable work.

Schwartz, William Leonard. "Molière's Theatre in 1672–73: Light from *Le Registre d'Hubert.*" *PMLA*, 56 (1941), 395. Details of production from the certified book of accounts for the Molière company, giving the title of each play performed, the size of the the audience, the income per play, and many other interesting details of the day-to-day operation of the company.

Taplin, Oliver. *Greek Tragedy in Action.* Berkeley and Los Angeles: University of California Press, 1978. Detailed examination of nine tragedies from a production standpoint: gestures, groupings, movement, stage properties, etc. as deduced from study of the texts.

Walton, Michael J. *Greek Theatre Practice.* Westport, Connecticut: Greenwood Press, 1980. The staging of the Electra plays from the fourth century on.

Webster, T.B.L. *Greek Theatre Production.* London: Methuen, 1956. Antiquarian survey of existing evidence of production, drawing upon vase and wall paintings, sculpture, surviving ruins, and quotations from contemporaries.

LANGUAGE, DICTION AND DELIVERY

Halstead, William P. *Shakespeare as Spoken: A Collation of 5,000 Acting Editions and Promptbooks of Shakespeare.* 12 vols. Ann Arbor, Michigan: University Microfilms International, 1977. A definitive compilation of Shakespearean production scripts, valuable for its examples of the art of cutting for performance.

Kökeritz, Helge. *Shakespeare's Pronunciation.* New Haven: Yale University Press, 1953. Priceless for understanding how Elizabethan speech sounded to its original audiences. Compares lists of puns, of rhymes, and gives phonetic transcriptions of a score of familiar speeches.

Prior, Moody E. *The Language of Tragedy*. New York: Columbia University Press, 1947. Although the discussion is limited to plays composed in English, many of the principles here given are applicable to serious drama in any language. A useful companion to Reynolds' works.

Reynolds, George Fullmer. "Plays as Literature for an Audience." *University of Colorado Studies*, Series in Language and Literature, No. 4 (1953), 1–51. A landmark work published in several forms and delivered as a lecture series at Stratford-Upon-Avon and the University of Birmingham in England and also at the University of Colorado. It explains the appeal which splendid language orally delivered possesses for audiences modern or premodern. Such factors as the actor's polarization and manipulation of his audience, the predispositions caused by emotion or by the sense of special occasion, and the reciprocal effect of audience response, are analyzed and described.

Rosenmeyer, Thomas G. *The Art of Aeschylus*. Berkeley: University of California Press, 1982. Excellent discussion of the text transmission of Aeschylus' plays, with detailed analysis of language and meaning much of which is applicable to all Greek tragic poets.

MUSIC AND DANCE

Arbeau, Thoinot. *Orchesography*. Trans. by Mary Stewart Evans, with a new Labanotation section by Mireille Backer and Julia Sutton. New York: Dover Publications, 1967. Basic reference for court dances of the sixteenth and seventeenth centuries.

Dolmetsch, Arnold. *The Interpretation of Music of the Seventeenth and Eighteenth Centuries*. New York: H.H. Gray Co., 1915. Useful to the musical director.

Dolmetsch, Mabel. *Dances of England and France, 1450–1600*. London: Routledge, 1949. Standard reference for early dances.

Emmanuel, Maurice. *The Antique Greek Dance*. Trans. by Harriet Jean Beauley. New York: John Lane Co., 1916. Excellent reconstructions of choral dances. Over five hundred illustrations from sculptures and vase paintings. Some dancers object to Emmanuel's use of ballet terminology to describe various attitudes and movements, but his meaning is always clear.

The English Dancing Master: or plaine and easie rules for the dancing of country dances, with the tune to each dance. London: Printed by Thomas Harper and sold by John Playford, 1651. Facsimile published by H. Mellor, London, 1933. Basic reference for country dances.

Galpin, Francis W. *Old English Instruments of Music, Their History and Character*. London: Methuen, 1911. Well illustrated, standard reference work.

Horst, Louis. *Pre-Classic Dance Forms*. New York: Dance Observer, 1937. Standard brief history. Describes the difference between court and country dancing, and gives steps, lists of composers, and history of popular dances from 1500 to 1750.

Lawler, Lillian B. *The Dance in Ancient Greece*. Middletown, Connecticut: Wesleyan University Press, 1964. Simple, clear, and well illustrated, with photos of dancers as shown on tombstones, monuments, and vase paintings.

Schlesinger, Kathleen. *The Greek Aulos*. London: Methuen, 1939. A study of the form and mechanism of the basic ancient Greek wind instrument and its relationship to the modal system. A good scholarly work, loaded with pictures, scales, and diagrams.

Winnington-Ingram, R.P. *Mode in Ancient Greek Music.* London: Cambridge University Press, 1936. Indispensable to an understanding of the nature and uses of Greek music.

STAGES, STAGE SETTING, AND STAGE MECHANICS

Beckerman, Bernard. *Shakespeare at the Globe.* New York: Macmillan, 1962. Excellent description of the style of production favored by Elizabethan outdoor theatres, of the operation of the repertory system and its effect on production. Valuable appendices on localization of scenes and on non-Shakespearean plays performed at the Globe.

Binet, Alfred. "The Psychology of Prestidigitation." *Smithsonian Institute Annual Report for 1894.* Washington, D.C.: Smithsonian Insitute, 1896, 555 ff. Binet's classic explanation of the means by which the magician manipulates and misleads his audience. Priceless for the director of plays featuring legerdemain, such as *Doctor Faustus, Macbeth,* and *The Tempest.*

Chambers, E.K. *The Elizabethan Stage.* London: Oxford University Press, 1923. Four Volumes. An encyclopedia of information about theatres, actors, playwrights, and production practices of the Elizabethan theatre.

Corsi, Mario. *Il teatro all'aperto in Italia.* Milan-Rome: Rizzoli, 1939. Magnificent illustrations showing the Greek tragedies subsidized by the Mussolini government and performed in ancient theatres restored for the purpose, examples of what imagination and unlimited resources can achieve.

Hainaux, Rene (editor). "Greek Tragedy, Its Production." *World Theatre,* 6 (1957), No. 4. A symposium of articles by producers of Greek tragedy in Greece, Italy, France, the United States and Great Britian. Abundantly illustrated.

Hewitt, Barnard (editor). *The Renassance Stage.* Coral Gables, Florida: University of Miami Press, 1958. The theatre writings of Sebastiano Serlio, Nicola Sabbattini, and Joseph Furtenbach the Elder, translated by Allerdyce Nicoll, John H. McDowell, and George R. Kernodle respectively. Profusely illustrated.

Hopkins, Albert Allis. *Magic: Stage Illusions and Scientific Diversions.* New York: Munn & Co., 1898. An encyclopedia of legerdemain, describing the mechanics of every kind of magical illusion, with fine illustraions. The necessary companion to Binet's work.

Pickard-Cambridge, A.W. *The Theatre of Dionysus in Athens.* Oxford: Clarendon Press, 1946. The first three chapters describe the theatre of the classical period and the manner in which it was used, with many canny speculations as to stage machinery and operation.

Southern, Richard. *Changeable Scenery.* London: Faber and Faber, 1951. The development of stage machinery in the English theatre from 1600 to the end of the nineteenth century, with diagrams and photos of models illustrating the wing-and-groove system which the English brought to perfection in the eighteenth century.

――――. *The Open Stage.* New York: Theatre Arts Books, 1959. Four good essays on the form and uses of the platform stage.

Bibliography of Texts and Translations of the Plays Discussed Here

There are many more editions of most of these plays than could be encompassed in a book of this size. I have therefore listed only the more recent editions, with from four to eight entries each, enough to give a prospective producer a sound basis for comparison.

THE ALCHEMIST (1610)

Facsimile of 1612 Edition. Noel Douglas Replicas. London: Douglas, 1927.

Brown, Douglas, ed. New Mermaid Series. New York: Norton, 1976.

Hereford, C.H. and Percy Simpson, eds. *The Works of Ben Jonson*. 8 vols. Oxford: Clarendon Press, 1925–1954. vol. 5.

Hollingsworth, Roger, ed. Plays in Performance Series. New York: B and N Imports, 1982.

Jamieson, Michael, ed. *Three Comedies by Ben Jonson*. Harmondsworth: Penguin Books, 1966.

Kernan, Alvin B., ed. New Haven: Yale University Press, 1974.

Steane, J.B., ed. Cambridge: The University Press, 1967.

ANTIGONE (c. 441 B.C.)

Banks, Theodore Howard, trans. and ed. *Three Theban Plays*. London: Oxford University Press, 1956.

Campbell, Lewis, trans. Oxford Classics Series. London: Oxford University Press, 1952.

Fitts, Dudley, and Robert Fitzgerald, trans. "An English Version." New York: Harcourt Brace, [1939].

Jebb, R.C., trans. In *The Complete Greek Drama*. Whitney J. Oates and Eugene O'Neill, eds. New York: Random House, 1938. vol. 1.

Kitto, H.D.F., trans. and ed. *Three Plays of Sophocles*. London: Oxford University Press, 1962.

Roche, Paul, trans. *The Oedipus Plays of Sophocles*. London: New English Library, 1958.

Wyckoff, Elizabeth, trans. In *The Complete Greek Tragedies*. David Grene and Richmond Lattimore, eds. Chicago: University of Chicago Press, 1959. vol. 2.

ELECTRA (c. 420 B.C.)

Banks, Theodore Howard, trans. and ed. *Four Plays by Sophocles*. London: Oxford University Press, 1966.

Ferguson, W.R. Scott, trans. In *Greek Plays in Modern Translation*. Dudley Fitts and Robert Fitzgerald, eds. New York: Dial Press, 1947.

Grene, David, trans. In *The Complete Greek Tragedies*. David Grene and Richmond Lattimore, eds. Chicago: University of Chicago Press, 1959. vol. 2.

Jebb, R.C., trans. In *The Complete Greek Drama*. Whitney J. Oates and Eugene O'Neill, Jr., eds. New York: Random House, 1938. vol. 1.

Kitto, H.D.F., trans. and ed. In *Three Tragedies of Sophocles*. London: Oxford University Press, 1962.

Sale, William, trans. New York: Prentice-Hall, [1973].

Schmitt, Gladys, trans. New York: Harcourt Brace, 1965.

Watling, E.F., trans. In *Electra and Other Plays*. Harmondsworth: Penguin Books, 1953.

DOCTOR FAUSTUS (c. 1588–1592)

Boas, Frederick S., ed. *The Tragical History of Doctor Faustus*. New York: Gordian Press, 1966.

Bowers, Fredson, ed. In *The Complete Works of Christopher Marlowe*. London: Cambridge University Press, 1966. vol. 2.

Brooke, C.F. Tucker, ed. In *The Works of Christopher Marlowe*. London: Oxford University Press, 1910.

Gill, Roma, ed. New Mermaid Series. New York: W.W. Norton, 1976.

Greg, W.W., ed. *Doctor Faustus. 1604–1616*. Oxford: Clarendon Press, 1930. Parallel texts of the two principal editions: the shorter "bad" text of 1604 and the "enlarged and altered" text of 1616.

Jump, John D., ed. London: Methuen, 1965.

Ribner, Irving, ed. *Doctor Faustus: Text and Major Criticism*. New York: Odyssey Press, 1966.

Steane, J.B., ed. *The Complete Plays of Christopher Marlowe*. Harmondsworth: Penguin Books, 1969.

LES FOURBERIES DE SCAPIN (1671)

Baker, H., and J. Miller, trans. (*The Cheats of Scapin*) in *Comedies of Molière*. London: J.M. Dent, 1929. vol. 2.

Frame, Donald, trans. In *The Misanthrope and Other Plays*. London: New English Library, 1968.

Gravely, George, trans. In *Six Comedies of Molière*. London: Oxford University Press, 1968.

Sutherland, Donald, trans. *Scapin*. Chandler Editions in Drama. San Francisco: Chandler Publishing Co., [1966].

Wood, John, trans. (*That Scoundrel Scapin*) in *The Miser and Other Plays*. Harmondsworth: Penguin Books, 1953.

FUENTE OVEJUNA (1611–1618)

Booty, Jill, trans. In *Lope de Vega: Five Plays*. New York: Hill and Wang, 1961.

Campbell, Roy, trans. An "English Version" in *The Classic Theatre*. Eric Bentley, ed. Garden City, N.Y.: Doubleday, 1959. vol. 3.

Colford, William E., trans. In Barron's Educational Series. New York: Barron, 1969.

Underhill, John Garrett, trans. In *Four Plays by Lope de Vega*. New York: Scribner's, 1936.

THE RIVALS (1775)

Bettenbender, J., ed. In *Three English Comedies*. New York: Dell, [1970].

Downer, Alan S., ed. In Crofts Classics Series. New York: Crofts, 1953.

Hampden, John, ed. New York: Dutton, [1930].

Levin, J., ed. New York: Norton, 1980.

Price, C.J., ed. In *Sheridan Plays*. New York: Oxford University Press, 1975.

SHE STOOPS TO CONQUER (1773)

Balderston, Katherine G., ed. Crofts Classics Series. New York: Crofts, 1951.

Bettenbender, J., ed. In *Three English Comedies*. New York: Dell, [1966] [1970].

Dent, J.M., ed. London: J.M. Dent, 1924.

Hopper, Vincent F., and Gerald B. Lahey, eds. New York: Barron, 1958.

Levin, J.A., ed. New Mermaid Series. New York: Norton, 1980.

TARTUFFE (1664)

Frame, Donald, trans. In *Tartuffe and Other Plays*. London: New English Library, 1967.

Rosenberg, James L., trans. Chandler Editions in Drama. San Francisco: Chandler Publishing Co., 1962. (In verse.)

Wilbur, Richard, trans. New York: Harcourt Brace and World, Inc., 1961. (In verse.)

Wood, John, trans. In *The Misanthrope and Other Plays*. Harmondsworth: Penguin Books, 1959.

THE TROJAN WOMEN (415 B.C.)

Hamilton, Edith., trans. In *Three Greek Plays*. New York: Norton, 1937.

Lattimore, Richmond, trans. In *The Complete Greek Tragedies*. 3 vols. Chicago: University of Chicago Press, 1959. vol. 3.

Murray, Gilbert, trans. In *The Complete Greek Drama*. 2 vols. Whitney J. Oates and Eugene O'Neill, Jr., eds. New York: Random House, 1938. vol. 1.

Vellacott, Philip, trans. (*The Women of Troy*) in *The Bacchae and Other Plays*. Harmondsworth: Penguin Books, 1954.

Way, A.S., trans. (*Daughters of Troy*) London: J.M. Dent, 1956.

VOLPONE (1605–1606)

Cook, David, ed. London: Methuen, 1967.

Dunn, Esther Cloudman, ed. In *Eight Famous Elizabethan Plays*. New York: Modern Library, 1932.

Hereford, C.H., and Percey Simpson, eds. *The Works of Ben Jonson*. 8 vols. Oxford: Clarendon Press, 1925–1954. vol. 5.

Jamieson, Michael, ed. In *Three Comedies by Ben Jonson*. Harmondsworth: Penguin Books, 1966.

Kronenberger, Louis, ed. Oxford: Limited Editions Club, 1952.

Index

Abel Drugger (*The Alchemist*), 143
Abraham and Isaac, 217
Abridgement of texts, 13-21
Accelerated progression, 66, 155
"Acting versions," of classics, 12
Adaptation of texts to modern tastes, xii
Aegisthus (*Electra*), 70
Aeschylus: *Oresteia*, 219; *Prometheus Bound*, 220
Aesthetics of the dirge, 77
Albright, H. Darkes, viii
El Alcalde de Zalamea, 217
Alcestis, 217
Alchemist, The: characters and casting, 138-145; costuming, 137; cutting, 137; disguises, 138, 139, 145, 146; exposition, problems of, 150; multiple-role characters, 145-146; productions of, 213; prologue and epilogue, 150; properties, 149; setting, physical requirements of, 148
Almagro, 105
American Conservatory Theatre, 215
Amphitryon, 30, 217
Andromache (*Trojan Women*), 81
Angels, Good, and Bad (Doctor Faustus), 98
Animal Farm, The, 134
Anne Frankford (*A Woman Killed with Kindness*), 25

Antigone: characters and casting, 57-61; chorus, age and sex, 57; commus, problem of, 56; costuming, 62; finale problem, 63; irony of first episode, 56; parodos, choral mime in, 45; productions of, 214; properties and costumes, 61-62; setting, physical requirements of, 61; silent central characters, 56; time lapses, 56; translation problems, 54; turning point, 64; unity of style lacking, 56
Antioch Shakespeare Festival, vii
Antistrophe, 45
Apron action, 135
Aristophanes: *Birds*, 218; *Frogs*, 218; *Lysistrata*, 219
Aristotle (*Poetics*): definition of comedy, 128; definition of tragedy, 37; function of music, 46
Artaxerxes, 186
Asides: 135, 184, 200
Association of Producing Artists, 215
As You Like It, 27
Athena (*Trojan Women*), 80
Aumont, Michel, 214
L'avare, 217

Bacchae, 46, 217
Balance of sympathies, 41, 55

Balance of voices, in casting, 24

Ball, William, 215

Barrymore, John, as *Hamlet*, vii, 17

Barton, John, 214, 215

Basics of directing, xiii

Bawtree, Michael, 215

Beaumont, Francis, and John Fletcher, 219

Beaux' Stratagem, The, 217

Becket, 29

Bedford, Brian, 215

Beggar's Opera, The, 218

Benet, Stephen Vincent, 93

Bi-polar scenes, 135, 136

Birds, 46, 218

Bob Acres *(The Rivals)*, 203

Bonario *(Volpone)*, 132

Le Bourgeois gentilhomme: costume period style, 161; dancing and fencing, 162; lightness of decor required, 161; producibility, 218

Browne, E. Martin, viii

Cacoyannis, Michael, 215

Calatrava, Knights of, 113

Calderón (Pedro Calderón de la Barca), 105, 217

Campbell, Douglas, 216

Cardinal of Lorraine *(Doctor Faustus)*, 101

Carnegie Tech (now Carnegie-Mellon University), vii

Cassandra *(Trojan Women)*, 80

Casting: for appearance and bearing, 25; of children's roles, 28; of choral groups, 47; diction, importance of, 23; doubling of minor roles, 31; for ensemble effect, 24; of female roles written for men, 26; for fencing, singing, and dancing ability, 25; of look-alikes, 29; of singing roles, 25; for the "twin" comedies, 30; of walk-ons and supers, 29

Catharsis, 41

Celia *(Volpone)*, 132

Censorship in England and Spain, 106

Century-of-Progress productions, 98

Changeling, The, 218

Changes of scenery and properties, 104

Characterization: of children in tragedy, 28; classical, in Molière's plays, 157; demands of plot, 39; generalized, 43

Cherry Orchard, The, 92

Children, problems in casting, 28, 87

Chorus, Greek: aesthetic function, 46; casting, 47; delivery, 48; grouping, 50; identity, 47; literary function, 45; mime, 44; movement and countermovement, 45, 50; musical accompaniment, 26, 50; rehearsal techniques, 49; size, 47; staging, 46; voice groupings, 48

Chorus in *Doctor Faustus*, 97

Chrysothemis *(Electra)*, 69

Cimbranos *(Fuente Ovejuna)*, 116

Cinema, influence on modern staging, 3

Circle in the Square, The: *Tartuffe*, 215; *Trojan Women*, 215

Ciudad Real, 113

Clandestine Marriage, The, 218

Classic Stage Company, 214

Clay, Jack, viii

Cléante *(Tartuffe)*, 176

Clytemnestra *(Electra)*, 69

Coates, Carolyn, 215

Cockpit-in-Court, 135

Colman, George, 218

Comédie-Française, 161, 213, 214

Comedy, Aristotle's definition, 128

Comedy of Errors, The, 30

Commander, The (Fernando Gómez de Guzmán) *(Fuente Ovejuna)*, 115

Commedia dell' Arte, 163

Commus: in Greek Tragedy, 44; in *Antigone* and *Electra*, 56

Comparison of texts and translations, 11

"Conflict" theory of drama, 53

Congreve, William, 220

Constance Neville *(She Stoops to Conquer)*, 194

Continuity: in premodern drama, 12; unbroken in *The Rivals* and *She Stoops to Conquer*, 206

Contrast, The, 218

Conventions: asides, 200; direct address, 200; hags and harridans played by men, 8; poetic speech, 5

Copyright restrictions on translations, 12

Corbaccio *(Volpone)*, 132

Corral de Comedias at Almagro, 105

Corvino *(Volpone)*, 132

Costuming: *The Alchemist*, 145; *Antigone*, 62; *Doctor Faustus*, 96; *Electra*, 73; *Les Fourberies de Scapin*, 166; *Fuente Ovejuna*, 116; Molière's plays, 161; *The Rivals*, 207; *She Stoops to Conquer*, 191; *Tartuffe*, 177; *Trojan Women*, 84; *Volpone*, 134

Country Wife, The, 218

Craig, Gordon: design for Eleanora Duse's *Electra*, 71; design for G. Tyler's production of *Macbeth*, 14

Creon *(Antigone)*, 55, 57

Cutting: Elizabethan plays, 15; general principles of, 15; intralinear, 16; prologue and epilogue in *The Rivals*, 211

Dame Pliant *(The Alchemist)*, 144

Dance: casting for ability in, 26; indispensable to Spanish drama, 107; integral in most early drama, 5

Dapper *(The Alchemist)*, 143

Darkness: imaginary, 8; symbolized by torch or candle, 7

Dawn-to-dusk cycle in Greek tragedies, 83

Daylight performances, outdoors, 7

Death of a Salesman, 149

Decor: of *Fuente Ovejuna*, 119; of *The Rivals*, 284; of *Volpone*, 135

Defects of speech. *See* Speech defects

Dekker, Thomas: *Old Fortunatus*, 219; *The Shoemakers' Holiday*, 220

Delivery, by Greek choruses, 47

Desdemona (Othello), singing ability, 25

Deus ex machina: endings in general, 156; in *She Stoops to Conquer*, 196; in *Tartuffe*, 177

Devil and Daniel Webster, The, 91, 93

Dialogue: reversed in *Les Fourberies de Scapin*, 167; stichomythic, 44; Spanish compared to English, 108

Diction: as a factor in casting, 23; poetic, 5

Direct-address convention, 3, 200

Directing for the Open Stage, vii

Disguise: as a feature of satire, 145; in the plays: *The Alchemist*, 145-147; *Doctor Faustus*, 96; *Les Fourberies de Scapin*, 166; *Volpone*, 134-135

Doctor Faustus (The Tragical History of Doctor Faustus): apparitions, 100-101; character change in Faustus, 95; characterization and casting, 97-102; doubling possibilities, 94; finale, staging, 104; imagery, 92; legerdemain, 103-104; missing middle, 92; musical accompaniment, 103; primacy of language, 92; productions of, 214; setting, physical requirements, 102; UFA staging, 98

Doll Common *(The Alchemist)*, 140

Dorine *(Tartuffe)*, 176

Doubling: in *Doctor Faustus*, 94; in general, 31-32; in *She Stoops to Conquer*, 193

Dramatic satire, contrasted with literary satire, 127

Duchess of Malfi, The, 29, 218

Dunnock, Mildred, 215

Echo phrasing, 158

L'Ecole des femmes, 218

L'Ecole des maris, 218

Elapsed time, in Greek tragedy, 57

Electra: accelerated progression, 66; characters and casting, 67-70; costuming, 73; "Electra complex," 67; productions of, 214; properties, 72; revelation scene in, vii, xiii, 76; set speeches, 44; setting, 71; "urn" scene, 76

Elmire *(Tartuffe)*, 176

Emotionality of Greek tragedy, 40

Emotional transparency, 194

Emperor *(Doctor Faustus)*, 101

Ensemble, oral, importance of contrasting voices, 24

Epicoene, or The Silent Woman, 218

Epilogues: *She Stoops to Conquer*, 197; *Volpone*, 136

Erasmus Montanus, 218

Esteban *(Fuente Ovejuna)*, 115

Euripides: *Alcestis*, 217; *Bacchae*, 217; *Iphigenia in Aulis*, 219
Evans, Bergen, viii
Evans, Maurice, 17
Everyman, 218
Externalized characters, 162

Face-Jeremy *(The Alchemist)*, 139, 146, 384
Farquhar, George, 217
Faulkland *(The Rivals)*, 201-205
Faust, the opera, 91
Fencing, casting for ability in, 26
Ferdinand and Isabella *(Fuente Ovejuna)*, 112
Fernando Gómez de Guzmán *(Fuente Ovejuna)*, 112
Feste *(Twelfth Night)*, 25
Final scene, problems of in *Antigone*, 63
Fletcher, John C., 215
Flores *(Fuente Ovejuna)*, 116
Foreknowledge in comedy, 4
Form in Greek tragedy, 43
Les Fourberies de Scapin: casting, 164-165; costuming, 166; finale, problems of, 168; "galley scene," 162, 168; "laughing scene," 168; mime, 168; music, and dance, 168; productions of, 214; "sack scene," 167, 168; setting, physical requirements of, 165; silent central character scenes, 159; Silvestre's disguise, 166; slap-sticks, use of, 167; temporal progression, 155; translating the title, 163
Freedman, Gerald, viii, 214
Frogs, 218
Frondoso *(Fuente Ovejuna)*, 115
Fuente Ovejuna: characters and casting, 114-116; climactic scene, 123; costuming, 116; decor, 119; doubling, 32; music and dance, 121; productions of, 214; properties, 120; rehearsal problems, 122; setting, physical requirements of, 118; translation problems, 108-111

Garrick, David, 143, 218
Gascon, Jean, 213, 215
Gate Theatre, N.Y., 213
Gay, John, 218

Generalized characters, 37, 43
Gielgud, John, 216
Glass Menagerie, The, 149
Gogol, Nikolai, 220
Goldoni, Carlo, 219, 220
Goldsmith, Oliver, 185-188
Granville-Barker, Harley, 6, 14
Greek National Theatre, 48, 213
Greek tragedy: concentration of plot, 44; definiteness of form, 43; emotionality, 40; *essence* in characterization, 43; familiar plots, 38; generalized characters, 43; ritual nature, 37; set speeches, 44
Greek Tragedy Theatre (Piraikon), 214
Grene, David, 68
Grizzard, George, 216
Guthrie, Tyrone, 149
Guthrie Theatre Company, 214, 215, 216

Haemon *(Antigone)*, 59
Hall, Peter, 216
Halstead, William P., viii
Hamlet, ii, 17
Hammond, David, 215
Hardcastle, Mrs. *(She Stoops to Conquer)*, 195
Hastings *(She Stoops to Conquer)*, 195
Haydon, Therese, 214
Hecuba *(Trojan Women, Hecuba)*, 78-79
Helen *(Doctor Faustus, Trojan Women)*, 100, 195
Henslowe, Philip, 93
Hepburn, Katherine, 27
Heston, Charlton, viii
Hirsch, John, 214, 215
Hirsch, Robert, 214
Holberg, Ludvig, 218, 219
Hutt, William, 215

Insect Comedy, The, 134
Intralinear cutting, principles of, 16
Ion, 40, 45, 218
Iphigenia at Aulis, 219
Irony, in tragedy, 38, 56
Irving, Jules, 213

Jacinta *(Fuente Ovejuna)*, 114
Jack Absolute *(The Rivals)*, 202

Jefford, Barbara, 28
Jeppe pa berget, 219
Jones, Inigo, 135, 150
Jonson, Ben, 127, 129, 137, 218
Jouvet, Louis, 173, 179
Julia Melville *(The Rivals)*, 204
Julius Caesar, 29, 31

Kastril *(The Alchemist)*, 143
Kate Hardcastle *(She Stoops to Conquer)*, 193, 197, 201
Kerr, Walter, viii
Knight of the Burning Pestle, The, 219
Kyd, Thomas, 220

Lady Would-Be *(Volpone)*, 133
Langham, Michael, 215
Laurencia *(Fuente Ovejuna)*, 114
LeGallienne, Eva, 84, 215
Legerdemain, 103
Length, cutting for, 14
Liaison, in Molière's plays, 156
Lighting: of Molière's comedies, 161; for mood in *The Trojan Women*, 83; problematic, in comedy night scenes, 190
"Lion Gate" at Mycenae, 71
Locale shifts in Greek tragedy, 57
La Locandiera, 219
Look-alikes, a hazard in casting, 29
Love, Greek idea of, 59
Lovewit *(The Alchemist)*, 144
Lucifer *(Doctor Faustus)*, 99
Lucius O'Trigger, Sir *(The Rivals)*, 204, 209, 212
Lucy *(The Rivals)*, 205
Lydia Languish *(The Rivals)*, 204
Lyric Studio, Hammersmith, 214
Lysistrata, 46, 219

Macbeth, xi, 7-8, 14
Machiavelli, Niccolò, 219
Le Malade imaginaire: mock death, 162; silent central characters, 159; tirades, 158, 162
Malaprop, Mrs. *(The Rivals)*, 203
Males in female roles, 6, 219
Mandragola, 219
Marceau, Marcel, 127

Maria Cortezo, Victor, 214
Marlborough, Duke of, 186
Martin, Christopher, 214
Mary Stuart 219
Mason, Marshall W., viii
Massinger, Philip, 219
Master of Calatrava *(Fuente Ovejuna)*, 116
Master of the Revels, as censor, 106
Le Médecin malgré lui, 162, 219
Menaechmi, 30, 219
Menelaus *(Trojan Women)*, 81
Mengo *(Fuente Ovejuna)*, 115
Mephistophilis *(Doctor Faustus)*, 96
Merrick, David, 29
Middleton, Thomas, 218
Midsummer Night's Dream, A, 29
Mime: choral in Greek tragedy, 45; illustrative of the oath in *Lysistrata*, 46; mimetic characterization in *Birds*, 46, in *Les Fourberies de Scapin*, 168
Minor parts, doubling, 31
Miser, The (L'avare), 149
Mitchell, Maurine Morgan, viii
Molière's comedy: accelerating action, 155; *deus ex machina* endings, 156; echo phrasing, 158; economies of means, 154; externalized characters; 162; liaison, 156; plays, 217-220; lighting for visibility, 161; settings, style of, 160; silent central characters, 158; symmetry of plotting, 155; temporal symmetry, 155; terminal scenes, 160; tirades, 157
Mosca *(Volpone)*, 131
Motivation, in *Tartuffe*, 170
Movement, choral: Strophe and Antistrophe, 45; where needed in Greek tragedy, 50
Mrs. Hardcastle *(She Stoops to Conquer)*, 195
Music: choral, Greek, 50; with dance in *Les Fourberies de Scapin*, 168, in *Fuente Ovejuna*, 121; integral in early drama, 5; required in *Doctor Faustus*, 103
Mycenae "rich in gold," 71

Nano *(Volpone)*, 25
National Repertory Theatre, 84, 215
National Theatre of Great Britain, 213, 216

National Theatre of Greece, 46
New Art of Writing Plays, The (Arte nuevo de hacer en este tiempo), 107, 113
New Way to Pay Old Debts, A, 219
New York Shakespeare Festival, 214
Night scenes, in comedy, 190
Northwestern University, vii, 214

Oedipus at Colonus (also *Oedipus Coloneus*), 44, 219
Oedipus the King (also *Oedipus Tyrannus)*: character determined by plot requirements, 39; children for emotional appeal, 40; doubling of principals, 32; messenger's set speech, 44; primacy of plot, 92; producibility, 219
Old Fortunatus, 219
Old Fox, The, 213
Old Hardcastle *(She Stoops to Conquer)*, 196
Old Man *(Doctor Faustus)*, 102
Old Vic, 28, 145
Oral ensemble, 24
Oregon Shakespeare Festival, vii, 214
Oresteia, 219
Orestes *(Electra)*, 68
Orgon *(Tartuffe)*, 174
Ortuño *(Fuente Ovejuna)*, 116
Othello: cutting of, 18-19; night scenes in, 7-8
Our Town, 186
Outdoor performances, advantages and disadvantages, 7

Paedagogus *(Electra)*, 69
Parodos, 45
Parrott, Thomas Marc, viii
Pascuala *(Fuente Ovejuna)*, 114
Pauses, between acts, 13
Payne, B. Iden, viii
El perro del hortelano, 220
Perspective of time in *She Stoops* and *Our Town*, 186
Pertinax Surly *(The Alchemist)*, 142, 146
Piraikon Theatre: chorus style, 46; tours, 48
Plautus, plays of, 217, 219
Plot: compression, 44; familiar plots, 38; linear, 3, 43; symmetry of, 155

Poetic speech, convention of, 5
Pope, The *(Doctor Faustus)*, 101
Porter, Stephen, 213, 215
Poseidon *(Trojan Women)*, 80
Les Précieuses ridicules, 161, 220
Prefaces to Shakespeare: cutting, 14; women in parts written for male performers, 7
Principles of Theatre Art, viii
Progression, temporal, 155
Prologue-Epilogue frame, 3, 136, 150, 211
Prometheus Bound, 220
Pronoun problem in Greek translation, 54
Properties: *The Alchemist*, 149; *Antigone*, 62; *Electra*, 72; *Les Fourberies de Scapin*, 167
Puritans, 106, 144

Rehearsal problems: in *Fuente Ovejuna*, 122; in *Volpone*, 136
Rehearsal techniques, applicable to Greek choruses, 49
Reinhardt, Max, staging of crowd scenes, 30
Repertory Theatre of Lincoln Centre, 213, 214
Repetition, in Moliére, 158
Revelations: in *Electra*, 76; in *Tartuffe*, 181
Reversed dialogue, 167
Revizor, 220
Reynolds, George Fullmer, viii
Richardson, Ralph, 215
Ritual, in Greek tragedy, 38
Rivals, The: characters and casting, 201-205; costuming, 207-210; duel scene, 211; general characteristics, 199; intralinear cutting, 20; productions of, 215; prologue and epilogue, 211; rehearsal characteristics, 201; scene changes, 206; type characters, 202; visual style, 205
Rondiris, Dimitri, 214
Royal Shakespeare Company, 214, 215
Ruta, Ken, 214
Rutherford, Margaret, 215

Sainz de la Peña, Vincente, 214
Satire, differences between dramatic and literary, 127
Scapino, 213

Scene changes: in *The Rivals*, 206; in *Tartuffe*, 180
Schiller, Friedrich, 219
Schliemann, Herman, 71
Schneideman, Robert I., viii
School for Scandal, The, 220
Scofield, Paul, 216
Seduction scenes: in *The Alchemist*, 151; in *Tartuffe*, 4, 181; in *Volpone*, 4, 136
Sequential plotting, 187
Il servatore de due padroni, 220
Set speeches, 44
Settings, physical requirements for: *The Alchemist*, 148; *Antigone*, 61; *Doctor Faustus*, 102; *Electra*, 72; *Les Fourberies de Scapin*, 165; *Fuente Ovejuna*, 118; *Tartuffe*, 180; *Trojan Women*, 82
Settings, style for: *Electra*, 71; Molière in general, 160
Seven Deadly Sins *(Doctor Faustus)*, 100
Shakespeare, compared with Lope de Vega, 106, 108
Shattuck, Charles, viii
Sheridan, Richard Brinsley, 199, 220
Sheridan Square Playhouse, 214
She Stoops to Conquer: basically narrative, 187; characters and casting, 193-196; common mistakes in staging, 184; costuming, 191; doubling minor parts, 193; language problems, 188; night scene problematic for comedy, 190; perspective of time, 186; productions of, 215; quotations from Shakespeare, 188; scene changes, 189; sequential plotting, 187; soliloquies, 187; songs, 197; special atmosphere, 185; two epilogues, 197; type characters, 202
Shift of locale, in Greek tragedy, 57
Shoemakers' Holiday, The, 220
Silent central character: in *Antigone*, 56, 64; a feature of premodern drama, xii; in Molière's plays, 158-159
Sir Anthony Absolute *(The Rivals)*, 202
Sir Charles Marlow *(She Stoops to Conquer)*, 196
Sir Epicure Mammon *(The Alchemist)*, 141
Sir Lucius O'Trigger *(The Rivals)*, 204, 209
Sir Politick Would-be *(Volpone)*, 133
Slap-sticks, 167

Soliloquies, in *She Stoops to Conquer*, 187
Spanish theatre: as compared to Elizabethan, 105; dances, 121; translation problems, 108
Spanish Tragedy, The, 220
Spectacle in Greek tragedy, 83
Speech defects, in casting, 24; limiting actor's usefulness, 24
Staging Greek choruses, 45-51
Stevens, T.W., 98
Stichomythic dialogue, 44
Stratford (Connecticut), Shakespeare Festival, vii
Stratford (Ontario), Festival, vii, 29, 213, 215
Strophe, 45
Style, in *The Rivals*, 205
Subtle *(The Alchemist)*, 138, 145
Suspense and surprise in early drama, 9
Sydow, Jack, 215
Symmetry, compositional and temporal, 155

Talthybius *(Trojan Women)*, 81
Tartuffe: characters and casting, 170-176; comparison of American and French productions, 172; costuming, 177; *deus ex machina*, 177; problems in staging, 181; productions of, 215; revelations, 181; revisions, 170; scene changes, 180; setting, physical requirements of, 180; silent central characters, 159; "table scene," vii, 160, 162
Teatro Español, 213, 214
Temporal progression, 155
Terminal scenes in Molière, 160
Texts: abridgement of, 13; comparison, 11
Time lapses, in Greek tragedy, 56
Tirade, the, a feature of Molière's comedy, 157
Tiresias *(Antigone)*, 60
Tony Lumpkin *(She Stoops to Conquer)*, 187, 195
Translation, 11, 12, 54, 108
Trojan Women: aesthetics of the dirge, 77; burning of Troy, 83; characters and casting, 78-81, 87; costuming, 84; emotional appeal, 40; lighting, 83; productions of, 215; properties, 84; reappear-

Trojan Women: (cont.)
    ance of the deities, 87; setting, physical requirements of, 82
Turner, Jerry, 214
Twelfth Night, 28
"Twin" comedies, casting, 30
Tyler, Royall, 218
Type characters, 202

UFA production of *Faust*, 98
Unity of style, 56
University of Texas, 214

Vaughan, Stuart, 215
de Vega, Lope (Lope de Vega Carpio), 105-107, 220
Vocal variety, in casting, 24
Voice groupings, in Greek choruses, 48
Volpone: bi-polar scenes, 136; Celia's incorruptibility, 4; characters and casting, 130-133; costuming, 134; court scene, vii, 136; cutting, 16, 129; multiple-role characters, 130; productions of, 216; prologue-epilogue frame, 136; rehearsal problems, 136; seduction scene, 136; setting, physical requirements, 135; singing roles, 25; style, 135; tortoise-shell scene, 159; turning point, 136

Wagner *(Doctor Faustus)*, 97
Walk-ons and supers, 29
Way of the World, The, 220
Webster, John, 218, 220
Western Kentucky University, vii
White Devil, The, 220
Wilbur, Richard, 171, 174
Woman Killed With Kindness, A, 25, 220
Women, in roles written for men, 6, 27
Wood, John, 173, 215
Wrede, Casper, 214
Wycherley, William, 218

Young Marlow *(She Stoops to Conquer)*, 195
Young Vic Company, 213

About the Author

LEE MITCHELL is best known for his memorable productions of premodern drama while Professor of Dramatic Production and Chairman of the Department of Theatre at Northwestern University. He is co-author of *Principles of Theatre Art* and author of numerous articles in *Theatre Arts, Educational Theatre Journal, Speech Monographs, Quarterly Journal of Speech, Philological Quarterly, Drama Critique, Players,* and other theatre magazines.